Fantasies of Nina Simone

Fantasies of Nina Simone

JORDAN ALEXANDER STEIN

DUKE UNIVERSITY PRESS
Durham and London 2024

Printed in the United States of America on acid-free paper ∞
Project Editor: Ihsan Taylor
Designed by Courtney Leigh Richardson
Typeset in Warnock Pro and Sophillia by
Westchester Publishing Services

Library of Congress Cataloging-in-Publication Data
Names: Stein, Jordan Alexander, author.
Title: Fantasies of Nina Simone / Jordan Alexander Stein.
Description: Durham : Duke University Press, 2024. | Includes
bibliographical references and index.
Identifiers: LCCN 2023046391 (print)
LCCN 2023046392 (ebook)
ISBN 9781478030706 (paperback)
ISBN 9781478026471 (hardcover)
ISBN 9781478059684 (ebook)
Subjects: LCSH: Simone, Nina, 1933–2003. | African American women
singers—Biography. | Women singers—United States—Biography. |
Singers—United States—Biography. | Feminism and music—United
States—History—20th century. | Womanism—United States. | BISAC:
SOCIAL SCIENCE / Ethnic Studies / American / African American &
Black Studies | SOCIAL SCIENCE / Women's Studies
Classification: LCC ML420.S5635 S74 2024 (print) | LCC ML420.S5635
(ebook) | DDC 782.42164092 [B]—dc23/eng/20240429
LC record available at https://lccn.loc.gov/2023046391
LC ebook record available at https://lccn.loc.gov/2023046392

Cover art: Nina Simone, ca. 1960. Photo by Herb Snitzer/Michael Ochs
Archives. Courtesy of Getty Images.

WHAT DO BLUES DO FOR YOU?
IT HELPS ME TO EXPLAIN WHAT
I CAN'T EXPLAIN.

—GAYL JONES,
CORREGIDORA

CONTENTS

Something

Listen for the ways Nina Simone signifies.

Listen from the beginning—to the rising, flowering tempo of her rendition of "Mood Indigo" or the Baroque counterpoint her dexterous piano infuses into a Broadway tune like "Love Me or Leave Me." Listen to the rich and billowy tones of "Feeling Good" and maybe hum along as they pepper your mood with their eager mischief; or else, listen to the aching downbeat of "Stars" as its melancholy slowly stresses your body, constricting your breath with a pain that isn't yours and also, now, isn't not. Listen to Simone's astonishing contralto as it rides across the bars of instrumental melody, intimating meaning beyond what any voice could ever just say. Listen to nearly any Nina Simone recording and hear it unfurl a legend told in real time.

Listen from now—to more than a dozen concert recordings and remixes posthumously released since 2003, feeding the fans' yearning for yet more from this someone who has already given so much. Listen to the nearly thirty compilations that remaster Simone's sound, tinker with its levels, and revise the order of her albums' tracks, offering up a fresh syntax in an old grammar that hints at the promise of meanings both new and familiar. Listen to the clips and sound bites that compress hours of interviews into viral, ten-second highlights: "That blackness," "No fear." Listen to the controversies that exploded in rapid succession as the Oscars snubbed the hit documentary *What Happened, Miss Simone?* (2015) and as the Hollywood biopic *Nina* (2016) cast the comparatively light-skinned Zoe Saldana as its lead. Listen to the black intellectuals who found resources, again, to name that pain—for example, Ta-Nehisi Coates, observing that Simone's dark skin and flat nose are caught up in the shameful logic by which "even today a young Nina Simone would have a hard time being cast in her own biopic"; for example, Daphne Brooks, contending that "until recently, the cards have been overwhelmingly stacked against black women musicians telling their own uncompromised, amanuensis-free stories—and importantly, telling stories that place craft at the center of their life ambitions and concerns."[1]

Listen to the then and the now, to their push and pull. To the ways Nina Simone is taken to be representative, even as she is also recognized to be in a class by herself. To the ways the past lays groundwork for the present, and the present, for its own reasons, can't help but renovate the past. To the ways the contradictory desires swirling around Simone's race, gender, and history refract the contradictory things that black womanhood, then and now, has been made to bear: beauty and dignity, but also abjection; empowerment, but also myriad forms of restriction; expansive room for individual talent, but structurally finite opportunity; authenticity, sincerity, realness, but also the ordinary emotional scars that heal and accrue as any person adapts to their world.[2]

Listen to the multiple rhythms being played simultaneously, to the ways *history* is another name for what happens when everybody is talking all at once.[3] It's no secret that US culture has long burdened blackness, and black womanhood especially, with such contradictory desires, though only lately has that same culture nominated Nina Simone as a candidate for the task of resolving them.[4] Something is taking place here. Our task will be to listen for it.[5]

THE SHELF OF BOOKS about Nina Simone grows heavy. In addition to Simone's autobiography and the documentaries and interviews in which she participated, a flurry of biographies, reams of scholarship, who knows how many exhibits, and a handful of both narrative and documentary films have appeared in the two decades since her death—in English, French, Dutch, Portuguese, German, Italian, Spanish, and Japanese—aimed variously at the uninitiated and the connoisseur, including fans, researchers, and children. Opportunities abound to learn the facts of Simone's story. And yet, though these facts certainly matter, the whole truth is almost never just a matter of fact. Truth is motivated, adumbrated, and expressed by and through irrational things too, like desire. Anybody who has wanted, which is also to say anybody, knows that wanting can make things real. So, in all that's already been said and seen and heard about Nina Simone, what else is true? What might still be worth listening for?

We might begin to hear an answer in "Please Read Me," Simone's cover of the Bee Gees' guitar-forward, psychedelic rock track about being a patient in treatment—the imperative of its title requesting explanation from a psychotherapist. Simone first recorded the song for 'Nuff Said! (1968), altering the opening line (such that Barry Gibb's "Many years ago I was a simple man" becomes "Many years ago I was a sinful girl") and stripping the psychedelic instrumentation all the way down to naked, with a tensely scaling piano and a voice that deliberately and plaintively holds its notes, delivering the titular line as an intimate, yearning, starving demand.

This performance is pretty clearly a matter of fact. Whether in the grooves of vinyl or the sequence frames of an MP3, the recording that archives the performance makes it difficult to dispute that it happened. But that facticity runs aground when we do nothing more imposing than consider the chorus. Is Simone actually asking to be "read"? On the one hand, her biographers incline toward no, documenting her ambivalent experiences and cautious suspicions of psychotherapy.[6] On the other hand, ambivalence and caution are not precisely what Simone's "Please Read Me" plays up, at least insofar as her arrangement and performance of this song brim instead with eloquent wanting and unassailable urgency.

But here's the thing: both can be right. The hunger of Simone's "Please Read Me" is something she expresses, maybe fictitiously in the first-person guise of a character, maybe authentically as herself, probably in combination, but in any case through her own conscious and, inevitably, unconscious process.[7] Behind both the biography and the performance is a person, and what's contradictory at the level of fact can nonetheless at a personal level be true.

It starts to make sense in psychological terms, where a person can express longing without having any clear object in sight, or where a person does not have to want literally to be read or analyzed by a professional in order to want to be attended to, to be understood, to feel attached in or to her life and her world. Or it can make sense in linguistic terms, where even propositionally unequivocal and to all appearances resolute statements of desire, of the kind for which Simone was and remains so widely admired, will inevitably be shaped by ambivalence and contradiction.[8] One consequence of the ordinary workings of both psychology and language is that anyone's conscious and deliberate expressions of feeling do not, and likely cannot, equal all that they themselves might feel. And such is the case not least because a person can feel more than one thing at a time—for instance, when a suggestion of hopefulness or optimism layers longing into the otherwise bargaining mood of "Please Read Me," as Simone shifts her emotional delivery from the hedging defection of Gibb's lyric "Maybe I've been lying on your couch too long" to the petitioning conditional of the next one, "I'll stay if you will see me through."[9]

Contradiction is a problem when you're sifting among facts, so let's not. The truth that exists beyond the facts might be found, instead, if we take contradiction seriously, not as a problem to be solved so much as an inexorable part of being a person. The work of this yet-one-more book on Nina Simone will, accordingly, be to listen when she expresses these kinds of contradictions. Doing so will be a way to learn something about Simone and, more generally, to learn something about listening for the operations—what psychologists sometimes describe with the more technical-sounding name "psychic mechanisms"—that hold these contradictions together. One of the principle such operations is fantasy.

III ● IIIII ● III

THE THEORY OF FANTASY that animates *Fantasies of Nina Simone* draws from the existing literature, mostly by psychoanalysts, psychologists, and others in conversation with them.[10] Why psychoanalysis? It's here as a framework, a heuristic, a way of thinking through the knots of language and affect in the human psyche. It is not the only way to do that work, but, through the accidents of education and experience, it is the space my understanding of these concepts happens to have grown in. As I suspect I am not alone there, I have hoped it would make for a decent intellectual scaffold for a study concerned with fantasy.[11]

Preliminarily, though, it's worth stressing that one reason there isn't much need here for any truly original theory of fantasy has to do with how extensively psychoanalytic theories of fantasy already reach into some of the most fundamental aspects of human experience. In the pages that follow, we will encounter theories and examples of both conscious and unconscious fantasies:

- concerning the bounds around the experience of being an individual (for example, fantasies of a person's omnipotence; of a person's relation, connection, and estimation of themself relative to others; of the distinction or integrity of one's self; or of how we can be consumed by others or they by us, even to the impossible degree of "if I were you")
- concerning the scale and scope of agency (for example, fantasies that grandiosely exaggerate, masochistically diminish, or indulgently excuse the significance, potential, or impact of a person's actions, including their capacity, aptitude, talent, or influence)
- concerning objectivity, or how much can or should be inside or outside any one person's experience (fantasies that a person or their actions can be comprehensive, total, impartial; or, by corollary, fantasies of the satisfaction that accompanies adequacy, being good enough)
- concerning violence (fantasies of our own or someone else's destruction and/or survival of destruction)
- concerning the habitation of space (fantasies of proximity or partition; of belonging or feeling at home in one's body or the world; or of what it might mean to get lost or be found)
- concerning the perception of time (fantasies of continuity, or of clearly delimited history, origin, telos; or, by corollary, fantasies that bend a linear perception of time around traumatic experience).

Because fantasies can have unconscious aspects—that is, because they can often go unrecognized in conscious thought or unrealized in social action—psychoanalytic theories have usually found that it makes little sense to hold them to moral designations like good or bad. Nor, for the same reason, is there much insight to be gained from pressing individual fantasies into diagnostic categories like normal or pathological, or from intellectualizing them into cryptonormative distinctions between something utopian like a relational subject or something flavorless like a liberal subject.

What makes fantasy matter analytically isn't its relation to goodness or normalcy—nor, as we saw with "Please Read Me," to any literal truth—so much as its almost invariable expression of honesty. Fantasies always express something that is at some psychic level genuine to the person expressing them. Yes, fantasies can contain lies, falsehoods, misdirections, deceptions, and any number of other conscious or unconscious delusions; yet the appearance of these dishonesties in our fantasies nonetheless tends very much to reflect things we honestly wish or desire. This is so because the unconscious does not abide negation, and so the presence of any refusals or denials is still a presence.[12] Thus, to commit a whole book to the study of fantasy is to commit to the astonishment of fantasy's capacity for expressive honesty—even when fantasy is unconscious, even when the person having a fantasy may not be aware that they are being honest. Listening for fantasy helps us hear the presence of a *something* that enables a person to bear any number of the contradictions attendant upon existence—which is to say, to bear the experience of being a person in the first place.

These preliminary and fairly sweeping points require some elaboration, but before we get there one final preliminary to keep in mind is that, in the case of a public figure like Simone, traffic on fantasy's street runs in both directions. We have already begun to see how our contemporary moment is busy wanting so many contradictory things from her, and so it can become too easy to forget that Simone wanted a lot of contradictory things herself. The pages that follow explore the very real possibility that those things she may have wanted for herself are not identical to the things we may want from her, that her coherence as a fantasy figure stands in tension with her desires and contradictions as an ordinary person. This study will, accordingly, insist on thinking through the space between our fantasies of Nina Simone and Nina Simone's fantasies of Nina Simone.[13]

LET'S WORK IT OUT through an example. For a consummate fantasy of Nina Simone, consider her cameo in the third season of the HBO serial *Insecure*. Protagonist Issa Dee (played by Issa Rae), reluctantly and in the wake of some significant personal setbacks, undertakes the abject task of cleaning out her apartment. To face her work, she dresses in a white T-shirt printed with an image of Nina Simone from the 1969 Jack Robinson photo shoot; the glamorous black-and-white Simone perches on a red rectangle, in which white letters spell out "MOOD."[14]

Issa's sartorial statement expresses a fantasy in that it holds together the contrast between the powerful image on the shirt and the menial tasks of domestic upkeep the woman sporting that image is obliged to perform. It's a scene of fantasy, moreover, because that suspended contrast is emotionally laden—some longing that dwells otherwise unspoken in Issa's mind or body, psyche or soma, finds outward expression, albeit through the fairly minimal gesture of an ironic caption that at once holds open and collapses the space between what is and what could be.[15] It's a scene of fantasy too because it disregards the ordinary rules of linear time, pulling 1969 into 2018, figuring Simone as both Issa's antecedent and her aspiration, fostering multiple connections and kinship between two women who otherwise lived history's permutations and possibilities differently. Above all, it's a scene of fantasy because it expresses itself without claiming or even necessarily knowing precisely what that expression amounts to, making something happen without doing any more than articulating, in Lauren Berlant's needful phrase, "something about something to someone."[16] The fantasy has meaning, but to ask what the fantasy really means is to ask the wrong question; the point, rather, is to recognize its meaningfulness.

Fantasy is a protean thing. Not all fantasies unerringly share these same qualities of suspended contradiction, emotional freight, temporal disregard, and meaningfulness without precision—but, however it happens, whatever its qualities, *fantasy* names the psychic process that secures your sense of the continuity of the world.[17] No matter what form a particular fantasy takes, in other words, that fantasy—its meaningfulness—helps to supply the person having it with coherence in an existential sense. *Fantasy* names the impulse, and at least one means, to continue existing in relation to a world whose phenomenal occurrence is fundamentally indifferent as to whether you do so.[18] More succinctly, we might say that fantasy's impetus and actions—for example, Issa's

||| ● ||||| ● |||

From *Insecure* (2018).

outfit and whatever it helps her to bear—condense into what D. W. Winnicott called the psychological operation of "going on being."[19]

Fantasy can help people to go on being in more ways than one. Even when the term is circumscribed within the fairly specialized registers of psychoanalysis or psychoanalytically inflected discourses, *fantasy* still has multiple referents, including conscious fantasies or daydreams, primal fantasies, and unconscious fantasies like those uncovered in analysis as the structures underlying a manifest content.[20] The German word *Phantasie* means "imagination," though less in the Kantian sense of the faculty of imagining (his term is *Einbildungskraft*) than in the sense of the world of the imagination, its contents and the creative activities that animate it.[21] When Sigmund Freud borrowed the plural, *Phantasien*, for his own writing, he most often used it to refer to daydreams, "scenes, episodes, romances or fictions which the subject creates and recounts to himself [*sic*] in the waking state."[22] In these conscious forms, fantasy tends to be able to work with, or be worked on by, logical thought.[23] Yet Freud also made allowance for the possibility that some fantasy could be unconscious, particularly in cases with children and in his late speculative anthropological writing.[24]

What fantasy isn't is desire. The condition of longing for an object or an outcome, desire is often theorized in terms of repetition, where it does not seek to capture the object of our longing so much as it seeks to recapture what the object of our longing stands in for.[25] Desire is by most accounts a ruthless and primal part of psychic life, and though the objects of our desire may change, desire's force is itself perduring, always running toward a finish line it never crosses, sometimes unfinishing us in the process.[26] Desire exerts its force at both conscious and unconscious levels, fixating on objects that can contraindicate one another, existing in tandem with other desires that contradict. The formula for desire is *who wants what*, and there's no question mark at the end. Its drive, however, belongs to time. The only rule that desire is bound to respect is difference in time: wanting anticipates, and therefore exists in temporal distinction from, satisfaction. Desire's watchword is *yet*.

Indeed, the very possibility of some ultimate satisfaction is, Freud conjectured, where desire comes from.[27] In his account, the body's needs drive our disposition toward things like water, food, and sex, but once we learn that our needs can be satisfied, we find we can long for a satisfaction that we do not yet feel. Enter desire. As proximate to the realm of necessity as this story of desire's origin might seem, once we've mastered the move of wanting something we don't yet have, we can just as easily desire things we don't yet have *and* don't yet need. And insofar as there is very likely more than one thing we don't have and for whose satisfaction we therefore could long, it is possible to desire more than one thing—even contradictory things—at once. Desire motivates, impels. Those impulses are multiple, messy, often uncompromising, and they heed only the distinction between the now-time of longing and the horizon time of satisfaction.

Freud tended to see fantasy's role as desire's helpmeet, its assistance made necessary by the fact that people "cannot subsist on the scanty satisfaction which they can extort from reality."[28] While desire can be ambivalent—it can, literally, pull in opposite directions—fantasy is not usually, in itself, ambivalent at all. On the contrary: fantasy takes the ambivalence of desire and makes it cohere. That coherence is typically comprehended by leaning on spatial metaphors. Freud locates fantasy in a "scene [*szene*]."[29] Jean Laplanche and J.-B. Pontalis call it a "setting [*mise en scène*]."[30] Cora Kaplan calls it a "presence" or even a "favoured spot."[31] For Nicolas Abraham and Maria Torok, it overlays, "mask[s] [*masquer*]."[32] Jacqueline Rose grants it viscosity: "Like blood, fantasy is thicker than water."[33] Joan Wallach Scott regards it as something "staged."[34]

Fantasy, we might say, is the stage on which desire's plot is rehearsed; it dramatizes the actions around wanting and getting or not.[35] Fantasy does more than complement desire by ordering it, however; that ordering can also loosen desire's obeisance to linear time.[36] Fantasy brings temporally distinct things like wanting and satisfaction into coherence by structuring the plot that shows them to coexist, just as the beginning of a story, in order to be identifiable as a beginning, requires lining up next to a middle or at least an end. In so doing, fantasy lends the actions around wanting and getting the coherence of an order or a narrative, in that sense making satisfaction seem real and thus making unsatisfied desires seem bearable.[37] Fantasy hews and orders the unruliness of desire; whether by reining it in or by letting it expand, fantasy gives desire, however provisionally, a shape.

In the earlier example, Issa, like all people, at all moments, wants something, but in this scene donning an image of Nina Simone isn't it; her outfit is not what satisfies her desire. Rather, her sartorial expression plots whatever she happens to desire—to be somewhere else, to be doing something else, to feel something else, to be someone else—into the present experience that is not anything else, that by definition does not contain what it lacks, and therefore that does not satisfy. Her fantasy resolves the distance between what is happening to her and what is not, connecting desire's dots into a line that smooths the roughness off its more jagged edges. Fantasy makes it possible not to be destroyed by the structuring, or else broken and unrepaired, conditions that create deficiencies in our experiences of satisfaction.[38]

Where desire may lead us to a questionable decision, an impulsive act, an indulgent flourish, fantasy picks us up and dusts us off and allows us to say to ourselves—certainly or guiltily or however we best recognize ourselves; the *how* matters—I am not (or, as the case may be, I am) that kind of person, this action is not (or, again, is) part of the pattern, often called a personality, that adds up to me as the person I recognize myself to be.[39] By the time we can narrate a fantasy to ourselves or others—as when, for example, we can imagine the details of a sexual fantasy, a dream job, a best-case scenario, a happy ending— fantasy has already built its bridge between the propelling force of desire and the world of social and linguistic conventionality. Such conscious narration is not, however, a requirement; fantasy's coherence can equally assume, and find articulation in, less linguistic, often more unconscious forms like intuition or vision. It all goes toward the same effect. The world that desire makes is urgent, immediate, but the world that fantasy makes belongs to a more durational timeline.

If all this makes fantasy sound like a generative resource, it may be surprising to recognize how often that generativity is characterized as a defense. In their authoritative dictionary of psychoanalytic vocabulary, Laplanche and Pontalis gloss *phantasy* as an "imaginary scene in which the subject is a protagonist, representing the fulfillment of a wish (in the last analysis, an unconscious wish) in a manner that is distorted to a greater or lesser extent by defensive processes."[40] Laplanche and Pontalis contribute to a consensus view that understands fantasy as proximate to, or even as a species of, defensive process; meanwhile, many more psychoanalytically inclined thinkers grant that in psychic life defensive processes—as the updated term *adaptive behaviors* already suggests—are a feature of the landscape. Nonetheless, both *defensive* and *adaptive* underdescribe the generative power of fantasy to shape people and the worlds they make, to add definition to the lives they live by exploring the ones they don't, to stretch the social baseline of reality, and to work apart from the ordinary rules of time. Clinical language like Laplanche and Pontalis's tells us from the perspective of the analyst what fantasy is, not, as in the more evocative scene of Issa wearing her Nina shirt, how, from the perspective of the person having it, fantasy can be sustaining, meaningful.

The meaningfulness of fantasy expression will be what matters for the pages that follow, but it's important to say up front that meaningfulness does not necessarily point to any unequivocal meaning. While fantasy lends desire the coherence of story and plot, some fantasies like some stories can still be unfiltered, disorganized. They can trail off. . . . There are also edges along which the categories "desire" and "fantasy" seem to blur, as, for example, when the kind of coherence that fantasy provides is itself the object on which your desire sets its sights. Who has not at moments wanted incoherently, wistfully, to feel organized by a coherence that has gone missing or, perhaps, didn't arrive at the expected time—why can't I get a break, why can't I meet someone, why isn't my life more together? Additionally, the relationship between what or how we fantasize and what or how (if anything) we act on or do with that fantasy is open-ended, variable, possibly contradictory. Freud sometimes implied that there was an element of wish to fantasy. Much like dreams—what he called the fulfillments of repressed wishes, shown to us in the theater of our minds as we sleep—fantasies can satisfy our wishes for coherence, even as our desires threaten to make us incoherent.[41] Fantasy, from this vantage, is very much the realm in which desire takes place.

But, you might reasonably ask, where doesn't desire take place? If people carry the potential incoherence of desire everywhere they go, it would follow logically that fantasy would be operative in the background everywhere as well. If you are committed to the notion that there is something called reality that's opposed to fantasy, this may be where you'll want to stop reading.[42] Notwithstanding, saying that fantasy operates everywhere doesn't mean that everything is a fantasy, so much as it means that fantasy is a part of, rather than opposed to, reality. Fantasy constitutes reality not as a conceptual opposite that lends reality definition but as a working partner in a person's psychic apprehension and expression. How much, how explicitly, how intensely fantasy operates in a given instance has to do with any number of factors, including how incoherent a person feels, how great their longing, how many directions their desire happens to be pulling them.

Fantasy may be able to suture a break in the world, but the nature of that break matters too. The world's fracture lines tend to have been designed long in advance of their break by structures that distribute risk and harm unequally, usually in the interest of protecting the powerful. In the United States, for those like Issa in the present tense of this writing, as well as for

III ● IIIII ● III

Nina Simone's reflection
(March 19, 1965). Photo by Sam
Falk/New York Times Co./
Getty Images.

those like Nina Simone who shaped and are shaped by its historical past, the pernicious, self-reproducing, and historically accumulating forces of racial capitalism have been among the more prominent things that etch the world's fault lines into place.[43] These forces enable anyone paying attention to recognize structural racism generally and antiblackness specifically as limiting factors on the horizon of life's possibilities. These forces, accordingly, unavoidably shaped Nina Simone's fantasies, for the same reasons, if not in exactly the same ways, that they shape and will shape Issa's as well as our own fantasies of Nina Simone. All people are capable of fantasy, but history is among the reasons why not all people have the same ones.[44]

ALREADY THERE'S SOME TENSION here. *Fantasy* belongs to a psychological vocabulary that appeals to universals, whereas *Nina Simone* belongs more to a tradition of black feminist thought and expression that critiques such aspirations to universality. The motive behind putting these terms together is that, for the disciplines in which fantasy is studied—psychoanalysis, literature, and critical theory, among them—Simone is not a canonical object and is not, therefore, the inevitable choice.

This study sits with that noninevitability in an effort to align itself with the corrective Hortense Spillers has described her own scholarship as aiming toward: undoing the circumstance by which "the history of black people was something you could use as a note of inspiration but it was never anything that had anything to do with you—you could never use it to explain something in theoretical terms. There was no discourse that it generated, in terms of the mainstream academy that gave it a kind of recognition."[45] Or, as Jennifer Morgan's paraphrase of Spillers's work succinctly summarizes, "There are people there who this entire field has attempted to erase. I just want to put them back out there."[46] That "just," though, indicates nothing simple because apart from some horrifying episodes in medical history, where a person gets stripped down until all that's left is a body, black women are rarely taken by academic knowledge-making practices as the starting point for broad claims about how aspects of being human work.[47] Such precedents alert us to the danger of instrumentalizing Simone, the possibility of reproducing the structures that use black women's lives and labors without compensation.

Fantasies of Nina Simone forces the point by imagining that what's specific or irreducible about Simone's life—including the intersection of her identities as an original genius and a black woman of her generation—is no more an obstacle to generalization than it would be for anyone else's.[48] The complex representational terrain through which Simone moved and struggled will certainly not be treated here as though it were beside the point, but neither will it be treated as if were the whole story.[49] Without ignoring any number of particular or even idiosyncratic aspects to Simone's life, work, and fantasy scenes, this study's method wagers that the detailed work of a case scales up to reveal itself as part of a pattern.

The assumption of case study–based research is that the single example is not a singular example, that instead it offers specifics on the basis of which something more general can be located, teased out, theorized, and tested against subsequent cases. Yet what counts as a legitimate case is always inflected by the consensus norms of the academic disciplines that build on them—what counts as a case, in other words, affects what counts as knowledge.[50] Accordingly, one of the utopian fantasies behind the present study and its choice of Nina Simone as a case is that committed antiracist scholarship could contribute to there being less racism in the structure of our knowledge but not thereby less of the human variety for which, especially in the contemporary United States, race is overwhelmingly, and reductively, the figure.[51] Part of what I understand antiracist scholarship can accomplish is that the full human complexity that shines through a black woman's expressions ought to be able to serve as a basis for knowledge about aspects of broadly human experience wound tight in the skeins of history and feeling. The fantasy here, which is also to say, one of the premises, is that all of us have something to learn from Nina Simone's example.

FANTASIES OF NINA SIMONE draws on existing theories of fantasy, but it assembles an original archive.[52] Necessarily so, as no collector has as yet put together a Nina Simone museum, and no library holds a collection called something like "The Nina Simone Papers," though at the time of this writing such things are in the works.[53] Accordingly, this book's archive consists of Simone's many albums and recordings, concert footage and documentaries, clippings and reviews, photographs in the public domain, published interviews, and declassified FBI documents. Additional consultations included the unofficial Nina Simone Database (http://www.boscarol.com/ninasimone), maintained by Mauro Boscarol; the Nina Simone clippings file at the New York Public Library for the Performing Arts; as well as what's been collected by Getty Images, put on YouTube, or tucked into the cataloged papers of others—Langston Hughes, Amiri Baraka, and James Baldwin among them.

The choice to rely on publicly available materials should make it easy for any reader who wants to follow up on or check my work. But this reliance also aims to defeat the idea that a diary, a letter, or a "private" document could, somehow, tell us the real truth behind the public figure. To say so is not entirely to deny that Simone came of age during a period in the twentieth century when the distinction between public and private selves was constructed and enforced very differently than now, nor entirely to concede the observation that Lisa Simone Kelly makes in *What Happened Miss Simone?*, that even offstage her mother was "Nina Simone 24/7."[54]

Rather, it is to dispute the idea that the archives and artifacts of private life tell the truth of the self—to dispute this idea because it contradicts the likelihood that however much we may construct our public selves, our images, and our self-presentations, in doing so we are, nonetheless, still expressing ourselves, consciously and otherwise. Think about it this way: the person committed to lying about who they are or what they do is not, of course, being truthful; but the act of lying turns out, itself, to be an honest expression of who they are and what they do. Every story told has a true history, even when that story isn't itself true.

THERE IS, INEVITABLY, a personal story. One impetus for centering a study of fantasy on Nina Simone is the Black Lives Matter Global Network (a member of the coalition Movement for Black Lives), a line of whose statement of self-declaration caught my eye sometime about 2014: "We affirm our contributions to this society, our humanity, and our resilience in the face of deadly oppression."[55] The same emphasis on humanity rings through in many subsequent statements. As Alicia Garza argued in her herstory of the movement: "Black Lives Matter is an ideological and political intervention in a world where Black lives are systematically and intentionally targeted for demise.... We've created space for the celebration and humanization of Black lives."[56] Or, again, as Patrisse Khan-Cullors writes in her memoir of the movement's emergence, black people "deserve to be our own gardeners and deserve to have gardeners. Mentors and teachers who bring the sunlight, the rain, the whispered voices above the seedling that says, Grow, baby, grow."[57]

As a humanities-based scholar, a central part of whose career had been devoted to studying, analyzing, and interpreting race in the United States, I found myself, upon reading these sentences, rather totally at a loss to locate what in my scholarly tool kit existed primarily or even effectively to do the work of affirming black humanity. My critical repertoire concentrated instead on analytics around structural racism, investigations into the politics of representation, and histories of racialization. These tools can and do generate all kinds of valuable knowledge, but though they may be compatible with the affirmation of black humanity, they do not exist to do the affirming. By their measure the claim for black humanity is, precisely, a claim.[58] It must be asserted because it cannot, in scholarly terms, be proven.

It's not clear what would solve this problem of proof—it's not inevitable that you think it is a problem in search of a solution—and the project of the book you are reading isn't to try. Yet one underlying assumption of this writing is instead that what can't be proven can still be elaborated.[59] Since about 2014, when I first read the initial Black Lives Matter statement, the interdisciplinary academic field of black studies has produced a robust critical and creative literature that makes, debates, and refines connections between structures of racism and antiblackness, on the one hand, and the claims of black humanity, on the other—a literature that the following pages cite, engage, learn from, and express gratitude toward. Such, then, is one conversation these pages seek to engage, and such is part of the decision to center Nina Simone in this study, for, what cannot be proven not only can be elaborated but also can most definitely be scrutinized in metacritical terms. We can ask why we might already "know" that Nina Simone doesn't exemplify the study of fantasy, why our knowledge has been arranged and received in such a way that would designate looking for a connection as a pretty foolish enterprise. We can wonder why, when disciplinary knowledge encourages us to dismiss foolish things, it so determinedly overlooks the awkward fact that the fool is usually the one who gets to tell the truth. We can and should ask, too, though, with our eye on this question of humanity, what it might take for such writing to create adequate space to really hear what Simone has to say honestly, without cryptically making her speak *as*?[60]

Of course Black Lives Matter is not the only available path to such questions. One might, for example, find one's way there through Sylvia Wynter's critical explorations of the human—the category, she argues persuasively, for which Western thought has over the last four centuries substituted and overrepresented the white, Euro-colonial category of "Man," with the consequence that "all other modes of being human would instead have to be seen not as the alternative modes of being human that they are 'out there,' but adaptively, as the lack of the West's ontologically absolute self-description."[61] Following from Wynter's analysis, one way into the question of what it might mean to investigate fantasy in terms of Nina Simone's humanity would be to draw out some of the alternative modes of being human, "with respect to ourselves and the nature-culture laws that govern our modes of being, of behaving, of mind, or of minding," and which our received ways of regarding fantasy have, therein, occluded.[62] Wynter gestures toward those alternatives, beyond the epistemological norms of rationality and thereby tied to a meaningfulness that isn't captured by scientific explanation, calling them at moments "invention" or "liminal."[63] Developing Wynter's alternatives, Alexander Weheliye has concurred that "enfleshment," the stripping away of multidimensional humanity until all that is left is a fungible body, gives meaning to the modern, capitalist, colonial version of "race," yet he argues that flesh and its "racializing assemblages of subjection . . . can never annihilate the lines of flight, freedom dreams, practices of liberation, and possibilities of other worlds."[64] It's not purely a question of alternatives in Weheliye's account; the way out is through.

This somewhat more dialectical development of Wynter's argument points to the likelihood that humans (let alone the category "the human") contain difference within themselves.[65] That capacity for self-difference, for the self to be in conflict with itself and the world, takes expressive forms like convolution, ambivalence, antagonism, or resistance, and these expressive forms can make the complexities of human psychic experience legible. In less philosophical terms, we might also note that even otherwise mundane activities undertaken while a person goes on being can, and often necessarily do, likewise involve more than one thing happening in the background. Self-difference registers at the levels of play, of gesture, of spontaneity, of creativity, of showing up—or, inversely, in the meaningfulness of failing to. Yes, fantasies can be grandiose, but they can also, like Issa's previously discussed, take the form of ordinary improvisations. Fantasy expression can assume a form no more or less complicated than getting dressed because, whether we consciously intend to or not, we are almost always expressing something.

Analysis of such ordinary expressions of the working of human minds often reveals the ordinary to be meaningful and, in its way, quite extraordinary. It's at this point, though, that things on the ground may stop looking dialectical. The contradictions we humans experience do not inevitably progress, transform, and settle into coherent epistemologies, instead often persisting as muddled truths.[66] Something can be—often is—meaningful without thereby resolving into something in particular. And it is on these lower frequencies that fantasy may speak for you.[67]

FANTASIES ARE SAYING SOMETHING, and so *something* is a significant term for the study of fantasy. Simone evoked *something* at her Westbury Music Fair performance on April 7, 1968, three days after Martin Luther King Jr. was assassinated in Memphis, Tennessee. With lilting alternations between what is specific and what cannot be specified, she told her audience, "I hope that we can provide some kind of, something, for you, this evening, this particular evening, this Sunday evening, at this particular time in 1968."[68] This *something* is a placeholder, a situation without precise specification, a happening on its way to becoming an event.

There are many reasons why a place might need to be held. *Something* can be tentative, an observation whose details stick out against the terrain of the expected or predictable, but whose significance isn't clear.[69] *Something* can also be tentative in a way that stokes excitement, a sense that the "half-formed trajectories are always the most compelling."[70] Or *something* can turn that tentativeness toward risk, toward making a demand, "not [as] the unvarnished truth of the unmediated real but rather something else riskily underdefined. The word that stands in for the pressure on *something* here is *need*."[71] *Something* can hover before consciousness as one of those things "our language has no words to describe, or even to indicate," which nonetheless "are there when the subject is not completely alone."[72] *Something* can name an unfamiliar synthesis of otherwise familiar components, a sign with the "capacity to absorb and organize all of these quite distinct anxieties together."[73] *Something* can instead be alternative, "the ephemeral instantiation of *something better than this*."[74] *Something* can be uncertain, "a frame for assuming responsibility even when one does not know with certainty that one has caused harm."[75] *Something* can also be inflected by longing, holding the place of "what you wanted but couldn't name, the resolute, stubborn desire for an elsewhere and an otherwise that had yet to emerge clearly, a notion of the possible whose outlines were fuzzy and amorphous, exerted a force no less powerful and tenacious."[76] Tentative, risky, demanding, hovering, alternative, unfamiliar, uncertain, desirous: Simone's "something" is any, maybe all, of these. The way she evokes *something* is the same way these pages will: to knowingly draw a circle around some of what can't be known.

When it comes to other people's fantasies, *something* is a way to hold the place of what isn't ours to know. Fantasy is an ineluctable part of psychic experience, and psychic experience, in V. N. Vološinov's impressively compact summary, "is something inner that becomes outer," just as social experiences, like language and ideology, are "something outer than becomes inner."[77] *Subjectivity*—that lofty philosophical word for the experiential condition of being a person—amounts to the weaving together of the inner and outer, the intrinsic and the extrinsic, the personal and the impersonal. The premise of psychoanalysis is that this weaving can be interpreted and discoursed upon, just as the premise of much humanistic scholarship is that any text can be.[78] (*Text*: from the Latin *textus* "style or texture of a work," literally "thing woven," from the past participle stem of *texere* "to weave, to join, fit together").

It's tempting to think interpretation looks like unweaving. A number of bread-and-butter knowledge-making activities instruct that any text can be read closely by isolating its most elemental words or notes or brushstrokes—the idea being that understanding its composition will tell us about its meaning. This method has good uses, but nonetheless the study of people runs it head-on into its limit, for although people can be read closely and their most elemental components, the inner and the outer, can be identified, those components cannot really be isolated.

Clinical psychoanalysis faces this challenge through the dynamic relationship between the analyst and the analysand, the doctor and the patient, which usually takes for granted that not all of a patient's interior world is, or is representable in terms of, language or narrative, and that analysis therefore must rely on the meanings made in the dance of transference and countertransference.[79] So let me be as clear as possible in stating that this clinical method is not mine: I am not, nor would I ever claim to be, a practicing analyst—Nina Simone's or anyone else's. Nor did I ever meet her, see her in person, or share space with her. Any relation between Simone and me is and will have to remain a fantasy of mine.

Instead, I am approaching Simone much as I have approached many of the other historical objects I have written about in my erstwhile career as a book historian—and, I would wager, much as many historians, literary critics, and other scholars who study texts approach their objects, and their fantasies of them, as well. The unusual challenge here is that my object was also a subject, a person. Accordingly, the main difference between this study and others I have elsewhere attempted isn't in approach so much as in, as it were, the final analysis: how well defended any interpretations of Simone can be.[80] It's true that a person is a weaving together of psychic experience and social or ideological signs, yet equally true that the meaningfulness of that relation does not depend on their being disentangled—often, in fact, depends on their *not* being disentangled.

How can we understand people if we can't unweave the ways they have been woven together? At some level, of course, we can't. There are things about other people that will always remain theirs, irreducible to them. There is a level of precision at which our knowledge of others rarely if ever arrives, because people are so unavoidably different from each other.[81] However, there are also aspects of other people that approximate aspects of our own experience and understanding, aspects about which we can therefore make solid guesses, thanks to some well-practiced tools like sense, observation, empathy, imagination. What results is a level at which our knowledge of others is approximate, general, but still accurate. How can we understand people if we can't take them apart in the ways they have been put together? We can commit to accuracy without precision. We can know *something*.

ANOTHER WORD FOR *something* might be *symptom*. The latter word belongs to a storied Marxist tradition, at the center of which sat Louis Althusser in the first months of 1965, reading *Capital* with students at the École Normale Supérieure, not only between the covers of Marx's volume but also, as he writes in the introduction to the book this seminar fostered, "transparently, in the dramas and dreams of our history."[82] Althusser's poetic opening prefigures the method of symptomatic reading that subsequent pages of his book develop, a reading that "divulges the undivulged event in the text it reads, and in the same movement relates it to *a different text*, present as a necessary absence in the first."[83] Symptomatic reading pursues a method of identifying these undivulged events—also called "lacunae"—in the text before rereading the same text again in their terms, a "second reading [that] presupposes the existence of *two texts*, and the measurement of the first against the second. But what distinguishes this new reading from the old one is the fact that in the new one the *second text* is articulated with the lapses in the first text."[84]

Symptomatic reading in Althusser's sense is not, as it is sometimes mistaken to be, the more general operation of uncovering meanings that are "hidden, repressed, deep, and in need of detection and disclosure by an interpreter"; its energy, rather, is more dialectical, a way of holding space for what history could not yet articulate, the future world that the present contains inchoate.[85] When Althusser writes of *meaning*, he does not use the usual French noun *sens* or the verb *signifier*; rather, the phrase translated as *meaning* is *vouloir dire*, literally, what the text *wants to say*.[86] Symptomatic reading holds the place of something.

There is every indication that Althusser and Simone were unaware of each other, even though it happens that she made her first tour of Europe in the summer of 1965 shortly after Althusser's seminar on *Capital* wound down. And though this coincidence may invite idle speculation as to the time, street, or café in which they could have brushed past each other like so many of history's strangers, it nevertheless remains the case that it was not Althusser who brought Simone to Marx, but Lorraine Hansberry. By all accounts the friendship between these two women was significant for each of them, and by Simone's own account, she and Hansberry "never talked about men or clothes or other such inconsequential things when we got together. It was always Marx, Lenin and revolution—real girls' talk."[87]

Citations to this last line appear endlessly in the scholarship on both Simone and Hansberry, and the line itself ranks easily among the most quoted

||| ● ||||| ● |||

"Singing in small group with
Lorraine Hansberry and Nina
Simone" (1963). Music Division,
New York Public Library.

that Simone ever wrote, spoke, or sang. Its arch irony is perhaps one reason that it attracts the attention of scholars, as the discourse for which Marx and Lenin synecdochically stand by nearly no other account goes by the name "girls' talk." The fact that nevertheless this discourse was what these two "girls" talked about—the fact, in other words, whereby Simone's quip at once holds open and collapses the space between what is and what could be—suggests that we may be proximate to a scene of fantasy.

Or, likely, more than one. Simone's fantasies may be here, but so may fantasies attached to and projected on Simone. The scholarly repetition of the line rereads Simone's fantasy wish, identifying the contradiction between "Marx, Lenin and revolution" and "girls' talk," and so marking the present absence that Simone's irony (creates, yes, but mainly) suspends. This abundance of quotation, in other words, performs an aggregative kind of symptomatic reading as it holds space for a future where "Marx, Lenin and revolution" would actually be the stuff of "girls' talk." Insofar as our present is not yet that future, quoting the line may also perform something of the scholars' own wishes to turn Simone's irony a few degrees closer toward truth by holding on to her initial fantasy and perpetuating it, making it last through our acts of citation, iteration, and, quite possibly, pleasure. The fact that when we're done, the dialectical turn isn't complete, and Simone's irony has not alchemically transformed into accuracy, doesn't make it not true, not meaningful. It still means *something*.

FANTASIES OF NINA SIMONE unfolds three closely related arguments. The first follows from a fairly straightforward historical observation. Beginning about 1968, the substance of Nina Simone's performance and recording material shifted away from early twentieth-century songbook standards, folk ballads, and jazz covers, as performed by an array of artists, and toward rearrangements and covers of songs by contemporary artists (including George Harrison, the Bee Gees, Randy Newman, Leonard Cohen, Pete Seeger, and especially Bob Dylan), nearly all of whom where white men. This shift takes place in adjacency to climactic moments in the mid-twentieth-century struggle for civil rights; in proximity to the dissolution of Simone's marriage to her second husband and full-time manager, Andy Stroud; and on the approach to the height of the international fame she achieved in her lifetime. My interpretation of this shift will be that Simone was exploring something about voice and authority, something about speaking to and through the power that adheres in race and gender privilege. Following quickly on these developments, beginning about 1971, her work evolves again, toward exploring Caribbean, African, and Afro-diasporic music, imagery, and sound (including a new emphasis on percussion, significant covers of three songs by Exuma, and multiple tributes to Bob Marley). I interpret all these shifts in her performance and recording material as fantasmatic expressions of her wanting—attempts at pursuing *something*.[88] For reasons that should already be clear, the emphasis will be on the act of exploration, not what it leads to. This first argument concentrates into the sections of this book titled "Covering," "1972," and "Obeah."

Second, this study makes a historiographical argument. In the past two decades or so, and as we have already begun to see, Simone has been the subject of an astonishing number of rereleased, remastered, and remixed albums and compilations, as well as biographies; films; cameos in theater, television, and fiction; scholarly studies; sound and music samples; multimedia citations; and a small cottage industry of artisanal crafts (shirts, pillows, posters, mugs, pins, keychains) sold and traded on websites like eBay and Etsy. Nearly all of these texts—here the previously mentioned example from *Insecure* is typical—identify Simone as a black woman, a powerful symbol of black womanhood, and, especially, an antecedent, as someone ahead of her time, as someone whose time has finally come. That is to say, I interpret these contemporary texts about Simone too as expressing fantasies, ones that allow them to locate themselves in the present by anchoring race and gender identities and related forms of social power in a usable past. The necessity and meaningfulness of these contemporary fantasies is not up for debate, but the following pages seek to unpack and understand the discrepancies between our contemporary fantasies of Nina Simone and Nina Simone's own historical fantasies of Nina Simone. Or, to put the issue in more concrete terms, these pages aim to sit with the likelihood that Nina Simone, in the wake of any number of significant personal setbacks, didn't have among her historically available resources a Nina Simone T-shirt to help set and sustain the atmosphere of her mood. This second, historiographical argument, then, will gather significance in this story from its tension with the first, historical argument. It is most clearly highlighted in the sections of this book titled "Audience" and "Fantasies."

The third argument frames both the historical and the historiographical points, and it concerns interpretation. Fantasies are meaningful—in the most basic sense, they contain something, and what they contain is usually significant somehow, more than incidental—but it would not be correct to insist that knowing what a fantasy *means* is necessary to its significance. Fantasies can be unconscious, unrealized, dreamed, misrecognized, denied, disavowed, or simply forgotten, all without mattering less for it. Armed with a meaningfulness whose precise meaning may be unavoidably obscure, fantasies can upset the more positivist or even descriptive claims about *what happened* that historically minded scholars and biographers tend to want to be able to make. Fantasy thereby differs from a lot of scholarly knowledge in that for scholarly knowledge to count as knowledge it must typically be social, shared. In the realm of knowledge we often speak of *explanation, demonstration, interpretation.* In the realm of fantasy, these things don't apply in the same ways. This third argument sustains the most focus in the early section of this book titled "Biography" but is threaded throughout.

These three arguments make up the backbone of *Fantasies of Nina Simone*, but by design they do not drive this study at a page-by-page level. The pace and motive of these pages are instead exploratory, and their aim is to raise questions, develop associations, and consider possible connections in the ranging and arguable evidence of another person's life and work. Nothing here is meant to be the last word on Nina Simone or anything else, and the success of this writing should be measured by whether some of what it suggests helps animate more sustained investigations down the road.

LASTLY, A NOTE on the form, which, you have probably begun to notice, fragments the larger narrative into chunks of varying length, grouped by theme. This chunkiness tries to capture something about the ways that fantasy's value is sustaining without necessarily being durational, even though these fragments do, by design, add up to a longer narrative, a larger interpretation, or rather a series of them. Nonetheless, it seemed worthwhile to pursue a short form that "gesture[s] to the so-much-more out there," that doesn't hide in the template of three or five chapters of six thousand to eight thousand words, each chapter with a coherent argument, a roughly equal number of endnotes, and a frame that disputes another critic or else claims fidelity to a grand theorist.[89] Such generic parameters serve a purpose, but one that is not identical to, and may not indeed be conducive toward, the present study's goal of trying to hold meaningfulness without trying to resolve exactly what it might mean. Therefore, it felt important to clear some space in this writing at a formal level, which would let interpretations more organically assume their size and shape instead of deciding long in advance which confines would make them legible. Imagine, if you will, that the form of these narrative chunks demonstrates an approach.

The stakes of this approach follow from the fact that if fantasy is psychically inevitable and unconsciously omnipresent for all people, that would include this author, me; and if fantasy bears ambivalence and contradiction, that would include this writing, mine. One contention behind the formal choices in *Fantasies of Nina Simone* is that even highly successful, generically normative works of scholarship and criticism are nonetheless domains in which fantasy successfully holds together subjective contradictions, though with the result of often making the presence of fantasy disappear.[90] The goal of writing in a formally nonstandard way is to see what happens when one makes that invisible labor visible.

The periodic recourse to first person in these pages likewise marks my attempt to call out some of how, when, and where my own scenes of fantasy get imposed on the fantasies already, inevitably lodged in the archive. It accordingly feels relevant to acknowledge at the outset that the lived experience of being black is not mine, that there are things about Nina Simone I can see but things I don't or couldn't or, more to the point, things that are not mine to see. Said the other way around, undoubtedly my own personal contradictions and the fantasies that resolve them are part of what led me to gravitate toward and identify with the moments in Nina Simone's life and career where she gravitates toward, arguably identifies with, but in any case gives voice to, kinds of power and authority that don't line up with the social consequences of her biographical accidents, either.[91] Part of my fantasy of Nina Simone, part of what I slowly realized I was trying to write my way into, was an identification with her own proclivity for cross-racial and cross-gendered identifications.[92] If this announcement makes you, the reader, feel as though you're being held hostage by my, the writer's, ego, the point here is something like: that would have been true even if I had not announced as much. It is a curious thing that academic writing often seems most self-indulgent at the moments it is being honest about its motives.

Be that as it may, and despite this awareness of my positionality as a writer, this writing proceeds with the assumption that what's true about me in this case is likely true about people who aren't me too: that what's at stake in any of our fantasies of Nina Simone is us as much as her. Our desire to know another person—to be adjacent to them, to be intimate with them, to listen to them, to celebrate them, to recover them, to narrate them, or even to condemn them—tangles them with us in complicated (sometimes mutual, sometimes very one-sided) fantasies. The point of what follows is not to speak for Nina Simone; rather, it is to understand how, among Nina Simone's many other gifts, she has become someone who enables us to speak for ourselves.

Biography

There are obvious reasons not to confuse ourselves with Nina Simone. Her biography is, like any biography, populated with circumstances and accidents that are or at least became irreducibly hers. The very name "Nina Simone" was itself a kind of accident, called into being only when Eunice Kathleen Waymon's narrative of upward mobility was leveling off in the summer of 1954, and she found herself playing a regular nightclub gig in Atlantic City. This wasn't the drama she wanted to star in, so she chose to recast.

Twenty-one years earlier, the person who would take the stage at the Midtown Bar and Grill under the name Nina Simone had been born, on February 21, 1933, in Tryon, North Carolina, the sixth child and third daughter of Mary Kate Waymon, a domestic worker and ordained minister in the Christian Methodist Episcopal Church, and John Divine "J. D." Waymon, a former musician, handyman, and sometime small-business owner who suffered from persistent health problems. Very early in life Eunice displayed prodigious musical skill, recognition of which led to the creation of a local scholarship fund so that this talented but underresourced child could have professional piano lessons.

Like many upward mobility stories, hers tried for a first. Hoping to become the country's first black classical-trained concert pianist, she studied for a year at Juilliard after graduating as high school valedictorian in 1949 but failed her entrance audition at the Curtis Institute of Music in Philadelphia in 1951, on the basis of what she said all the way to her grave was discrimination. A one-take, favor-to-a-friend recording of George Gershwin's "I Loves You, Porgy" in 1954 led to an album deal with Bethlehem Records and subsequently to multialbum contracts with Colpix, then Dutch Phillips, then RCA Victor. For a while she thought she was still training to be a classical musician. Only gradually did the accident become the plot. Managed for a decade by her second husband, Andy Stroud, Simone became a popular musician, between 1959 and 1993 releasing more than thirty live and studio albums, routinely doing as many as three a year during the 1960s while also maintaining a consistent touring schedule.[1] In 1962, she gave birth to her only child, Lisa.

The trajectory of the narrative shifted again. Beginning in the early 1960s, partially through her friendships with Lorraine Hansberry, James Baldwin, and Betty Shabazz, Simone became immersed in the civil rights movement and later the Black Power movement. After about 1964, her musical output shifted determinedly in this direction, providing a soundtrack for the Black Power generation as it was turning the volume down on canonical protest songs from the 1950s. After a decade of fierce and vocal activism, recording, and touring, which exacted their costs, Simone left the United States in September 1970, living first in Barbados, then Liberia, Switzerland, the Netherlands, Paris, and, after 1993, Southern France, where she died on April 21, 2003, at age seventy, from complications of breast cancer.

Simone herself put all but these final details together in the account she gave to the British filmmaker Stephen Cleary, with whom she cowrote *I Put a Spell on You: The Autobiography of Nina Simone*, published in 1991.[2] This memoir is notable, not least because its emphasis on her early poverty, later financial exigency, and general disdain for popular music seems deliberately to depart from the prevailing conventions among those of her generation for representing the life of a black entertainer.[3] Yet however carefully crafted this self-portrait was, its account didn't exactly become the definitive one.[4] Simone's death a dozen years later was followed with a spate of biographies, including David Brun-Lambert's breezy *Nina Simone: The Biography* (2009) and Nadine Cohodas's thorough if somewhat impatient *Princess Noire: The Tumultuous Reign of Nina Simone* (2010).[5] These were preceded by several illustrated short tributes, including the memoir/biography hybrid *Nina Simone: Break Down and Let It All Out* (2004), written by longtime friends Sylvia

Hampton and David Nathan; *Nina Simone, "Black Is the Color..."* (2005), a mostly pictorial tribute compiled by ex-husband Andy Stroud; and *Nina Simone*, by Kerry Acker (2004), a volume for juvenile readers in the Women in the Arts series published by Chelsea House. This first wave of biographies was succeeded by A. Loudermilk's thoughtful review essay in the *Journal of International Women's Studies* (2013), Jennifer Warner's compact *Keeper of the Flame* (2014), and Alan Light's *What Happened, Miss Simone? A Biography* (2016), a print tie-in to the Netflix documentary with which it shares a name. Most recently four volumes have appeared in French—two novelizations (Gilles Leroy's *Nina Simone, roman* [2010] and Sophie Adriansen's *Nina Simone, mélodie de la lutte* [2022]) and two biographies (Mathilde Hirsch and Florence Noiville's *Nina Simone: Love Me or Leave Me* [2019] and Frédéric Adrian's more tightly balanced *Nina Simone* [2021]).

The biographies are favorable and often honest about the complexities of their subject. There's a lot to be learned from them, and Simone's autobiography in particular offers material that's worth listening to. One major limitation of these biographies, however, has to do with the ends toward which their genre makes them push. Biographies traffic in facts, things that can be consciously, explicitly, socially known—which is also to say, shared. But it is not facts so much as accidents that accumulate into a life. When a biographer looks back on an accident, knowing full well that it was, in retrospect, a turning point, it can be difficult to appreciate how much it may, at the time, to the person experiencing it, have looked or felt like something more open-ended.

Biographical facts aren't usually allowed to be subjective in this way, even though the experience of the life that a biography aims to capture almost inevitably was. It gets especially murky because the subjective experience of a person's life often contains elements of the lives that person didn't live, as when we're animated by the thing we didn't do, the opportunity we waited for that never came, the connection we didn't make, the better world that wasn't, the decision we regret, the one that got away.[6] As when Simone didn't get admitted to the Curtis Institute, or didn't become the first black classical-trained concert pianist.

The most subjective parts of a person's experience sometimes show up in the artifacts that make up the biographer's archive: letters, images, and recordings, performances, declarations, and testimonies. But they show up there as traces—of doubts, hopes, moods, emotions, illusions, dreams, aspirations, desires—and these kinds of subjective experiences, like most subjective experiences, don't archive well. Their traces can easily get diluted, or even lost, as biography turns artifacts into story. The problem doesn't register just

IN RECITAL . . .

EUNICE WAYMON, PIANIST

NEW CENTURY AUDITORIUM
One Twenty-four South Twelfth Street
Friday Evening, February 19th, 1954
at 8:30 o'clock

SUBSCRIPTION   (INCLUDING TAX) $1.30

SPONSORS
**Philadelphia Branch N. A. N. M., Inc.
and Young People's Music Club**

||| ● ||||| ● |||

Advertising card for a piano
recital performed by Eunice
Waymon at age twenty-one
(1954). Collection of the
Smithsonian National Museum
of African American History
and Culture.

as method but also in the craft. As no less skilled a writer than C. L. R. James once put it, "The realities to which the historian is condemned will at times simplify the tragic alternatives with which he is faced."[7] Like historians, biographers are charged with narrating the meaning of events in terms of how they ended, where they led. Theirs is the unenviable task of molding subjective experiences into the shape of a woman's life.

Relevant too is the very long history, especially in the United States, of consigning black writers to the genre of life writing. Dating all the way back to the eighteenth century, white audiences and publishers have often studiously ignored the evidence of black creativity and instead made precious little room in official literary worlds for black people to tell stories about anything other than themselves. And those selves, moreover, have often been narrowly edited to emphasize the boundaries that might discipline black experience in a white supremacist world—from pious platitudes to near-pornographic spectacles of black pain.

None of this is to say that black writers, and indeed many black women, haven't found their voices, whether in creative genres (including friends of Simone's such as Lorraine Hansberry or Toni Morrison) or by reclaiming life writing for their own purposes (including contemporaries of Simone's such as Angela Davis or Anne Moody). Nor is it to say that biography can't be redeemed. It's more to insist that not only has biography, generically, made it difficult to register some of the more minor but still meaningful experiences in a person's life, but that biography, historically, has made it even more difficult if one happens to have been, as Nina Simone was, an upwardly mobile black woman genius in the twentieth-century United States. That the biographers do a good job doesn't counter the limits of their enterprise.

FACTS PROVE TO BE a strange measure of a life, and few lives really steer into a single territory designated as fact or fiction. Living phenomena have a way of blunting these edges. If someone tells you a lie, for instance, it would of course not be true, but the fact that they told it always would. That thing to which a lie refers may be verified externally and found to be false, but the expression of the lie—like all expression—is always immanent to itself, enacted in time and space that we can't take back. Yes, we can dispute the veracity of an expression, like whether something happened or what something means, and we can try to amplify its effect or mitigate its consequences, but we cannot undo the expression if we agree that it's been done.

Something other than biography in its usual sense, then, is more likely to be sufficient to the task of understanding someone like Nina Simone, someone whose language often mattered not just for what it said but how. Put down the biographies and listen to the opening lines of Simone's cover of George Gershwin's "My Man's Gone Now," and you can tell immediately that she expresses so much more than her words literally say. Unmistakably, in these sounds, there is feeling and longing and needing and wanting, a world that is here and maybe a world that isn't.

One of Simone's most circulated songs, this same recording of "My Man's Gone Now," from *Nina Simone Sings the Blues* (1967), appears on at least fifteen different compilations and reissues. It is iconic in its representation of who she was and what she did. As it happens, this cover is itself an accident, a warm-up or wind-down, spontaneously thrown off during an RCA recording session in 1967, captured in one take. Nadine Cohodas quotes the session producer Danny Davis, who praised Simone's "stamina to deliver with even more intensity and spirit a rare, perfect performance."[8] Alan Light calls it "a spare and languid reading," part of a set "that encompassed blues history."[9] Both, in other words, succumb to the biographer's temptation to take the once-off of the perfect performance as what matters. Neither considers that because it can and did happen once, it might have happened many more times, and the part where it didn't therefore means something too—at the general level of fact that it didn't, but also in the moment-to-moment choices that, only retrospectively, add up to that general fact. The biographers' words capture what the performance is for us, but not how the performance felt for Simone. And it's not their fault, really, so much as what they signed up for. Biography often requires that facts weigh more than feelings.

Where else can we look to begin to establish a rapport between what is said or known or documented, on the one hand, and what is only felt or (what oddly often counts as the same thing) unknown, on the other? In the case of "My Man's Gone Now," Simone's version is not necessarily, in and of itself, a fantasy expression, but her act of singing it is one place to look for fantasy's traces. Singing may also be a better candidate for the evidence of fantasy than writing or other creative acts, at least inasmuch as a performance has a phenomenological element—something more than words or music, something singular, however maximal or minimal, however spontaneous or rehearsed. This one-of-a-kindness that imbues any performance comes from somewhere other than the source material, other than the song as it is written. Follow that iteration to fantasy's door.

||| ● ||||| ● |||

PAYING ATTENTION TO FANTASY can raise questions about our objectivity. Fantasy isn't self-evidently present in any archive, not the way that more artifactual elements are thought to be. How can we know that what appears to be traces of Nina Simone's fantasy aren't in fact projections of our own? Certainly, as we wander away from the facts, toward fantasy, things can get subjective in more than one way. And if we let things get subjective, we might in the end reposition what we're studying so that it sits at an angle that reflects back the good light in which we'd prefer to see ourselves. In so doing, we might distort the object of our study and the knowledge that our study makes about it. We might.

But what's the actual alternative here? Making knowledge isn't the same as making truth. We can treat our projections responsibly without pretending—indeed, by not pretending—that *responsibly* means *objectively*. The things we're trying to know about Nina Simone can never be known perfectly, and can never quite be known in the way she knew them, because we're the ones trying to do the knowing, because our ways of knowing are ineluctably partial, and because, as we'll see later on, ethical listening requires that we make room for some amount of opacity.[10] To insist otherwise, to insist that we really can know something totally, participates in its own fantasy—the one where reality brooks no alternative meanings.[11]

At moments, as we study Nina Simone, we may want to nail down what happened and guess about what it might mean, as the biographers do; and there are good reasons why we might want that. But at other moments, if we're going to capture the *how* and not just the words, we should try to listen for the fantasies that don't become biography's facts. We should listen for what Hortense Spillers has called "the singer's *attitude* toward her material, her audience, and, ultimately, her own ego status in the world as it is interpreted thorough form."[12] And by implication: we should listen too for the parts of her unconscious the ego may not know, as it is interpreted through form as well as whatever doesn't accede to form. Nothing is just about what it adds up to, important as the latter may be. And so our task is in not letting what things add up to blot out the something that is part of the process even if it doesn't factor into the final equation.

This, as I would like to imagine it, may have been what attracted Simone to recording a cover of a Richie Havens song that begins:

Step out in the night
When you're lonely
Listening for the sounds
That your ears don't hear[13]

This, as I would like to understand it, is an ethics of listening.

LISTENING TO THE SPACES between words also means we'd be following Simone's lead. At least, what goes unsaid is something she notices again and again in her autobiography, *I Put a Spell on You*. Most frequently it is associated with her father. She recalls that when she was a child, for example, "I saw how Daddy was when he was in pain, how he kept his feelings close to his heart and lived alone with his hurt."[14] Or, again, "Daddy knew how much harder things were because he was black but he never mentioned it to anyone."[15] On her wedding day, it became clear that J. D. Waymon didn't appear to much like Andy Stroud, but "he didn't say anything . . . when we got alone together I asked him about it. . . . He kind of looked away and said if I was sure then go ahead, he wouldn't say anything more about it."[16] After she was married, when her autophile father came to visit and she let him drive her Mercedes, "he didn't say much, just sucked his teeth as he felt the power of the car, smiled and started to whistle."[17] In Simone's telling, her father wove language and feeling together, but inversely, so that silence became meaningful insofar as it was a way that intensities, whether of pain or pleasure, found their expression.

Though *I Put a Spell on You* most often associates silence with Simone's father, it seems, to some extent, to have been an aspect of her natal family life more generally, and particularly with regard to her consciousness around race. She says she knew, for example, that her mother wanted her to become the country's first classically trained black concert pianist, but she also insists that her mother never said such a thing: "At home we never talked about race, ever. It was the great unspoken that we lived with but never brought out into the open."[18] It's a familiar enough domestic scene: mother and father, each not saying all of what they mean, both complicit in a silence so loud that their daughter could hear it plainly. Intervals of speech and silence become a pattern, a rhythm, to which domestic life moves. Silence negotiates as much as speech does. (*Negotiate*: from the Latin for "business," literally meaning "not leisure": silent negotiation, business as usual.)

In her 1991 telling, Simone retrospectively granted agency to her childhood silences: "I had not made a connection between the fights I had and any wider struggle for justice because of how I was raised: the Waymon way was to turn away from prejudice and live your life the best you could, as if acknowledging the existence of racism was in itself a kind of defeat."[19] In addition to being expressive of emotional intensities, silence also enacts the power of making meaning in a far less intense, more denotative register. Silence, in such cases, amounts to the opposite of nothing, and as such takes up the kind of space that can contour a boundary or define the parameters of a something. Silence in these examples wields the power of what doesn't happen, and what doesn't happen is something too.

LISTENING FOR SILENCE is one way to register how meaningful expressions aren't always literal. But words aren't always literal, either. *I Put a Spell On You* reverses the story of Simone's father's silence on the occasion sometime around 1970 when she overheard him speaking a little too much, in a conversation with her baby brother and sometime collaborator, Samuel Waymon:

> I stood there in the dark and listened to Daddy tell lie after lie after lie. It wasn't true, none of it, and even Sam, the baby, the youngest, had eyes and ears and a brain enough to know what Momma did and how she worked day after day. I stood there numb, unable to believe that Daddy would try to deceive Sam in this way. Daddy, who never lied about anything.
>
> I had been misused and cheated all my life, and up to that point the one person I could rely on had been my father. The realization that he lied as well, like everybody else in the world, just crushed me. I felt the same disgust as when I heard the news of the Birmingham church bomb, and like then it was the final straw. I had spent years fighting for a lost cause; my marriage was over and my future was uncertain. After all the work I had done I didn't have financial security, and I couldn't even find out where most of the money I earned had gone. Of all the people I respected most had tricked and betrayed me—and now here was my father, who never lied, never, doing the same thing. If I had had a gun in my hand I might have killed him right there where he sat. As it was I walked into the kitchen and told him he wasn't my Daddy any more because I disowned him. From that moment I had no father. Then I walked out. Daddy didn't say a word.[20]

Simone was listening to her father talk, but what are we listening to in her telling? One answer has to do with how the part of this story that's based in facts gets torqued by Simone's expression of how this moment feels. I don't mean that she tells us some of what she feels, although she does. I mean that Simone's language, *how* she tells the story, seems to express something in excess of what the words literally say.

There's the way the grammar buckles. These paragraphs are full of Simone's outrage, but the nature of her father's offense is inexactly described. She faults him for lies, but she also sees, fairly, that he lies "like everybody else in the world." It seems unlikely that a woman of nearly forty would never before have considered the possibility that her father, like anyone, occasionally fibbed or exaggerated or claimed credit for something he didn't do. It's not hard to imagine that even good fathers sometimes rely on their children to prop up stories of paternal glory, fictional or otherwise. Yet at least at the level of expression, what's not hard to imagine congeals into something that isn't expressed in a straightforward way. "Of all the people I respected most had tricked and betrayed me—and now here was my father" conjoins clauses paratactically, jumbling coordination and subordination. The logic and, at this moment, the grammar of these paragraphs struggle toward intelligibility. The gravity of the episode is clearly enormous, and yet, at a literal level, what is at stake doesn't quite get said.

There are also the suggestions that meanings may be superimposed. Describing herself confronting a series of stresses, Simone's stated anxieties about this moment of her life ("my marriage was over and my future was uncertain") are complicated by a simile: the comparison she makes to the bombing of the 16th Street Baptist Church in Birmingham and the resultant murder of Addie Mae Collins (aged 14), Carole Robertson (aged 14), Cynthia Wesley (aged 14), and Denise McNair (aged 11). Simone's syntax compares that moment to this one in terms of her reaction ("I felt the same disgust as when . . ."). Maybe that's all she meant—extreme disgust. But if the comparison is over-determined, if there's more than one thing happening in her expression, there may be something unstated but meaningfully imposed here as well, such that the comparison is to the action and not just her reaction. If that's the case, it would seem that she is characterizing her father's comments not merely as explosive and destructive but, more pointedly, as harmful to little girls.

What we're listening for, in other words, is how literalness doesn't monopolize truth. Simone's language in this passage strains in a couple of ways, but given the severity of the pain evoked here, who can blame her? We might even posit her linguistic imprecision as an expression itself, a means by which something churning inside finds a way to get out, to make itself known, whether she fully knows it or not. However, what that something is exactly remains elusive. The associations I'm teasing out are my associations, ways it makes sense to me to connect what I hear when I listen to what Simone said, using some of her words to patch a hole that other of her words opened up. I could easily be making a mistake, and there is no way to find out if I'm correct or not. So let correctness not be the measure. We can't know why her language and feelings happen the way they do or where they come from, and, that said, we'd be a bit callous to insist that we had to know exactly what something means before we could acknowledge that it was meaningful. Suffice it to say: *something happened.*

Anytime anyone puts feelings into words, they're substituting something that can't exactly be communicated (something inner) for something that more exactly can (something outer). It all rides on the "exactly." Some thoughts are governed by concept metaphors, making them unthinkable without the words we have for them.[21] Other words get us efficiently enough where we need to go, while still others get displaced, only skimming the asymptote of a thought or feeling that cannot fully be externalized in its own guise. This quality of substitution that lives in language means that all we can ever know about a moment like this one is that it expresses some something, some excess whose more-than-literal content is part of why literal language breaks down. Simone's words express a meaningfulness that we can register without needing to know exactly what they mean—without thinking that *knowing exactly* is what would count as knowing.

||| ● ||||| ● |||

FANTASY EXPRESSIONS MAY not be literally true, but they are almost in-variably honest. The story that Simone tells in *I Put a Spell on You* about the rupture with her father has the aura of fantasy's operation not because it didn't happen, and not because it is in some sense *merely* a fantasy, but rather because her conflicting feelings in the moment add up to a meaningfulness that appears to strain the ordering impulses—in this case, the logic and the grammar—of her usual modes of self-expression. Fantasy's traces appear to move from background to foreground at the moment that it's working most strenuously to make things cohere.[22] We saw in this example that Simone's parataxis aligns her with vulnerable positions—little girl, dead girl—which may bespeak some proximity to a pain that is expressed without being explained, pain that belongs to this moment but possibly without originating there. This expression of vulnerability peeks out between words that are apparently trying to say something else. Indeed, the position she most boldly claims here is not a vulnerable one but an aggressive one, "If I had had a gun in my hand I might have killed [my father] right there where he sat."[23] Her aggression, her bold-ness, complements the more vulnerable adjacent claim with which, in content and expression, it contrasts. It's not that she *really* means one thing and not the other; not that the anger is a screen for the pain or vice versa. No, it's that the desires in these claims contradict, but fantasy pushes their expression toward coherence.

It cannot be overstated how ordinary a feature of psychic life this kind of contradiction is: a *something* that resolves unto itself. None of this is a prob-lem, and yet interpretation so often volunteers to solve it.

BIOGRAPHY STRAINS TO CAPTURE silence, but it also strains to capture excess—those moments that feel or sound large to our experience because we know even as they're happening what they're larger than. Simone certainly tuned in to both frequencies. And she spoke about at least one time they came together, on September 15, 1963, when she learned of the bombing of the 16th Street Baptist Church: "It was more than I could take, and I sat struck dumb in my den like St Paul on the road to Damascus," and then, "An hour later I came out of my apartment with the sheet music for 'Mississippi Goddam' in my hand. It was my first civil rights song, and it erupted out of me quicker than I could write it down."[24] Music "erupts" out of her "dumb"-ness, an alternative to speech, a way of saying something. As if the music correctly answered a question that had been asked of someone else in a room down the hall.

The best-known recording of this song comes from a live performance at Carnegie Hall, one of Simone's three in that venue between March 21 and April 6, 1964, and there she opens with a declaration, "The name of this tune is 'Mississippi Goddam,' and I mean every word of it." The song's defiance is right there in the title. Daphne Books calls it Simone's "legendary cursing anthem," and southern radio stations banned it, allegedly on the grounds of profanity.[25] But the sincerity evoked in the first-person "I mean every word of it" sits uneasily next to the more syntactically roundabout "of . . . is" clause, this first "Goddam" that is not spoken by an "I" who means it, so much as a "Goddam" embedded in a title—a proper noun, not an exclamation. Something comes forward here as something (maybe something else?) also recedes. This tension, these two movements, seem to rhyme with the eruption and dumbness that together midwifed the song into this world.

Musically too "Mississippi Goddam" carries complex formal tensions, modulating between spoken and sung, switching melodies, changing tempos like a show tune.[26] The upbeat opening sound is reminiscent of the kinds of show numbers that vaudeville audiences would have known. Simone then switches from the major chord to the relative minor.[27] As it proceeds, the song quite literally strikes its chord. It's not a key change, which would be the more expected way to accomplish the song's feel. Instead, she plays two ends of the same key, moving from what, within the fairly expansive genre of the show tune, are considered sunshiny tones to more melancholy ones. You don't need this technical description, though, to know that a lot is going on here—listening to the music makes that unequivocal.

MISSISSIPPI ✳⊙‼?✳⊙!

BY NINA SIMONE

· FROM THE ALBUM "NINA SIMONE IN CONCERT" PHS 600-135/PHM 200-135

This single has been issued for DJ's in answer to your many requests. It has been specially edited for air play, featuring the "BEEP-BEEP" in place of ⊙✳?‼??.

"NINA SIMONE IN CONCERT" is proving to be a big exciting album. **MISSISSIPPI** ⊙✳?‼?? is receiving tremendous recognition. It may be the most topical selection in years. This outstanding message song, with the great "SIMONE" feel and rhythm, makes this a ⊙✳?‼?? hot disc.

40216

b/w SEA-LION WOMAN

⫶ ● ⦀⦀ ● ⫶

"Mississippi Goddam," 7-inch
single sleeve (ca. 1964).
Wikimedia Commons.

In the Carnegie Hall recording, Simone peppers her piano modulations and chord changes with a number of spoken asides. Perhaps most memorably, she tells her audience, "This is a show tune, but the show hasn't been written for it yet." It sounds like a declaration, an explanation, but like everything else in this performance, it is deceptive in its clarity, an instance perhaps of the "dialectic of luxuriant withholding" on which black aesthetics have been known to turn.[28] Simone offers up a genre (show tune) in which the audience can locate what it is hearing, at the same time that she yanks away any more precise context (the show, which hasn't been written). Hers is not, however, *not* an explanation, as genre can itself be a way of saying something.[29] Show tunes signify as demotic, lacking the cultural prestige of other compositions, very much including the ones that had been the substance of Simone's classical training. And while the control and precision of classical composition is often socially coded white (just as improvisations in jazz are often socially coded black), Simone's performance, as we have seen, is at once masterfully controlled and yet deliberately framed to her audience by the improvisational "yet."[30]

In its origin, its words, its sound, its genre, "Mississippi Goddam" holds together tensions and contradictions. It makes something cohere. It is, in every sense, pretty fantastic.

FANTASY RECONCILES WHAT is here and what is not. When Simone covered Judy Collins's "My Father" on *Baltimore* (1978), she was very likely aware that she was not singing about her own father. Earlier, at an RCA recording session in 1971, Simone tried to perform the song but interrupted herself on the grounds of nonrecognition. Partway into the second verse, having sung of a father who worked the mines in Ohio and promised the song's "me" that "we" would someday live in France, Simone stops playing piano and announces, "I don't want to sing this song. It's not me. My father always promised me that we would be free, but he did not promise me that we would live in France [laughter]." Someone in the recording booth patches through to ask, "How about Brooklyn?" and Simone replies, "No, my father knew nothing about New York, at all. He promised me that we would live in peace, and that, maybe I'll still get. OK we'll have to skip that one."[31]

More than one boundary seems to strain here: between the performance of a song and the biography of the performer, between "It's not me" and "he did not." By 1971, Simone wasn't speaking to her father, but in this recording she was certainly speaking about him and, to some extent, for him. Michael Boyce Gillespie observes too that whatever boundaries were straining in this 1971 session strain further following J. D. Waymon's death in the fall of 1972. From then on, he writes, "Traces of 'My Father' appeared as a part of her own autobiography when reflecting on him. In an article for *Jet Magazine* that detailed her performance in New York City at Town Hall (3.8.85) where she made her NYC concert debut in 1959 the allusions to the Judy Collins song are evident, 'My father used to say to me, "One day, I promise you, you will see the world. You'll go to far distant places. . . . Along the way, you'll have your joy and you'll have your pain." I've experienced some of that.'"[32] It's become difficult to tell who is speaking for whom. But the point isn't to sort it out.

These slips of position can get psychic work done. They allow what maybe happened to substitute for what maybe didn't, and vice versa. They allow whatever was present for Simone to be there, to register, even if what's present for her isn't anything we who are not her can agree was there. Of course, we could insist on disputing the nature of reality. We could say, *that's not what really happened*. We could say, *that's not your father, that's someone else's*. But what are we doing, trying to prove someone wrong? If we're in the realm of fact, we can dig in there, however pedantic doing so might make us seem. But if we're in the realm of feeling, we'd be out of line. Someone's feelings cannot be false exactly—that's the wrong measure. If "My father used to say to me" is a proposition, it may be inaccurate, but if it expresses a wish, a sentiment, a hope, a summary, a metaphor, then it stands.

But let's not lay this logic of substitution at the feet of words alone. Recall that fantasy's theorists try to comprehend it spatially—scene, setting, stage, spot, layer. Recall that fantasies allow us to switch positions. It's a substitution game, but unlike in the case of a linguistic substitution such as metaphor (where one can identify the vehicle and the tenor) and unlike the language of dream interpretation (where a manifest content stands in for a latent content), what stands in for what in fantasy is much slipperier, much more reversible all of a sudden, much more resistant to analytical pinpointing.

Another example: in 1957 Simone recorded "Don't Smoke in Bed," which begins "I left a note on his dresser / and my old wedding ring."[33] She reprised the song onstage at Carnegie Hall in 1964. But in 1991 she seems to have reprised it again, at least somewhat, as she recalled in her autobiography: "I walked out on Andy. I left my wedding ring on the bedroom dressing table and caught a plane to Barbados."[34] It's possible to say that Simone jumbled the song's lyrics with her own experience. But it's also possible to say that her attraction to the song in the first place was an attraction to what it expressed, even if she didn't have occasion or, perhaps, any conscious desire yet to express herself in its terms. These possibilities offer opposed explanations, but they may equally be true—and, in any case, we have no way to prove whether they are. It is accordingly going to be more accurate in the long run to say that something is happening than to say x is happening to y. Whereas, in grammar, a verb is transitive or it's not, in fantasy, transitivity is the very condition we're working in.

Part of the lesson here may be that thoughts and feelings are just as susceptible to miscommunication as any words; they too are subject to substitutions from time to time. Simone's friend and chronicler David Nathan recalled seeing her in London sometime around 1985: "I'd always known that Nina lived in her own reality and in that reality, she was indeed a real African queen reincarnate. I came up with the term 'bleedthrough' to describe the condition she was manifesting, a state in which people operate as if they were still in a past life."[35] The term is suggestive, but it may also be unnecessary.[36] Isn't what *bleedthrough* describes just an extreme version of what we all do, of what fantasy is? We're in the domain of fantasy when we come across an expression that is not obviously or actually describing *social* reality. That expression is still real, still at some level true, but not for everyone involved, at least not in the same ways.

This is not to say that every time we disagree it is a matter of fantasy. But it is to suggest that disagreements can be bound with fantasies, if we're psychically invested in them—whether that investment is in our position, or in the fact of opposition itself if the parties we're opposed to do not at some level mirror our opposition. More simply put, getting to live in your own reality can be the whole point. Disputing reality can be as real to us as anything.

III ● IIIII ● III

FANTASY CAN BE VIOLENT. We can fantasize about destroying ourselves, or destroying parts of ourselves, destroying others, or destroying the
parts of ourselves that others represent to us. Doing so can feel gratifying or
pleasurable.[37] Freud located the onset of such things early in life, "not later
than in the fifth or sixth year."[38] Subsequent commentators have located the
violent or destructive aspect of fantasy much earlier in development, and also
consistent with conflicts that persist much later. D. W. Winnicott described it
as a child's overcoming the space between me and not me.[39] Melanie Klein located it at the origins of sexuality and posited its overcoming as the condition
on whose basis we can experience love.[40] Serge Leclaire has argued that there
can be no life without a child "killing" the dreams and desires of the parents
to which anyone born cannot help but bear witness.[41]

One of the ways we destroy is with words. Hortense Spillers is the rare
scholar who set out to understand what *daughter* means to the mommy-
son-heavy discourse of psychoanalysis, arriving at the suggestive conclusion
that the way "'daughter' escapes patriarchy [is] by mutilation and effacement
only."[42] Simone would not, I think, have said she escaped patriarchy, but if
anything gets mutilated or effaced in Simone's case, it would appear to be
her father's name.

In her own telling, though, it wasn't her father Simone was trying to
evade, so much as her mother. Simone writes that she sought a stage name
when she started at the Midtown Bar and Grill because she imagined that
her nightclub act wouldn't sit well with her mother the minister, for whom
"that wouldn't be any different than working in the fires of hell."[43] And so, she
recalled, "When summer came I left Philly as Eunice Waymon and arrived
in Atlantic City as Nina Simone."[44] The choice of a stage name is part of the
lore—it comes up in all the biographies, including, here, Simone's own. But
even there, whatever happens in the sixty-two miles between Philadelphia
and Atlantic City, this short space of transformation, is edited out in favor of
the point of arrival. So much is in a name, yet so little of it gets spelled out.

For starters, what did this show business sacrifice of the patronymic, in
Spillers's terms, efface? Fathers may be part of it, but in Simone's telling: "I'd
had a Hispanic boyfriend one time, Chico, who had christened me Niña, pronounced Neen-ya, which was the Spanish for 'little one.' Chico had called me
that all the time, and I really loved the way it sounded. And I liked the name
Simone too, ever since I'd seen Simone Signoret in those French movies. So
there it was, Nina Simone."[45] She stops being a Waymon not by the conven-

tions of the patriarchal law—not, in other words, when she trades her father's name for her husband's—but in the more casual space of a lover's call and an actress's allure. In this passage, she phoneticizes the name in her lover's language, yet passes over the agency by which we all came to pronounce her name differently than he. The silences speak loudly to one conclusion, though: Nina Simone names herself Nina Simone. Part of what's *not* being effaced is her power to choose the terms. Nearly half a century later, when her now-grown daughter Lisa joined her on the stage of the Wiltern Theater in Los Angeles in 2000, Simone beamed and boomed: "This is my baby, my baby Lisa. She's a superstar you know, don't forget, now: her name's *Simone* and she can sing!"[46] Lisa's given name is Stroud, and her married name is Kelly. But her stage name is Simone, and her mother emphasized this name that doubly stands in the place of the patronymic. It seems to have meant something to her.[47]

Is that what Spillers calls an escape? It very well may be as good an escape as anyone gets to make. But the act of self-definition, by which Simone rejects her father's name, or perhaps her parents' language (what she elsewhere had called "the Waymon way"), is also reminiscent of the part the hero assumes in Freud's most famous complex. Typically, the drama of Oedipus is, like all Greek tragedy, received as a parable for how you can't outrun fate, and one of Freud's more indelible insights was to switch the emphasis, suggesting that what you really can't escape is history.[48] We remain connected even to the things we reject, often in the very act of rejecting them.[49] Langston Hughes celebrated the point playfully in a 1962 publicity notice: "Why should anybody like Nina Simone simply because her name is not Nina Simone? Answer: Because she had the nerve to take a name like Nina Simone which bears no relation to anyone living or dead—formerly not Nina Simone."[50]

Simone's longtime friend Gerrit de Bruin told a more serious story after her death: "Another thing about Nina was that she really wanted her parents to be proud of her, especially her mother. She had an early publicity photograph sent to her parents that she had signed 'Eunice.' Years later when she became a doctor of music and a doctor of humanities, she began signing her name Dr Nina Simone. This meant a lot to her and she had the inscription on the photograph changed to Dr Nina Simone. It was rather strange."[51] Yes, rather strange, but largely from the perspective by which your name is supposed to stay the same, by which renaming isn't re-creating, by which you don't get to escape.[52] That may not have been Simone's perspective. Maybe indeed "she really wanted her parents to be proud of her," maybe that never changes. But what *can* change is who "her" is.[53] Simone seems to be saying, at least in part, that "her" is someone who gets to name herself.

‖ ● ‖‖ ● ‖

Nina Simone, Netherlands
(ca. 1980s).

III ● IIIII ● III

IF DESIRE IS ABOUT wanting a satisfaction that's not present, here and now, and if fantasy is about bringing a sense of that satisfaction into the here and now, nothing stops fantasy from presenting us with satisfaction in factually impossible forms. Nothing stops it, and often we stoke it. If the satisfaction we desire is from others, we can fantasize about them giving it to us. Common-sense boundaries between *me* and *not me* don't hold here, however, because we are in effect, through the operation of fantasy, giving ourselves what we want from others, from a position of the other that we occupy with our mind.[54] A range of terminological nuance exists to describe how we take other people into ourselves psychically—identification, incorporation, introjection, internalization—but my point just now is only that taking them in sometimes looks like standing in their spot. It sounds clunkier than it often feels.

Fantasies can, accordingly, be scenes of watching one's self.[55] When Simone's father was dying in 1972, she didn't go to see him, did not call or speak to him. The day he died, she wore black onstage and performed a cover of Gilbert O'Sullivan's "Alone Again (Naturally)," with rewritten lyrics.[56] The opening verse begins:

> I remember this afternoon
> When my sister came into the room
> She refused to say how my father was
> But I knew he'd be dying soon.[57]

Simone here sings about a knowledge of life and death that goes unspoken. It's an act of linguistic betrayal, and it works at more than one level. There is what she refused to say to her father. There is what she says about her father. There is the way that what she says about her father contains a refusal to speak. In this scene, she occupies the positions of speaking and not speaking. She and her father substitute for each other, more than once, but she plays all the parts. *I Put a Spell on You* tells this story and in the act of telling expresses something, lays some emphasis on the moment. Again, it's no less meaningful, and no less complete, because it stops short of saying what it means.

My own emphasis is on the inevitability of it all. Others have pointed to something more intentional. Malik Gaines, for instance, writes that "in Simone's performance methodology, multiple positionality is a source of provisional power, a way to act in excess of the permanent exclusion experienced in any one location."[58] Likewise, Emily J. Lordi describes how "Simone's survivorship was 'warrior-like' in that it was precisely *about* doing everything, about claiming a home on multiple stages, and in myriad styles."[59] They're right. But just because multiple positionality is a method doesn't mean it's only ever a method—that it is always engaged methodically, with deliberateness, intention, or strategy. It feels likely that, at least sometimes, when we need support we simply reach for the thing that's close, even if it is (in?) our own head.

FANTASY ISN'T LITERAL. One song in Simone's repertoire, in particular, seems premised on an intimacy it equally may or may not reveal. She twice recorded "Stars," Janis Ian's weary lament about fame and its loneliness, first at the Montreux Jazz Festival in 1976, released on video, and again at the Vine Street Bar and Grill in 1987, released on *Let It Be Me*. The two performances bear notable similarities to each other, in a way Simone's rerecordings often do not, but in this case it is the former that one would be hard-pressed to characterize as something other than an absolutely perfect performance—of this too-much-covered song, as well as within Simone's oeuvre. Every element hits just right: the piano's tempo, the quiet jazz percussion that accompanies, Simone's delivery and its almost theatrical understatement, her vocal modulations, the lyrics sung with a sadness that is so painfully tangible yet landing somewhere on the near side of overwhelming, as if to remind us that the unbearable is defined by the formal fact that it must be borne.[60] It's not easy to listen to Simone sing this song and not believe it to be true.

At the same time, many of the lyrics fail to check out against Simone's life story. She did make it when she was young, as the song portends, but in showbiz, not classical, and in any case, as she recorded "Stars" at ages forty-three and fifty-four, it seems no one with any authority had told her, "You've had your day / Now you must make way." The performance's sheer perfection likewise renders ironic the line "I guess there isn't anything to put up on display." Simone didn't precisely "lust for fame." She did not live her life "in sad cafés and music halls." Most crucially, perhaps, she did not "know the pain of living with a name you never owned," because, as we've seen, she did own it.[61]

Yet the details of a life do not have to be literal to be real, and what Simone expresses here so powerfully is a truth that's more emotional than in any other way actual. She voices that emotional truth, she commands it and submits to it. In doing so, Simone gets to be herself, even if the song's protagonist isn't, or isn't merely.

III ● IIIII ● III

NOT EVERYTHING THAT GOES unshared in our minds is a fantasy. In 1966, Simone went on a nationwide tour as an opening act for Bill Cosby, the experience of which exhausted her to the point of instability: "Wave after wave of tiredness broke over me and I felt like any minute I would fall asleep for a hundred years. I looked over at Andy and for a moment I could see right through his skin, right through as if he were covered in plastic, and I saw the blood pushing around, and the organs of his body twitching and throbbing, his heart beating. And then it was gone, and I was near to my normal self again."[62] Simone opted not to leave the tour, despite the strain it was clearly presenting her with, and "carried on, and the weirdness carried on too, coming and going. I had visions of laser beams and heaven, with skin—always skin—involved in there somewhere."[63] Whatever Simone may have been experiencing—daydream, hallucination, fugue, absence—is not, I think, what we mean by fantasy. And yet the object to which her experience tethers does seem to secure for her a sense of continuity. What does skin signify? Why *always skin*?

One obvious possibility, of course, is that skin color acts socially as a master signifier of race.[64] A consciousness of skin, a perception not of the embodied self but of how the embodied self is itself perceived, shows up in many other accounts of black being. In one well-known example, Frantz Fanon attributed this consciousness to what he dubbed "sociogeny," the production of social phenomena.[65] In a less abstract register, he dramatized sociogeny with the scene of a (white) child shouting to his (white) mother, "Look, a Negro! [Tiens, un nègre!]"[66] The language of the (white, child) other attaches to the (black) subject, and this external stimulus tenders a meaning that, quickly or slowly but unwaveringly, seeps into the (black) self and accumulates there. It's a form of self-consciousness that works double time for the same pay.

Fanon's understanding of race as a sociogenic principle has invited comparison to Louis Althusser's explanation of ideology, anchored as it is around a similarly concrete utterance, spoken by an officer of the law, "Hey, you there! [Hé vous, là-bas!]"[67] But the comparison isn't quite right because there's a real difference in the way self-consciousness can register when one is being spoken to versus being spoken about. To be hailed, in Althusser's sense, may make you aware of the power of the police, and in so doing may bring you into line with part of a social system in which labor and power are reproduced, but it doesn't make you, sociogenically speaking, you. To be hailed is to learn that you can and may be hailed, not to learn that you will only ever be hailed. Sociogenic subject-making goes deeper than interpellation, getting under the skin and settling there, never dreaming of the time it lived anywhere else. There's an echolalic, echoic aspect to these antagonisms that make you.[68] The experience has happened, in a time and a way that feels remote enough from experience to seem instead like a condition or, as one of Fanon's translators would have it, a fact of blackness, leaving a person to live in the aftereffects of some original transgression that has been felt and maybe forgotten but has never gone.[69] Christina Sharpe, with poetic precision, calls this phenomenon "the residence time of the wake."[70]

This meaning for skin is surely at play in Simone's experience, but there are other meanings that may be too. Everyone has skin, after all, and so no matter how its color signifies, no matter how that color registers in our or another's psyche, skin is also, inevitably, the envelope for that psyche, literally holding us together.[71] Simone's visions involving "always skin" seem to retain skin's holding function without the racialized, pigmented surface.[72] At least this would seem to be part of what appears in the vision of Andy without his skin—a functioning body with only a plastic cover—that allows her to see the contents inside the body's envelope without them splattering to the floor. The body's meaning becomes, as it were, transparent, yet she rightly describes that transparency as unreal.

Gender matters too. To some extent, skin is a site where race undoes gender. Angela Davis has argued that the demands for labor value placed on black women's bodies under slavery were comparable to the demands placed on men's, and so "they might as well have been gender-less as far as slave holders were concerned."[73] Moving in a more theoretical direction, Hortense Spillers conjectured that the experience of the Middle Passage was for many an experience of female "flesh" becoming "ungendered."[74] Christina Sharpe extends these insights into the afterlife of slavery: "That oceanic ungendering repeats."[75] Gender shakes off skin like water, which coats, perhaps, but does not seep in.

At other moments, gender's intersection with skin feels more perpendicular. Simone's "problems" on the tour started, she relates, "when Andy walked into my dressing room and found me staring into the mirror putting make-up in my hair, brown make-up, because I wanted to be the same colour all over. I was wearing a white gown and all I could think about was how the colour of my gown should contrast with the rest of me, which had to be the same all over."[76] Here is arguably a moment where Simone's "weirdness" is again signified by skin, though admittedly that skin shows up displaced by a metonym, the makeup that is usually applied to that part of the corporeal surface and now is being applied elsewhere on the body. I don't know what the gesture means, and I'm reluctant to guess. It's neither possible nor advisable to parse the logic of a space like this, where logic breaks down. But if we stay with the description as she offers it, I can speak personally and tell you that what catches my attention isn't just the application of makeup to hair—an attempt to treat the whole body as if its surface were skin?—so much as the fact that "the rest of me" to which the makeup is applied, and the gown with which it's meant to contrast, don't register a division by sex or gender. Trappings of the feminine—makeup, the gown—live on both sides of the brown-and-white contrast Simone, in her telling anyway, is trying with this gesture to pronounce.

SKIN WAS ON THE BRAIN. After Simone was introduced to Lorraine Hansberry in the early 1960s, she began "thinking of myself as a black person in a country run by white people and a woman in a world run by men."[77] Later, "By the time the sixties ended I'd look in the mirror and see two faces, knowing that on the one hand I loved being black and being a woman, and that on the other it was my colour and sex which had fucked me up in the first place."[78] In an undated note she wrote to herself during the same decade, she made the point in more personal terms: "I can't be white and I'm the kind of colored girl who looks like everything white people despise or have been taught to despise. . . . If I were a boy, it wouldn't matter so much, but I'm a girl and in front of the public all the time wide open for them to jeer and approve of or disapprove of."[79]

Somewhere amid these realizations, in 1966, Simone released a recording of "Four Women," a song she'd written a few years prior about skin tone and self-worth.[80] Each of four verses traces the story of a different black woman, contemplating her skin tone and her sexuality, often in relation to each woman's social horizons for labor or power. The song's take on the status of black women in the United States was critical, and rare—as there were few testimonies in any medium in 1966, let alone songs recorded by contemporaries, that even tried for serious consideration of black women's experiences.[81] Yet the song was sometimes misunderstood and condemned for its traffic in stereotypes embodied by its characters, Aunt Sarah, Saffronia, Sweet Thing, and Peaches.[82] The song's sheer accessibility may have been part of the problem. Unlike "Mississippi Goddam," "Four Women" is a highly rhythmic composition, repeating twelve bars with a four-bar tag on each chorus, a simple melody with piano, flute, electric guitar, and bass guitar accompaniment—that is, until the end of the final verse, when the music dramatically crescendos with frenzied piano playing, dissonant harmonies, and a final lyric screeching toward unintelligibility.[83]

In concert, Simone sometimes paired "Four Women" with "Images," a poem by the Harlem Renaissance poet Waring Cuney, which Simone tended to sing a cappella. One such recording appears on *Let It All Out* (1966). Another appears in a concert video from Holland the same year.[84] In its entirety, the poem reads:

She does not know
Her beauty,
She thinks her brown body
Has no glory.

If she could dance
Naked,
Under palm trees
And see her image in the river

She would know.
But there are no palm trees
On the street,
And dishwater gives back no images.[85]

Sung a cappella, Simone's performance of "Images" is unique in her repertoire, as well as intimate, raw. But the poem's nameless "she" is an impersonal
figure in a song sung about her, while the stereotypically named narrators of
"Four Women" tell their stories in the first person. And so, though Simone
sometimes paired "Images" and "Four Women," the pairing can feel like one
song acting as the foil for the other.[86]

The tension across this pairing—the tension between speaking for and
speaking as—arguably runs through Simone's ruminations on her skin ("that
on the one hand I loved being black and being a woman, and that on the other
it was my colour and sex which had fucked me up in the first place"). It even
more apparently runs through her 1965 Holland concert, where she introduces
"Four Women" as a song about "Four Negro women. Each one with a different
color. Each one with a different grain of hair. And one of the women's hair is
like mine."[87] We have yet to talk about the ways Simone's embodiment was part
of her performance, and we will. Suffice it to say for now that she didn't often
use that embodiment with quite so much deliberate literalness, as she does in
this moment from the 1965 Holland concert, to supply a song with illustrations.

Between audio and video, "Four Women" ranks among Simone's most
recorded songs, and often, as we have already seen with the Holland performance, she sought to further situate its context and elaborate the details of its
characters. Doing so isn't necessarily correcting for the condemnations and
misunderstanding of the song, which, in 1965, the year before it was released
on an album, have not yet come. Something else is happening.

In a nearly nine-minute performance of the song in Berkeley in 1969,
Simone introduces "Four Women" with an unusually long, apparently im-
promptu monologue. As the song's rhythmic melody loops six or eight times,
she tells her audience:

We've done this song a million times for you, so we don't need to explain
Aunt Sarah too much to you. Except to tell you that she's still going to

work every morning about seven thirty, walking the streets of Harlem. She's 107, and she's still struggling on, but it's OK, it's OK, she doesn't have too long to wait now. Aunt Sarah. She wears a rag on her head. Head rags are fashionable these days, [audience laughter] they're all in *Vogue* and everywhere. Aunt Jemima is in style [audience laughter]. [Simone laughs] Aunt Sarah has lived long enough to see the full circle come 'round!

After the song's first verse, about Aunt Sarah, Simone makes another aside, letting the bars of melody loop again:

I could tell you a story about my mama. In the South they call her Auntie, in these grocery stores. I only wish I had been there when they called her Auntie. No *Mrs.* [pause] You see I know Berkeley's on fire. I know that anyway. You see, I say that in a positive way. But I kinda have to hold myself down here, because the vibrations are so strong. I tell you this, if I had been there when they called my mama Auntie I would have burned the whole *goddam* place down, I'll tell you that [audience cheers].[88]

A lot is happening in these asides, but one thing to notice is their effective personalization of the four women's experiences in the song. "Auntie" and "Aunt Jemima" and "Aunt Sarah" are stereotypes, but Simone makes quite plain that they are also women—similar at the level of type, perhaps similar in complexion, but quite individual in their biographies. They have elaboratable lives and experiences, and they require relief from their pains, as in the first aside, or defenses of their dignity, as in the second. What's stereotypical isn't less real, Simone seems to say. Or perhaps, a person who fits a stereotype nonetheless deserves recognition as a person. These asides and embellishments in the telling drive the performance toward something more personal than stereotypes, but in the 1966 album recording it's arguably there already, in the astounding, cringing, almost embarrassing pain that animates the last screeched lyric, the fourth woman's cry and demand, "My name is Peaches!"[89]

I've always wondered how directly this song hovered behind Hortense Spillers's introduction of herself, twenty years later, as a figure stereotyped in discourse, a "marked woman," with a list of names that begins "'Peaches' and 'Brown Sugar.'"[90] It seems more obvious, however, that the Simone of "Four Women" and the Spillers of "Interstices: A Small Drama of Words" are seeing the same things about black women, skin, sexuality, and power, when the latter writes that "the lives of black American women . . . relegated them to the marketplace of flesh, an act of commodifying so thoroughgoing that the daughters labor even now under the outcome."[91]

ONCE YOU BEGIN to notice it, skin is everywhere in Simone's oeuvre. It shows up in her "problems," in her self-reflections, in her song lyrics, in her stage presence, in her political anger. And it shows up quite a few times in the biographical stories she tells us about herself.

One that stands out is from age eleven, about a recital in segregated Tryon, North Carolina, where her parents were asked to give up their front-row seats for a white family she "had never seen before."[92] Simone recalls that she "stood up in my starched dress and said if anyone expected to hear me play they better make sure my family was sitting right there in the front row where I could see them, and to hell with poise and elegance. So they moved them back."[93] The price of making her desire known was humiliation all around. "The day after the recital I walked around feeling as if I had been flayed and every slight, real or imagined, cut me raw. But the skin grew back again a little tougher, a little less innocent, a little more black."[94]

Skin is the metaphor Simone lights upon for the wounding and healing of this childhood trauma—the metaphor that holds together this story, but also perhaps holds together something for the person telling it. Yet insofar as skin color is also the signifier of race in her segregated childhood, it's an arrestingly literal vehicle, one that seems to substitute for its tenor even as it aims for metaphor. Feeling "flayed," feeling "cut . . . raw," these too are metaphors, though inasmuch as her pain was both real and bodily, they likewise stretch in the direction of literalness. Her telling of it, like the moment itself, is clearly meaningful, though again it's less clear exactly what it means. Simone's language turns away from itself, as language will, and we're left to listen as carefully as we can.

Richard Elliott, in his excellent book-length critical study, *Nina Simone*, connects this traumatic childhood episode to the conclusion of the French biopic *La Légende* (1992), in which Simone's daughter and family are seen sitting in the front row of a circa-1990 concert, played just to them.[95] As critical interpretations go, it strikes me as both subtle and beautiful, a well-spotted symmetry between the beginning of one autobiography and the conclusion of another, released just a year apart. It's the kind of full-circle payoff that leaves us—readers, viewers, critics, fans—with a sense of redemption, a happier ending. In short, I like this interpretation a lot, and all the lessons of my professional training as a writer and critic affirm that this is how you do it. For the very same reasons, though, I do wonder whether this interpretation represents Simone's fantasies, or just her critics! I have the same wonder

From *La Légende*, dir. Frank
Lords (1992).

about both *What Happened Miss Simone?* and *The Amazing Nina Simone,* two documentaries that end with title cards informing the viewer that at her death Simone was awarded an honorary degree from the Curtis Institute, the same institution that had rejected her more than forty years before.[96] I wonder whether redemption exists outside of narratives like the ones we interpreters spin.

Whose sense of continuity is held together by a scene that may or may not recall another scene, whose subject may or may not be conscious? Who has skin in the game?

SOMETIMES WE DO TRY to go back and tie it together. *Here Comes the Sun* (1971) is the first album Simone released after she stopped speaking to her father and after her divorce from Andy Stroud; and this first album not to list Stroud as her producer, lists Simone herself as a little girl. The majority of the album's back cover, below the track listing and credits, is the reproduction of a photo signed, "Lovingly,—Eunice Waymon—Age 12," to whom it attributes a poem:

> "All music is what
> awakes within us when we
> are reminded by the instruments;
> It is not the violins or the clarinets—
> It is not the beating of the drums—
> Nor the score of the baritone singing
> his sweet romanza; nor that of the men's chorus,
> Nor that of the women's chorus—
> It is nearer and farther than they.—"

This image of Simone as a child would seem to contrast with the album's tracks, none of which assume a juvenile position or perspective, some of which (covers of Bob Dylan's "Just Like a Woman" or Frank Sinatra's "My Way") could only be spoken by adults, and others of which ("O-o-h Child") are nominally spoken to children.[97] The words of this poem, too, would seem to create contrast, as violins, clarinets, romanza guitars, or a men's chorus do not make the sounds this album features. Yet if this image and these words are meant in some way to caption or at least exist in association with *Here Comes the Sun*, what appears to be a contrast would have to be a component, would have to be present even if it was not otherwise legible.

The appearance of pieces of the past in our present, especially in the form of associations or invocations that don't follow from it, is typically called *regression*. In psychoanalysis, this term names a defensive process, though how it works has been the matter of some debate, following from, and even within, Freud's writings.[98] As with fantasy, however, calling regression "defensive" may underdescribe how it feels to be in a situation that might require you, or allow you, to be pulled toward another part of yourself that offers something copacetic.

No matter what we call it, though, it's difficult to know whether the image on the back of *Here Comes the Sun* can be understood as a regression in a

HERE COMES THE SUN   Nina Simone   Stereo MOVLP1037

SIDE 1

Here Comes the Sun (3:31) / Just Like a Woman (4:58) / O-O-H Child (3:14) / Mr. Bojangles (4:56)

SIDE 2

New World Coming (4:05) / Angel of the Morning (3:29) / How Long Must I Wander (6:16) / My Way (5:06)

Arranged by Nina Simone
and Harold Wheeler
Conducted by Harold Wheeler
A C.T.N.S. Production
Produced by Harold Wheeler
and Nat Shapiro
Production Coordinator: Sam Waymon
Front cover design: Bernie Casey

Orchestra assembled by Kermit Moore / Background voices assembled by Howard Roberts / Special thanks to Corky Hale for bringing her harp to our sessions.
Recorded in RCA's Studio B, New York City / Recording Engineer: Ed Begley

RCA STEREO RECORDS may be played on any modern phonograph with a lightweight tone arm. You will hear excellent sound reproduction on a stereo player and full stereo sound on a stereo player.

Originally released ℗ & © 1971 RCA Records, a division of Sony Music Entertainment. This release ℗ & © 2014 Sony Music Entertainment; manufactured & distributed by Music On Vinyl B.V. for Sony Music Entertainment. Warning: All rights reserved. Unauthorized duplication is a violation of applicable laws. Made in the EU.

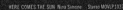

Here Comes the Sun, album
back cover (1971).

significant sense, or whether, more minimally, it is a glance toward the past from a tenuous present. Whatever is happening here does seem to play with time, in a way that seems to say something about the points it moves between, though whether that something is a change over time or a collapse, or both, seems impossible to determine. If anything, the movement would seem to rhyme with José Esteban Muñoz's account of the pockets of utopia in his own brown childhood, where "I was able to imagine a time and a place that was not yet there, a place where I tried to live."[99] It's also unclear what exactly might be sought by whichever kind of looking back this is. A return, a place to hide out? A reset that would allow Simone to move forward on a different trajectory? The backward glance may also offer, as we saw in her attempted recording of "My Father" for this same album, a fantasy of multiple positions, a chance to be present to a past self—maybe to retreat into her, but maybe to talk to her, to tell her what one wishes someone else had, or perhaps to offer comfort, to say, "Some day / We'll get it together and we'll get it undone."[100]

It would very likely be more satisfying if I were better able to say what the image means, to make an educated guess, to stake an argument or an interpretation. The interpreter's temptation, in every instance, is to catch hold of the elusive, to pin the meaning down, to resolve the multiplicities of fantasy space into a single meaning—and, in this instance, to use the details of Simone's biography to explain her gesture of reproducing this image. The temptation is to imagine that a contradiction is a problem to be solved, as though the life that fills a biography added up to a whole sum without remainders. It's tempting, and a lot of things that count as knowledge encourage us to give in to it. Indeed, maybe it's not wrong to give in to the temptation of fixing meaning. Maybe what's dishonest about it, in the scheme of knowledge, is quite negligible.

Resisting this temptation becomes easier, however, if we imagine that the elusiveness of other people's fantasy isn't the key to its complexity.[101] For one, that equation between the elusive and the complex denies that we build complexity out of the familiar—that in the production of complexity we typically take what we know and assemble it, ornament it, add to it, invite its components to interact, affect, and alter one another, and reproduce it or perhaps mutate or synthesize it, but in any case grow it. Complex things aren't necessarily hard to know, they're just large and so must be approached with an energy suited to their scale. It's more building out than pinning down.

While complexity is large, what's elusive is usually more foreign. Things that are genuinely elusive to our thought are ones that can't readily be metabolized; or, to choose another metaphor, they're the ones that live at such a distance from the familiar as to rarely visit or appear on its scene. But that means they are elusive relative to us, not in and of themselves. The amount of difficulty in getting to know an elusive thing has less to do with any necessary largeness on its part, so much as the vastness of our distance from it.[102] Sometimes—I'd wager often—things that are difficult to know are in and of themselves quite simple. Simplicity, meanwhile, is sometimes what regression fantasizes when it imagines a backward glance in the service of self-defense, when regression to childhood invites romantic notions of an elsewhere for the complexities of adulthood, a childhood often figured, however distortedly, as less complex— with the projected lessening of complexity there making it all feel elusive.

Trying to pin down the supposedly elusive meaning of *Here Comes the Sun*'s back-cover image can lead us to ignore what the image is. We could, for instance, indulge in the poetical speculation that "Eunice Waymon—Age 12" appears as a child in a literally black-and-white (and, in that metaphoric sense, simpler) world; but to do so, we'd have to ignore that this world frames her in an image that washed her skin of its blackness. It's not that the photo is overexposed, since it registers shadow and luster in reasonable gradation. It looks more like the photograph was originally shot with three or four harsh portrait lights (one of which you can see, if you look closely, reflected in her eyes), a studio setup lit in such a way as not to illuminate her complexion but to fade it.[103] Such techniques for rendering black skin on a kind of film that was never designed to capture its beauty were more or less standard in 1945 when this image was taken, and they hadn't changed much by 1971 when this image was reproduced.[104] What had changed was the dignity that black girl-hood might be afforded—for example, with the publication, also in 1971, of Joyce Ladner's poignant study of the choices and circumstances that navigate black girlhood toward black womanhood, *Tomorrow's Tomorrow*.[105] What had changed was whether holding a black girl under harsh lights was some-thing everyone might be expected to agree to. We can say it more simply, or in other words, with greater respect for its complexity, than interpretation of the elusive requires: to refind one's self in black girlhood isn't a thing to be dismissed as regressive.[106]

Fred Moten, as usual, says it better: "What is often overlooked in black-ness is bound up with what has often been overseen."[107]

THE WAY WE MAKE a point expresses something about our sense of that point. Toni Morrison conjured the scene of the 16th Street Baptist Church bombing by slowing the moment deliberately, musically: "The bits of Sunday dresses . . . did not fly; they hung in the air quietly, like the whole notes in the last measure of an Easter hymn."[108] Simone, by contrast, wrote of a truth that syncopated like so many slaps in the face: "The bombing of the little girls in Alabama and the murder of Medgar Evers were like the final pieces of a jigsaw that made no sense until you had fitted the whole thing together. I suddenly realized what it was to be black in America in 1963, but it wasn't an intellectual connection of the type Lorraine [Hansberry] had been repeating to me over and over—it came as a rush of fury, hatred and determination. In church language, the Truth entered me and I 'came through.'"[109] Simone wrote of revelation, of the "until," of the "rush," of the "suddenly." Of "what it was to be black in America in 1963." Of how the mundane coexists with the unimaginable.[110] Of having to take in all at once something that . . . what? Shouldn't have to be imagined in the first place? What is the alternative Simone might have fantasized about, if she fantasized about alternatives at all? What don't the biographies say?

(Perhaps what Simone saw was the annihilation of four little girls.

Perhaps what she couldn't help but see was this cruelest sociogeny, marking little girls as black little girls at the moment, in the act, of their ceasing to go on being little girls at all.

Perhaps this is part of what Simone meant when she said she was herself the target of assassination, whether by white supremacists or the FBI.[111]

Perhaps to go on working and singing and fighting when she was tired, she had to imagine that the alternative was fatal.

Perhaps it was fate she was trying to fight, as much as anything else.

Perhaps she wasn't afraid to fight, didn't consider or didn't care that she might lose.

Perhaps losing something is too often the thing that makes us recognize what we had.

Perhaps some recognition of whatever *something* is here is what Daphne Brooks means when she writes of Simone singing "blacker-than-blue notes."[112] Perhaps it's a version of what Fred Moten means when he writes, "These material degradations—fissures or invaginations of a foreclosed universality, a heroic but bounded eroticism—are black performances.")[113]

I will insist that there is so much we can't know, and yet I am at pains to show that there is so much here.

Covering

Fantasies open up positions that we, or some part of us, then get to occupy. In fantasy, we can stage a relation with someone else, or stage their relation to us. We get to be in their shoes, their heads, their bodies, their lives, their voice, their place—or what we imagine those things are, or what we wish those things were. We get to shift away from this present scene where our desires are unsatisfied to another scene where that satisfaction can be imagined, envisioned, apprehended—where it can in those ways be real. Fantasy positions don't always endure, but they sustain. The effect is to make things bearable, and in many cases that amounts to making things expansive, making us or the world we inhabit feel larger, more abundant, more alive with possibility, more.

Within the mutable boundaries of fantasy space, speaking *for* someone else and speaking *as* someone else can line up, run together, break away again. In fantasy, our perceptions of the life we're living and of the life we're not—the life we're sure we're not living because we imagine someone else is—have the potential to fold into each other, at least in some way, at least for some time. Of course, it matters very much to us which other life, which of its qualities, which "someone else" we're fantasizing about. That someone else could be someone personally unknown to us just as easily as it could be someone with whom we're reciprocally intimate; either way, it's someone we've invested with something. That process of investment, the how and why someone else matters, can, however, be elusive to our thought, can be a source of ambivalence, can be something we absorb and then reject, or vice versa.

We arrive at a sense of self by taking other people into ourselves. Fantasy is just one of the many ways we do so, but it's one worth listening to. Something is being voiced.

III ● IIII ● III

NINA SIMONE'S CATALOG is full of standards spanning multiple genres. Coming out of the late 1950s, she covered a number of traditional songs ("Children Go Where I Send You," "Black Is the Color of My True Love's Hair," "Cotton-Eyed Joe"), as well as show numbers from composers such as George Gershwin, Irving Berlin, and Richard Rodgers and Oscar Hammerstein, and also from other popular songwriters of the 1920s and 1930s, such as Cole Porter, Hoagy Carmichael, and Dorothy Fields and Jimmy McHugh.[1] An album's worth of covers of Duke Ellington's compositions fills *Nina Sings Ellington* (1962). Her final album that tended in this direction was *Broadway-Blues-Ballads* (1964), though by the same point in time she had already begun recording protest songs. "Mississippi Goddamn" is arguably Simone's most well-known song, and it is one of those most frequently evoked by biographers and scholars. It is, however, one of the very few of her recorded songs that she wrote herself.

Depending on how one counts, the songs Simone wrote in her most prolific years (1959–74) can be added up on one or two hands.[2] These include of course "Mississippi Goddam" and "Four Women." She gets writing credit for "Old Jim Crow" on *Nina Simone in Concert* (1964), "Blackbird" on *Nina Simone with Strings* (1966), "Real, Real" on *Nina Simone Sings the Blues* (1967), and "Consummation" on *Silk and Soul* (1967), as well as three instrumentals: "Central Park Blues" on *Little Girl Blue* (1959), "African Mailman" on *Nina Simone and Her Friends* (1959), and "Under the Lowest" on *Nina Simone at Town Hall* (1959).[3] She also did a lot of rearranging. Simone rewrote and rearranged "Go Limp" (by Alex Comfort, later the author of *The Joy of Sex* [1972]), a mock ballad about a young woman who gets pregnant at a protest march, on *Nina Simone in Concert* (1964), and she effected a similar transformation on Bessie Smith's "Need a Little Sugar in My Bowl," first recorded as "I Want a Little Sugar in My Bowl" for *Nina Simone Sings the Blues*. She set poetry to music, as with Waring Cuney's "No Images," which became "Images" on *Let It All Out* (1966), and Paul Laurence Dunbar's "Compensation" on *Nina Simone and Piano* (1969).[4] She also collaborated. "Backlash Blues," cowritten with Langston Hughes, appears on *Nina Simone Sings the Blues*, as does "Blues for Mama," cowritten with Abbey Lincoln.[5] "Why? (The King of Love Is Dead)," an original song written by Simone's bass player Gene Taylor, was recorded live at the Westbury Music Fair on April 7, 1968—that is, three days after Martin Luther King Jr. was assassinated—and released on her only album that year, *'Nuff Said!* (1968).[6] Meanwhile, the two parts of "Revolution" on *To Love Somebody* (1969) and "To Be Young, Gifted and Black" on *Black Gold* (1970) were cowritten with Weldon Irvine Jr. A few other of her recorded songs were written by band members or producers. For example, "It Be's That Way Sometime" was written by her brother and bandmate Samuel Waymon, and "Love O Love" by Andy Stroud, both on *Silk and Soul*; and a handful of songs were composed by the writing duo Bennie Benjamin and Sol Marcus, in conjunction with her recordings for Phillips, on *Broadway-Blues-Ballads* and *Wild Is the Wind* (1966).

But that's about it. Nearly every other song on every other album had been written by someone else, and the majority of which had previously been recorded by someone else. To an easily forgotten extent, Simone's practice here tracks with the norms of the US recording industry before the rise of the singer-songwriter—the likes of Laura Nyro or Joni Mitchell—in the later 1960s, and Simone was not the only performer to continue with covers well into the 1970s, Linda Ronstadt being chief among the most commercially successful examples.[7] Still, some critics find Simone's covering embarrassing, though they shouldn't; it seems narrow to suppose originality adheres only or even primarily in new source material.[8]

Besides, listening to Simone cover a song, you never doubt that it is, in every sense, *hers*. One big reason why is her voice. It sounds "soft and hazy," according to one critic, like "hot chocolate or angostura bitters" according to another; it "lent status to female surrender, and romance to blunt transgressions," according to a third.[9] In less metaphoric terms, and even to a musically untrained ear, Simone's voice is the standout feature of an otherwise distinctive performer, appearing on album after album as rich, low, and ponderously sad. Simone's vocal sound tends deep, even for a contralto, and though she trained for more than a decade as a pianist and never as a singer, her voice nonetheless carries a tune effortlessly, meriting frequent and favorable comparisons to a slew of soulful chanteuses such as Bessie Smith, Sarah Vaughn, and Della Reese. But if Simone's voice was deep, it was also long. And this may be its real performance signature: to hold notes, elongating them in dynamic tension with the progress of a song's instrumental melodies. Simone frequently held notes, if not exactly too long, than at least long enough to make her audience feel like she didn't always want to let them go.[10]

This vocal elongation colors the emotional character of many of her best-known performance numbers. The tenacious vibrato of her cover of Gershwin's "My Man's Gone Now"—a song normatively performed in *Porgy and Bess* by an operatic soprano—proves a clear instance, as its minimal piano accompaniment (just a single chord repeated rhythmically for most of the song's middle) is held together by Simone's trailing vocal notes that harmonize and ache across the piano's pauses.[11] (Even Ella Fitzgerald's 1957 recording, likely the model for Simone's own, enunciates its words.) But there are dozens of other examples, and indeed one would be hard-pressed to find, among Simone's copious recordings, any real staccato articulations. Her talent for elongating notes appears in songs written to accomplish this very feat of swelling melody, such as "I Loves You, Porgy." But it also appears to great effect in tunes composed for other ends, such as the upbeat melody of "My Baby Just Cares for Me" or in the monosyllabic rhythms of "Here Comes the Sun," a song that George Harrison delivers as a dose of percussive pop optimism, but that Simone delivers instead with dynamic vocal tension across the piano's staccato, transforming the sunniness of the titular chorus into the kind of incantation you might repeat when there are no more tears left to cry.

There's theory behind the way she worked.[12] Vocal elongation lends a sad feeling to many of Simone's songs because, aurally, it adds tension to a sound. That tension, moreover, tends to be resolved with acoustic attenuation, or, in less technical terms, it tends to get resolved gradually. The result feels languid, melancholy, the sonic equivalent of a kind of pathos-laden understatement. This particular technique of vocal elongation stands in contrast with other ways of diluting musical tension—say, the appoggiatura for which someone like Adele is famous, wherein a note is elongated in a way that borrows time from a subsequent note, creating a tense attenuation followed by an abrupt resolution (the chorus from "Someone Like You" provides a ready example, where "like" is held long with "you" delivered abruptly; the emotion of Adele's songs comes arguably not with sadness but with a sense of relief).[13] Simone's elongated notes, by contrast, string together and then trail off, giving these vocal performances a tension that doesn't really resolve so much as it wears out, adding a richly dejected feel.

Simone's vocal stylings and arrangements enabled her conclusively to shape the mood of the otherwise widely circulating songs she performed and, in so doing, to change their meaning. "Black Is the Color of My True Love's Hair," an Appalachian folk song about a beautiful woman, becomes in Simone's rendition, with her minimalist piano composition and characteristic vocal moves, a song about blackness itself.[14] Her version's suggestion that the color of the lover's hair were its own cause for celebration resonated with the emerging insistence in the 1960s that, in a phrase activists like Stokely Carmichael and Miriam Makeba helped popularize, "Black Is Beautiful," while at the same time bearing this message in mood and suggestion rather than at the literal level of its lyrics (which instead praise the lover for "his face so soft and

III ● IIIII ● III

Nina Simone (ca. 1960). Photo
by Herb Snitzer/Michael Ochs
Archives/Getty Images.

wondrous fair").[15] The result was a song that could be appreciated as striking and political, yet not necessarily threatening to (especially white) album buyers who may have spared few thoughts for civil rights.

Given this signature technique, and the throaty contralto that flavors it, it's no surprise that Simone's songs are so distinctly *hers*. She owns her work musically—leaving other people's songs, as one reviewer described them, "Simone-ized"—and one might go so far as to underscore the singular quality of this route to ownership, as her more than thirty albums include so many original arrangements and singular interpretations, and yet so few songs for which she herself wrote the music or lyrics.[16] The material may often have been secondhand, but Simone's delivery is unquestionably first-rate.

COVER SONGS OFFER GLIMPSES of the ways that artists can also be fans.[17] They are often locations where something about fantasy (ours, someone else's) can be staged. As one artist absorbs another's words, moods, and sounds by translating these into their own idiom, we can sense an implied intimacy between artists that reflects (stimulates, gratifies) the audience's desire for more of them than we've otherwise been offered. Our longing supplies the plot. The interesting thing about a cover, therefore, is almost never why it happens, but rather who covers whom—not the nature of the relation, which can be presumed, so much as who gets to be in relation. It's no wonder that the most knowledgeable students of covers are often fans, for covers allow fans the excitement of mapping relationships (of influence, between personalities) in unexpected ways—the pleasure and surprise that can be evoked, for instance, when one mentions that Simone, when recording for her final studio album in 1993, covered Prince's "Sign o' the Times."[18]

In this respect, the most self-reflexive cover of all time is arguably "Killing Me Softly with His Song," about the experience of listening to a stranger sing a different song and identifying so personally with it as to be intimidated by the artist and embarrassed by the crowd.[19] Allegedly about Don McLean's "Empty Chairs" (which, notably, is about the almost completely inverse experience of not having listened to an intimate lover), "Killing Me Softly with His Song" was first recorded by Lori Lieberman on her eponymous 1972 album before becoming a hit the next year for Roberta Flack.[20] It is surely Roberta Flack whom Lauryn Hill was covering when she sang most of the same lyrics in the reimagined version of the song, "Killing Me Softly," on The Fugees' final album, *The Score* (1996). But whom was Roberta Flack singing about? Not Lori Lieberman. Probably not Don McLean. Her most iconic version of the song not only is a cover but, in being a cover, offers the most abstracted take on the song, no longer about a personal experience of identification with a particular song and instead about the experience of identification itself. What "Killing Me Softly with His Song" shows in can't-make-this-up detail, however, is what we arguably see in any cover song: the layers of desire and fantasy projection that suggest a collaboration between two parties who aren't otherwise present to each other.[21] Those two parties are equally the artist who records first and the artist who records second, and the artist who records second and us, their fans.

Should there be any doubts that covering gestures toward intimacy, toward a kind of imitation that expresses some desire, it's worth noticing that Flack modeled her early career partly on Simone's, covering Simone's covers a number of times, including renditions of Leonard Cohen's "Suzanne," the Bee Gees' "To Love Somebody," Al Wilson's "Do What You Gotta Do," and the spiritual "If He Changed My Name," which Flack recorded under the title "I Told Jesus."[22] It's also true that Simone covered a few covers that Flack had recorded first, including Bob Dylan's "Just Like a Woman," though there's no indication here of reciprocal influence.[23] As we'll see, Simone knew she was covering Dylan and had eyes for no one else.

Simone meanwhile reports resentment toward the attention other artists received for songs she'd also recorded. *I Put a Spell on You* recalls the tour in Europe in the summer of 1968, following the assassination of Martin Luther King Jr., which Simone did not cancel only because her cover of "Ain't Got No/I Got Life" had become a long-desired hit single there. The tour became motivated by something like jealousy: "In Europe other people had been having hits for years using songs I first recorded: 'Please Don't Let Me Be Misunderstood' hit for The Animals, 'I Don't Want Him' for Nancy Wilson, 'I Put a Spell on You' for Alan Price, and 'The Other Woman' for Shirley Bassey."[24] All of these songs were in fact written and nearly all recorded by others before Simone made them hers, though originality is perhaps not the brass ring she's reaching for.[25] It seems she desires not so much to be original as to be definitive. At the very least, it's clear Simone could not stand to be seen in the opposite light, as derivative, "as if I only covered other artists' hits like some second-rate cabaret singer."[26] If one of the features of a cover song is fantastic, to project or create an intimacy, Simone's comments remind us that destruction too is one of fantasy's reliable modes for resolving conflict. To be definitive is to vanquish both the original and the subsequent.

HERE'S WHAT COVERS aren't: stealing. As Michael Awkward has written, in one of the best explorations of this tricky musical phenomenon, "The concept of theft seems inadequate to describe what, by the mid-1960s, had become a *cultural exchange* of musical texts."[27] Sure, it's reasonable enough to speak of theft in the early 1950s, when Elvis Presley achieved his fame with songs and dance moves smuggled across the color line, but it's trickier to call it theft by 1978 when Art Garfunkel, James Taylor, and Paul Simon hit number one on the Billboard Easy Listening chart with a cover of Sam Cooke's "Wonderful World."[28] The differences, as Awkward rightly argues, are the social and sonic measures of desegregation that took place in US culture on either side of the mid-1960s.

But just because something hasn't been stolen doesn't mean that it was exactly on offer. Accordingly, what covers indisputably are, are acts of appropriation. One way that appropriation typically works is through mechanisms of power so uneven that the powerful can claim to have invented something they in fact took from someone else. It's not news that in exactly this way, white people quite consistently treat the creative resources of blacks in diaspora as extractable raw materials for the production of cultural phenomena.[29] And so I want to be as clear as possible that what's being staked out here is a very slender point: while white liftings of black sound, or musical style, or dance are textbook examples of this centuries-long dialectic of "love and theft," covers aren't usually—at least not in the same ways.[30]

The differences have to do with the fantastic aspect of covers, the intimacies at which they hint. Covers typically want to be seen *as* borrowed. That doesn't mean that they're innocent of the dynamics of racial appropriation, so much as it has meant that many successful white artists performing songs or styles previously developed by black artists do so in ways that deliberately signify miscegenation. Covers tend to offer the erotics of relation, the thrill of crossing, rather than a game of whitewashing. Amiri Baraka (writing as LeRoi Jones) grumbled about this tactic among white musicians in 1966: "They steals, minstrelizes (but here a minstrelsy that 'hippens' with cats like Stones and Beatles saying, 'Yeh, I got everything I know from Chuck Berry,' is a scream dropping the final . . . 'But I got all the dough . . .')."[31] Baraka's complaint has to do not with stealing but with a tactic of deliberate and avowed borrowing—the ways white artists give credit in order to score credit.

Unlike outright theft, covering moves—often, wants to be seen to move—across the sonic color line, and, as such, it has the potential to meddle with expected social hierarchies.[32] The point can be demonstrated most readily in the difference between a cover of a song and what might be called a "version" of a song.[33] Because music is a performance medium, any song is, phenomenologically speaking, a version of a song; so when we specify a cover, we are making a claim about authority. There may be an intimacy or an erotics to covers, as we've seen, and these may reflect the performers' and the audiences' fantasies, or not, but intimacy and erotics too are inflected by power, inequality. To come first signifies. Putting the matter another way, the strength of a cover, and what distinguishes it from just another version, is the extent to which it can upend the who-came-first hierarchy.[34] A truly successful cover song doesn't feel like a mere derivation but something that stands on its own. And this, as we have seen, was the game Simone preferred to play.

It's also a game she often won outright, as the songs she covered so totally became hers. The cover of "Lilac Wine" that appears on Jeff Buckley's *Grace* (1994) is, he averred, his attempt at a Nina Simone song.[35] As with so many other songs that Simone recorded, however, it's a cover. "Lilac Wine" was written by James Shelton and first performed by Hope Foye in the short-lived musical theater review *Dance Me a Song*. It was then recorded by Eartha Kitt (1953), Helen Merrill (1955), and Judy Henske (1963), all before Simone covered it on *Wild Is the Wind*. But without question Simone's aching vocals and tempo changes were what Buckley sought to transform into the "distortion and excess" of his electric guitar.[36] He was covering a Nina Simone song, doing a cover version of what he recognized not even as a cover but as something definitive.

III ● IIIII ● III

NOBODY THINKS THAT what we do when we practice and perform classical music is "covering," even though it's not *not* that. Yet the language for talking about classical couches in very different idioms. You don't cover Bach; we say that you practice him, you recite him. You don't make a Bach movement yours so much as you learn from it and perhaps, if you play well, exemplify it. We reserve words like *imitation, inspiration*, and *mastery* for learning and playing this repertoire. The same actions are rarely described as a fantasy of finding ourselves through someone else's expression, but that difference in description is, so far as the present discussion is concerned, just a matter of custom.

And, in small degrees, terms like *imitation, inspiration*, and *mastery* do gesture in the direction of fantasy. Consider how Roland Barthes heard a movement by Bach on the radio one day in 1979, which he didn't at first recognize because the harpsichordist, Blandine Verlet, played "three or four times faster" than Barthes was used to playing it himself, "for all that I play badly."[37] He disdained the effect: "All the characteristics that I usually associate with the piece had disappeared; they were *lost*, had vanished, as if down a trapdoor; such and such a melodious 'little phrase' no longer sang; it wasn't even identifiable; a song has been silenced, and with it Desire." This disappointment, Barthes says, was not conceitedness "but an Amateur's truth." To be able to love Bach's movement, Barthes had to make it his, had to have it in the way he knew and wanted it, a way that was less correct than the harpsichordist's professional standards and yet was, for Barthes, better, because his own. Whether or not we play Bach, by Barthes's reasoning, we all love like amateurs sometimes, because we all love things according to criteria that matter quite a bit more to us than to the ways a more "objective" standard-bearer might estimate those things.

Far from being an amateur, Simone was a professionally trained classical pianist. When she began that training as a child, "we only played Bach," and, writes Simone, "soon I loved him. . . . Once I understood Bach's music I never wanted to be anything other than a concert pianist; Bach made me dedicate my life to music."[38] She learned from Bach's compositions and mastered them and no doubt exemplified them. But that professional dedication is where her love for Bach leads, not where her love for Bach begins. The latter happened earlier, in a fledgling moment before the amateur had worked herself into being the professional she would become. It would be, accordingly, inaccurate to read these sentences where Simone describes her training and come away with the implication that she only held the perfect or professional performances to her heart.

Professional training can make professionals, but it can't make those professionals un-have their amateur loves. To wit, that tender cover of Bob Dylan's "To Love Somebody" at the Antibes Jazz Festival in 1969, where Simone, seated at her piano and at the height of her performance power, extended the song to more than seven minutes by repeating the piano melody in a symmetrical arrangement reminiscent, at least technically speaking, of a Bach cantata. "I'm gonna do the last verse again," she sing-songed into the mic, "just for myself."[39]

III ● IIIII ● III

FANTASY CAN BE a hall of mirrors. The speaker of "Seeräuber-Jenny," in Bertolt Brecht and Kurt Weill's *Die Dreigroschenoper* (*The Threepenny Opera*), imagines avenging herself on the townspeople she serves, once a ship of pirates under her command sails in. Translated into English by Marc Blitzstein for the show's 1954 New York production, "Pirate Jenny" expresses the song's fantasy space through lyrics that in each verse use the modal verb *can*, followed by other verbs in present participle. For example:

> You gentlemen can watch while I'm scrubbin' the floors
> And I'm scrubbin' the floors while you're gawking
> And maybe once you tipped me and it makes you feel swell
> In a ratty waterfront in a ratty-old hotel

Or later:

> You gentlemen can say, "Hey girl, finish the floors
> Get upstairs, make the beds, earn your keep here"
> You toss me your tips and look out at the ships
> But I'm countin' your heads
> While I make up the beds
> 'Cuz there's nobody gonna sleep here
> Tonight, none of you will sleep here

Or again:

> Then you gentlemen can wipe off the laugh from your face
> Every building in town is a flat one
> Your whole stinking place will be down to the ground
> Only this cheap hotel standin' up safe and sound
> And you yell, "Why do they spare that one?"[40]

Something possible (the gentlemen can watch, can say, can wipe off) transitions into something that is happening (scrubbing floors, counting heads, making beds, standing up). None of it, of course, *is* happening; or, rather, it's happening in the way stories happen, rather than the way other kinds of events do. Jenny gives voice in this song to a fantasy, a future occasion whose satisfaction she conjures into her present.

When Simone performed "Pirate Jenny" at Carnegie Hall in 1964, she amplified the fantasy's mirroring by shifting the fantasy's terms. Where Blitzstein's translation of the first verse had given "In a ratty waterfront / in a ratty old hotel" for Brecht and Weill's "Und Sie sehen meine Lumpen und dies lumpiege Hotel," Simone instead sang with revised lyrics, "In this crummy Southern town / In this crummy old hotel."[41] There's no mistaking what she was doing. Daphne Brooks makes the case summarily: "Simone's cover of 'Pirate Jenny' would, in the midst of evolving black enfranchisement struggles, generate all sorts of rich historical allusions to the trajectory of African American forced migration, with a 'Black Freighter' coming and going, making a passage in the middle of the song toward our heroine who prophesies her own reversed stowage of escape on board the ship."[42]

Simone's "Pirate Jenny" firmly locates its setting in the US South and delivers a performance rich with theatrical emotion. It's extraordinary, not least for its deviations from an expected Brechtian mode. While the complexities of Brecht's aesthetic philosophy defy easy summary, suffice it to say that beginning with Lotte Lenya's origination of the role of Jenny in 1928, early performances of *Die Dreigroschenoper* typically emphasized the abstractedness of its setting and delivered songs with detached emotion.[43] Simone's performance moves in exactly the opposite directions. Her signature vocal moves are on display in the song, as in the bridge when she attenuates the *i*'s and *e*'s in the line "The ship, the Black Freighter" with stunning emphasis across the menacing drum roll that erupts behind her vibrato. More than this, however, Simone's delivery is pure theatricality, as she carefully calibrates her volume, enunciation, and sound patterns to give the song's lyrics unmistakable suggestions of vindictive pleasure, cruel anger, and, in the final chorus, an unsettling tenderness that contrasts with her earlier expressions. Simone's version introduces specificity, pronounces emotion, and grants politics a different confrontational form than in a Brechtian scheme.[44] While she accordingly offers a highly original rendition of "Pirate Jenny," there is a lot about how she did so that is consistent with other of her performances and performance styles. What sticks out here, in other words, is not Simone's sonic and political performance so much as the choice of this particular, not-at-all-obvious song through which to showcase it—her choice to layer such a performance over a song about someone else's fantasies.

It would certainly be possible to imagine that adapting a high-culture object like "Pirate Jenny" would be an effective way for Simone to bring politics into an elite venue like Carnegie Hall in 1964. She's on record with an instance of that strategy the next year, on her first European tour, when she introduces "Tomorrow Is My Turn," an English adaptation of Charles Aznavour's love song "L'amour, c'est comme un jour," by telling her Dutch audience that when she sings it, "I make it a protest song."[45] Multiple commentators have likewise noticed that Simone's "Pirate Jenny" indisputably talks about racism without actually saying the word.[46] As Ruth Feldstein writes, for instance, music and vocals "were the means through which [Simone] exposed the socioeconomic and gendered dimensions of racism and expressed a fantasy about vengeance."[47]

But if Simone didn't literally talk about racism here, there are other ways that she could not but have signified something proximate to it. Standing on the stage at Carnegie Hall, all eyes on her, Simone inevitably, perhaps deliberately, as Malik Gaines puts it, "fills Brecht's intended gaps with her physical intelligibility."[48] At the very least, this song about subterfuge isn't performed as one, and for the audience watching Simone, it becomes instead a performance shot through with dramatic irony. What for Brecht and Weill—for their character Jenny—was a fantasy about vengeance becomes, in Simone's performance, an insistence that the person who could enact vengeance is also a person who could look like her. Simone's "Pirate Jenny" asks its audience to imagine that Simone could play this character, could perhaps play any character—we might push so far as to say the audience is asked to imagine that blackness neither creates nor imposes any limits on speech. A fantasy of vengeance becomes a fantasy of the conditions of vengeance's possibility, a fantasy that a black woman could speak from anywhere, could stand universally as a representative of a subject, the "I" of enunciation. It's an efficacious fantasy, too, at least insofar as it translates fairly well across media. Simone's performance ensures the disembodiment of its sound-only recording doesn't at all leave the social meanings of embodiment behind.

III ● IIII ● III

SIMONE REPORTEDLY DIDN'T THINK much of her voice. Her vocal stylings may have been one route by which her covers made those songs definitively hers, but her career and training had been as a pianist, after all. In
her own telling it was the gig at the Midtown Bar and Grill that pushed her
to sing. The most detailed description comes in a 1970 interview: "In spite
of my limited range and limited voice, I sang everything I heard. The piano
helped because I have perfect pitch. I would play the songs in the easiest key
to sing in, so that nobody could detect that my voice was limited. By the time
I got into show business, I had studied the piano seriously for fourteen years,
practicing for about six hours a day. I never studied voice, but I had been
around people who had studied voice, so I knew a little about it. I just used
whatever came naturally to me."[49] The emphasis falls on professionalism, on
training. Its opposite is "whatever came naturally," a sly signal, perhaps, that
for her piano comes first and singing second. It's clear that Simone imagines
herself to be a serious pianist, which of course she was. But as we listen to
Simone play and sing, is this sense of herself as a singer second what we take
in, or is it something else? No doubt there's more than one answer, but my
point is that the answer we give depends on who we happen to be and what
we happen to hear, not who she was or, entirely, on how she's making music.

WE ARE NOT the only thing that people hear in our voice. Other things sound there, echo, resonate, and certainly this was true in Simone's case. For example, Geneva Smitherman begins *Talkin and Testifyin: The Language of Black America* (1977) with Simone's "It be's dat way sometime," the chorus from the song of the same title that opens *Silk and Soul*. According to Smitherman, the phrase both exemplifies the language and style of black English, using "the verb *be* to indicate a recurring event or habitual condition, rather than a one-time-only occurrence," and further exemplifies "a point of view, a way of looking at life, and a method of adapting to life's realities."[50] Put (perhaps too) simply, Simone's voice sounds black.

But that's not the only thing that could be heard. Joe Hagan, one of the very few critics to get a look at Simone's unpublished papers (in 2010 these were in possession of an eighty-four-year-old Andy Stroud), notes that "what is immediately striking is how lucid and candid Nina Simone could be, how easily she could tap her emotions in writing, and how, occasionally, she seemed to take great solace in getting thoughts on paper, often in her most desperate hours."[51] It's not obvious, reading Hagan's essay, why it should be so striking that Simone might be capable of clear self-expression, until he ventures a further explanation: "Having studied at an all-girls boarding school as a teenager, her grammar and spelling are flawless."[52] What's striking about her expression, it seems, is its correctness, its propriety. Put (perhaps too) simply, Simone's voice sounds white.

Obviously, a person can sound like either and both, can code-switch with finesse. But what's worth noting here isn't the likelihood of Simone's accomplishments in code-switching so much as the exemplarity with which Simone is credited in each register. Her interpreters arrive at contradictory conclusions, but in each of them she is being heard as voicing the language of others perfectly.

Whose voice is hers? It's a rhetorical question, in part because it would seem that Simone herself spent time debating the answer. Her experiments with voicing others show up across her output in the 1960s. They arguably begin in earnest not with the cover songs she'd been performing and recording since the late 1950s, but with *Nina Simone in Concert* (1964), her first record with Philips. This album includes three tracks—"Don't Smoke in Bed," "Plain Gold Ring," and her breakout single, "I Loves You, Porgy"—all of which she'd previously recorded for her first album with Bethlehem Records, *Little Girl Blue*. There may be practical reasons for having redone them—working with a different label, under a different contract, she perhaps wanted to have versions of some of her early hits more firmly under her creative or financial control. But such practicality has a way of also containing within itself less self-evidently practical things. At the very least, it's unlikely that this rerecording didn't at some level register, to her or someone around her, as a reprisal, a doing-again-differently, even if not necessarily a do-over.[53] It cannot be without some meaning that, at this juncture in the mid-1960s, after so many years and so many albums spent working her voice through other people's songs and words, Simone now took to covering herself.

‖ ● ‖‖ ● ‖

THERE'S ALWAYS A LAG in the meanings and desires that constitute us. Freud called it *Nachträglichkeit*. His translator James Strachey called it "deferred action."[54] I've heard people say "afterwardsness" or "après coup." Lauren Berlant memorably calls it the dialectic of "Hey, you!" and "Wait up!"[55] All these terms point toward how the part of us that wants, and the part of us that understands what-how-why we want, can't quite keep pace with one another. The lag or nonalignment happens in psychic life, but, experientially, it also happens across time. It's not a contradiction, at least inasmuch as one thing being the case one moment and another thing being the case another moment isn't, strictly speaking, a contradiction. But, for the same reason, it's not something that fantasy can resolve.

A lot of things were shifting in the early 1960s. Civil rights was shifting toward Black Power. One generation of activists was shifting toward the leadership of another. Simone's aesthetics started to shift too. She put away the wigs, appeared in public and onstage with her hair natural, her body draped in African prints.[56] Black women were incorporating the symbolic language of beauty and fashion into their activism, and Simone was leading the trend.[57] This aesthetic shift in Simone's self-presentation was more pronounced and more consistent after about 1965, but it was not new at that point.[58] An interest in Africa had taken hold with her trip to the Dinizulu Festival sponsored by the American Society for African Culture in Lagos, Nigeria, in 1961. Shortly upon her return Simone met and began a longtime friendship with Miriam Makeba, whom she lovingly described on first meeting as "so African."[59] In other people or places, we can recognize ourselves—both who we are and who we want to become.

To say the same thing another way, our ability to recognize ourselves can depend on our audience. Simone took the stage at Carnegie Hall for the first time on April 12, 1963, wearing a wig that appeared to tame and straighten her natural hair. She wears another on the album cover of *Nina Simone in Concert*, in a photo presumably taken on the same stage a year later, though by this time the venue's halls, and the album's side-B, were echoing with the modulations of "Mississippi Goddam." The sounds of that concert were what was recorded and circulated. The sounds were what mattered to history and protest far more than their singer's headpiece. Yet some pathos might be glimpsed in the discrepancy between the hair that had to be tamed and the protest song that didn't.

Sometimes, muses Claudia Roth Pierpont regarding the 1963 concert, "the small personal freedoms are harder to speak up for than the larger political

||| ● |||| ● |||

Nina Simone (1952). Photo by
Herb Snitzer/Michael Ochs
Archives/Getty Images.

ones."[60] If Simone's wigs or dresses, and their variance from how she may have wanted to present herself, could indicate that perhaps she was retreating from something, holding back, not presenting herself as who she wanted to be but instead as who she thought she needed to be seen as—well, who hasn't? There's something profoundly ordinary about wanting to be received by our audiences, even if the price of that reception is to insist that one part of our self walks into the room first while another slinks in later, more or less unnoticed. Our expressions—very much including our self-presentations—contain traces of our fantasies about ourselves. Fantasies, moreover, can contain traces of something like our wishes. It make the most sense if you don't insist that what we might wish for is, purely or simply, what we want.

III ● IIIII ● III

VOICING CAN BE a strategy. Desire may make us who we are, and fantasy may allow us not to be broken by desire's unmet demands, but fantasy's processes are often unconscious—something that we express without fully understanding what we're expressing, or even that we're doing so. The more conscious or intentional version of this work has sometimes been called thinking. Such, at least, is W. R. Bion's formulation in an influential 1962 paper, that thinking has to be called into existence to cope with thoughts.[61] He writes that thought begins in infancy, a way of comprehending or conceiving of our experience as it happens in our development. Thinking is thought driven toward systematicity—toward things like preconception, expectation, communication. These are ways of coping, to use Bion's word, because what we preconceive, what we expect, what we communicate is often rooted in frustration. Thinking has to be called into existence to cope with thoughts, in other words, because thoughts are often bummers.

Simone says she was thinking as she wrote to Langston Hughes in 1965 from London, in belated reply to the copy of his autobiography, *The Big Sea* (1940), that he'd previously sent. In part, her letter says:

> I use the book—what I mean is I underline all meaningful sentences to me—I make comments in pencil about certain paragraphs etc. And as I said there is a wealth of knowledge concerning the negro problem, especially if one wants to <u>trace</u> the many many areas that we've had it rough in all these years—Sometimes when I'm with white "liberals" who want to know why we're so bitter—I forget (I don't forget—I just get tongue-tied) how <u>complete</u> has been the white race's rejection of us all these years and then when this happens I go get your book. I'm looking forward to using it more & more in this way as times go on.

III ● IIIII ● III

Overleaf: Nina Simone, letter to
Langston Hughes, July 6?, [1965].
Langston Hughes Papers. James
Weldon Johnson Collection in
the Yale Collection of American
Literature, Beinecke Rare Book
and Manuscript Library.

Dear Langston — ①   London, sunday
                                    night
    I've owed you this letter 6?!   July
for some time now — so I'm finally
doing it.

    Thank you — thank you for the
books (your autobiographies) you gave
us — I'm reading "~~the big~~ The Big Sea", right
now and it gives me such pleasure —
you have no idea! It is so funny —
I read chapters over & over
again — 'cause certain ones
paint complete pictures for
me and I get completely
absorbed:

    Then too, if I'm in a
negative mood and want to get
more negative (about the racial
problem, I mean) if I want to get
down right mean and violent I go
straight to this book and there is
also material for that. Amazing —

    I use the book — what I
mean is I underline all meaningful
sentences to me — I make comments
in pencil

About certain paragraphs etc. And as
I said there is a wealth of knowledge concerning the negro
problem, especially if one wants
to trace the many many areas
that we've had it rough in all
these years — Sometimes when I'm
with white "liberals" who want to
know why we're so bitter — I forget
(I don't forget — I Just get
tongue-tied) how complete has
been the white races rejection
of us all these years And then
when this happens I go get
your book. I'm looking forward
to using it more & more in this
way as times go on.
        As a matter of fact, Langston,
I feel sorta' tongue-tied now
for there's so much I'd like
to say to you And I can't possibly
write as fast as I think And
even if I did I'd be here all
night writing this letter.

As a matter of fact, Langston, I feel sorta' tongue-tied now for there's so much I'd like to say to you and I can't possibly write as fast as I think and even if I did I'd be here all night writing this letter.[62]

Simone's claim to feel "tongue-tied" here is itself highly articulate, expressed in the complex verbal construction of an analogy, and written with what appears to be a degree of self-awareness. It is of course more than possible to map one's experience in terms of what lives at its edges, the ways it could go on but won't. It is therefore perfectly clear what Simone might mean when she writes that she can't possibly write as fast as she thinks, and if she did she's be here all night writing this letter. There's always more to thinking than we can say—fast enough or at once. It's also the case, as well, that how we express our thoughts may thereby to some degree end up contradicting all that we feel.

Fantasy, we have seen, works to reconcile such contradictions. But if thinking across the gap between how we express ourselves and how we feel is, as Bion suggests, a coping mechanism, thinking begins to sound like the negative of fantasy, a reconciliation not between desire and satisfaction but between desire and the expectation of frustration or dissatisfaction.[63] Rather than the expansiveness of fantasy, thinking begins to sound a lot like the resignation of calling the game before it's ended, of cutting off the flow before the water runs out, of not being able to say it all. Of course Bion is not the last word here, and surely there are those of us who fantasize about a kind of thinking that is something other than resigned. But, in any case, it's possible that the intentional, deliberate, or purposeful routes to reconciling our contradictions don't always feel that good. The unconscious ones, the ones we don't in any sense intend, these may bring us less pain.[64] It's important not to overthink it.

|‖| ● ‖‖| ● ‖|

WHETHER SIMONE INTENDED it or not, it would seem that, like most of us, she tried at moments to speak her voice through someone else's words or position, even if, unlike many of us, in so doing she often managed to elevate covering and rearranging to exquisite heights of originality and self-expression. One might push further, though, and insist that covering underdescribes not only what she did with other people's songs, which aimed—often success-fully—to stake out the songs as hers. If we're looking more longitudinally, we might also notice that covering underdescribes the subtleties of a creative process that looked different as Simone's interests and objects, and, quite pos-sibly, her sense of herself and her art, evolved over the course of the 1960s. By 1969, it had become something.

Her first album that year, *Nina Simone and Piano*, represents a departure and, arguably, a return.[65] Billed on its record sleeve as "Pure Nina," the album features Simone accompanying herself on the piano, and the album's few other sounds—an overdubbed organ, clapping, tambourine—were all done by Simone as well. It's a "first," declares Tom (The Master Blaster) Reed, in the album's liner notes, though my inclination is to debate that assessment.[66] While this solo production is indeed a first among Simone's recorded out-put, we've elsewhere seen her capacity to strip complex songs and interpret them in minimal registers—such as "My Man's Gone Now" on *Nina Simone Sings the Blues*—and, of course, we've heard that she played by herself at the Midtown Bar and Grill in Atlantic City in the summer of 1954. She tells that episode like this:

> That first night the only thing I wasn't nervous about was what to play. I knew hundreds of popular songs and dozens of classical pieces, so what I did was combine them. I arrived prepared with classical pieces, hymns and gospel songs and improvised on those, occasionally slip-ping in a part from a popular tune. Each song—which isn't the right way to describe what I was playing—lasted anywhere between thirty and ninety minutes. I just sat down, closed my eyes and drifted away on the music.
>
> . . .
>
> So the next night I sang as well. It wasn't hard to fit it to the im-provisation because I used my voice as a third layer, complementing the other two layers, my right and left hands. When I got to the part where I used elements of popular songs I would simply sing the lyric

and play around with it, repeating single lines over again, repeating verses, changing the order of words.[67]

The practice she describes here from fifteen years before *Nina Simone and Piano* is clearly not characteristic of that later album, as even a cursory listen will immediately show. Nonetheless, the creativity and improvisation of that earlier solo practice are the clearest precedents for this album that showcases Simone in three layers—right hand, left hand, and voice—and, in light of this earlier practice, *Nina Simone and Piano* could be considered less a "first" and more a back-to-basics. It's in this same spirit that Joshua Chambers-Letson identifies the improvisations in the summer of 1954 as Simone "transforming her work at the Midtown into a condition of possibility."[68] No wonder one reviewer, offering superlative praise, sensed something excessive in the album's minimalism and kept calling it "too much."[69]

Yet another way *Nina Simone and Piano* recalls Simone's description of her work at the Midtown is in its emphasis on popular music. Several of the album's tracks are from contemporary shows—"The Desperate Ones" from *Jacques Brel Is Alive and Well and Living in Paris*, which premiered off-Broadway in 1968 (at the Village Gate, where Simone was also a regular); "Everyone's Gone to the Moon" was a hit for Jonathan King in 1965; and "I Think It's Going to Rain Today," written by Randy Newman, had been previously released on his 1968 debut album but had also been recorded by various artists at least a dozen times since 1966. Elsewhere on the album, Simone continues with what she had been doing so successfully for most of the decade—including covers of Hoagy Carmichael's standard "I Get Along without You Very Well (Except Sometimes)" and of Leonard Bernstein's "Who Am I?" from the Broadway production of *Peter Pan* (1950), her originally arranged blues standard, "It's Nobody's Fault but Mine," and her rendition of Paul Lawrence Dunbar's poem "Compensation" set to music.[70] But the interest in contemporary songs is relatively pronounced and, in any case, seems to add something that hadn't been part of her mix before.[71]

When Simone had covered contemporaries, or at least peers, they were very often black men. In addition to Ellington, for example, she covered Oscar Brown Jr.'s "Brown Baby" (1960) on *Nina Simone at the Village Gate* (1962); Johnny Mathis's "The Twelfth of Never" (1957) on *Folksy Nina* (1964); Jalacy "Screamin' Jay" Hawkins's "I Put a Spell on You" (1956) on her album of the same name (1965); and Chuck Berry's "Brown Eyed Handsome Man" (1956) on *High Priestess of Soul* (1967). Covering Randy Newman, a white male contemporary ten years her junior, was something relatively new, even though it was not totally unprecedented. Following on Simone's cover of Bob Dylan's "Ballad of Hollis Brown" (1964) on *Let It All Out* (1966), and of the Bee Gees' "In the Morning" (1966) and "Please Read Me" (1967) on *'Nuff Said!*, however, "I Think It's Going to Rain Today" was one of the very few times in nearly two dozen albums that Simone recorded a song previously written and performed by a contemporary.[72]

The year's next album, *To Love Somebody* (1969), took a hard turn in this direction, as it included nothing but contemporary songs, marking the single most significant departure of her career to date in terms of source material. *To Love Somebody* opened with a cover of Leonard Cohen's "Suzanne," followed by Pete Seeger's "Turn, Turn, Turn"; two songs from the Bee Gees ("I Can't See Nobody" and the titular "To Love Somebody"); and three songs by Bob Dylan ("I Shall Be Released," "Just Like Tom Thumb's Blues," and "The Times They Are a-Changing").[73] In the middle of the album is the two-part anthem "Revolution" that Simone cowrote with Weldon Irvine Jr. From this point at the end of the 1960s, covers of contemporary songs find their way prominently onto nearly all of Simone's subsequent albums. *Black Gold* (1970) includes Simone's cover-medley of "Ain't Got No/I Got Life" from the musical *Hair*, as well as two songs by British folk artists, "Who Knows Where the Time Goes?," written and recorded by Sandy Denny in 1967, and "The Assignment Sequence," written by Jan Hendin and recorded by her duo Jan & Lorraine in 1969.[74] *Here Comes the Sun* (1971) includes a cover of the George Harrison song after which it is titled, as well as Dylan's "Just Like a Woman"; the Five Stairsteps's "O-o-h Child"; "Angel of the Morning" (written by Chip Taylor and recorded by various artists after 1967); and the Paul Anka/Claude François collaboration "My Way" that hit for Frank Sinatra in 1969. *Emergency Ward* (1972) includes a medley based on George Harrison's "My Sweet Lord" and an interpretation of Harrison's "Isn't It a Pity."[75] The Nitty Gritty Dirt Band's "Mr. Bojangles" appears on *It Is Finished* (1974), as do covers of Ike and Tina Turner's "Funkier Than a Mosquito's Tweeter" and the Everly Brothers' "Let It Be Me."[76] *Baltimore* (1978) takes its title from the Randy Newman song and also features a cover of Hall and Oates's "Rich Girl."

If Simone's voice is her most distinctive attribute, it's worth pausing to notice that her career's second decade involves her voicing an unprecedented number of contemporary artists, most of them white and male. To some extent, these covers proceed very much like her covers of Gershwin or Ellington in the first part of her career—a song rearranged and made hers through sound and vocal styling. Simone's cover of "Just Like Tom Thumb's Blues," for example, gives that song a lamenting sadness, almost a ballad quality, which

Dylan's original lacks. Simone accomplishes this effect with attenuated vocal notes, as well as by slowing the tempo of the song and replacing the dominant guitar of the original with a piano melody, backed by the rhythms of a hand drum and a guitar that comes in late in the first verse. Where Dylan's original is sympathetic to its protagonist, Simone's version collapses the protagonist and the speaker, making the song a personal lament as much as a story.

Indeed, what's curious about this cover is its perspective, the way it aligns Simone, as speaker, with the young man about whom the story is being told. Her cover, in other words, contracts the space between speaker and subject that Dylan, no stranger to imposture or playing characters, tries to hold open. Simone's "Just Like Tom Thumb's Blues" not only places her signature on the feel of the song but, furthermore, allows her to speak in the voice of a young man homesick and whoring in Juarez, Mexico—a set of subjective positions into which no one has tried to emplot details from Nina Simone's biography.[77] The effect of this cover, then, is fantastic, in both colloquial senses of the word: it is extraordinarily good, and it is fanciful, remote from reality. Simone's voice was unmistakably hers, but it was also something she used to ventriloquize, to project into the position of others.

It's never easy to say whether a particular fantasy is a cause or an effect. No less an authority on fantasy than Freud himself hesitated over this question. Ever eager to work backward, Sherlock Holmes–like, and uncover the events for which the presenting symptoms of his patients were clues, Freud nonetheless admitted that the difficulty of this task stemmed from the fact that the unconscious didn't respect the chronology of progressive time.[78] Even in a case like Simone's, where a fantasy of speaking her voice in a masculine position clearly comes to the fore of her archive around 1969, it is still not easy to determine whether this fantasy is the cause or the effect of any number of other shifts in her life that ripple in all directions around this one point in time. It's not easy, and maybe it's not advisable.

Fantasy can't be picked apart, parsed into vehicle and tenor like so many metaphors. Instead, fantasy blurs the edges between the things it compares, sometimes making them into each other, sometimes not, and most often partially so—though, maddeningly, there aren't many rules about which parts will run together in a given instance. As we listen to Simone's performance of "Just Like Tom Thumb's Blues," we may notice that she doesn't share much biographically with the song's subject, but when she collapses that subject with the song's speaker, when she speaks in his voice, she claims nonliterally to be expressing something literal about herself. Doing so perhaps sounds like what people do when they pretend or act—but in this case the lines she delivers are not as they had been written, and, rather, she's gone off script to express something else. What that *something* happens to be, however, is not clear, and to frustrate the interpreters further, it doesn't have to be. A lack of clarity may be the point, as insistence without specification is often the prerogative of fantasy expression.

FANTASY CAN BE a matter of emphasis—not a radical break or a new discovery, but more often a way to lean into a curve, to tilt toward something. For this reason, it can be challenging to interpret. This problem of interpretation—the difficulty of knowing what a fantasy is trying to express—becomes particularly pronounced in Simone's cover of Leonard Cohen's "Suzanne," the opening track on *To Love Somebody.* Cohen had written the song—a kind of modern blazon, describing not only a woman's body but also many of her attractive and idiosyncratic personality traits—as a poem in 1966, and he recorded it as a song on *Songs of Leonard Cohen* in 1967. His version draws clearly on a modern tradition of heterosexual love songs, though more than many such songs of its time, "Suzanne" offers a particularly rounded portrait of its eponymous subject—she is a character, not a type. The song is animated by a profound libidinal investment in a woman whom the speaker nonetheless evinces little desire to possess in any too-conventional way. And the not-quite quality of this song's heterosexuality may be the reason that Simone was not the first woman to cover it; Judy Collins had released a version, based on Cohen's published poem, in 1966, the year before Cohen's own recording.

As with so many of Simone's covers, her strategy with "Suzanne" was to transfer the original's guitar melodies to piano and to use her voice to create rich, elongated harmonies with the music. Her rendition includes one of the most syncopated rhythms among her recorded songs, with the piano punctuating the end of verses with arpeggio notes in a high key. (Concert performances sometimes reallocate this effect to hand drums, giving the song a deeper rhythm, more reminiscent of West African percussion styles.)[79] Simone's "Suzanne" is harmonically much more complex than Cohen's original. One reviewer, reporting on a 1969 concert, posited, "She may do Leonard Cohen's haunting 'Suzanne' but, while it still comes out haunting, it is Nina's own haunt—simmering, burning and eventually bursting with passion."[80] Her haunt, yes; but whose passion?

Simone's own position as speaker maintains ambiguity around its emotional investments. The song—ambivalent about desire in its original version—is not apparently homoerotic once it's told with one woman singing about another. If anything, Simone's cover seems to become more descriptive of Suzanne, minimizing her status as a woman to be seen and wanted, and emphasizing instead her status as a person with a point of view. But if that is Simone's goal, why speak *about* Suzanne and not *as* her, as she had done when covering "Just Like Tom Thumb's Blues"?

AMBIGUITIES EMERGE TOO as lyrics change: Who is she, and who is I? Simone's cover of Dylan's "Just Like a Woman" follows his original into the third person: "She takes just like a woman / yes she does." Simone's sticking-to-the-script here may also harbor shades of rejection toward Roberta Flack's version of the song, released the summer prior to Simone's 1971 album recording, as Flack not only uses the first-person "I" but takes liberties by reordering the song's verses, so that "I take just like a woman" becomes more chorus than verse. Simone's cover deviates from Dylan's only in the final lyrics (well, that and the pretty glorious translation of Dylan's rustic drums and harmonica into Simone's elegant piano playing), where his line "She fakes just like a woman" becomes her first-person claim "I take just like a woman / yes I do." The song's stated desire to have a woman yields in the end to a vocal desire to be one.

This move toward a first-person identification amped up when Simone recorded "Just Like a Woman" live in 1987 for *Let It Be Me*, but it becomes most pronounced at one of her late concerts, in São Paulo, Brazil, in April 2000, where Simone belts the "I" in nearly every verse before laying acoustic stress on the corresponding possessive pronoun as she sings "lately you see *my* ribbons and *my* bows."[81] More extraordinary still is the near-final chorus, where, with the full showmanship of her singularly controlled spontaneity, Simone sings:

But I break
I used to break
I don't break anymore
They can't do anything else bad to me anymore
Anything worse they've done before
So I don't break
I'm not a little girl

Even without the crowd going wild, the choice of words has a stunning effect—a powerful, declarative, near-definitive rewriting that owns what it claims and claims what it owns.

This performance is too deliberate, too willful and aware, to be called fantasy, at least not in the sense we've been using. But if it is Simone's choice to sing the song this way, it may well be that the 1971 version was also a choice, one that perhaps finds itself or its authority or its territory in the less willful and aware, more impersonal space of possession—in the projected space where one talks about a "she" in order only more indirectly to talk about an "I" that goes largely implied. It works that way for Dylan in 1966. It works that way for the heteromisogynist goggles through which his songs so often view women. And it seems like it could work that way for Simone too until, eventually, it doesn't anymore.

SEX IS THE ONE thing that nearly everyone agrees is also a metaphor. The sexual meanings of fantasy expressions, thereby, are often neither literal nor transparent. It's certainly possible that in singing a love song about Suzanne, or about the "she" who's just like a woman, Simone was expressing her own desire for a woman—just as, years later, the Indigo Girls did in their cover of Dylan's "Tangled Up in Blue."[82] But it's also possible to desire someone's body—to envy, emulate, admire—without desiring them sexually.[83] It's possible too to be confused or contradictory in one's wanting. The unevenness of power inflects the conditions of these expressions as well, and more generally we do well to heed Omise'eke Natasha Tinsley's words, that "black queerness itself becomes a crosscurrent through which to view hybrid, resistant subjectivities—opaquely, not transparently."[84] I take Tinsley to mean that it's fine to raise possibilities, as long as we don't mistake them for conclusions. We have no way, nor should we pretend that we do, to resolve fantasies of Simone's when they spell out no resolution for themselves.

But of course people do pretend. After Simone's death, a number of rumors surfaced of her lesbian affairs, mostly articulated in homophobic terms by Andy Stroud.[85] These were largely based on his recollections of the company she kept around 1960, the people he remembered meeting as her friends before they were married more than forty years earlier, and based as well on the fact that Simone in the same period frequented Trude Heller's, an in-the-know lesbian hangout in the Village.[86] That nearly the entire biographical account of Simone's sexuality is based on her ex-husband's speculative report of what she may have done with other people is, to say the absolute least, irresponsible.

Even if we could prove that Simone had sex with women, we do not therefore know what doing so meant to her. Or to make the case the other way around, even if we could prove that Simone didn't have sex with women, that shouldn't lead us to conclude that her relationships with women weren't a kind of love, which is also to say, a context in which it was possible for Simone to admit a desire to be different.[87] Consider her relationship with Lorraine Hansberry. As recounted by Nikki Giovanni, who had been close to Simone in the late 1960s, "What is important is that [Simone] loved [Hansberry] and she was loved in return. She never had to watch her back. With Andy, she watches her back."[88] To love and be loved usually does add up to something, but again that something, to be meaningful, doesn't have to be something in particular.

Meanwhile, queerer strains of psychoanalytically informed thinking sometimes observe that even the more public-facing part of sexuality called gender is

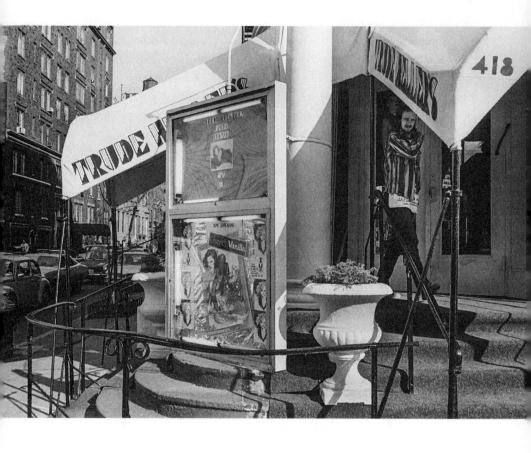

III ● IIIII ● III

Trude Heller's, Sixth Avenue
and West Ninth Street,
Manhattan (ca. 1970s). Photo
by Arthur Nager.

often defined not as Freud would have it, by its fatality, but rather by its mutability.[89] "Masculine and feminine are not dispositions," posits Judith Butler, "but accomplishments."[90] More poetically, muses Robert Glück, "gender is the extent we go to in order to be loved."[91] Sometimes we go to that extent and stay there. Other times, the meanings of sexuality and sexual identity shift—over a lifetime, but also within a single moment, also within a single person. Some people find themselves in sexual identities that endure and that they themselves can endure; others recognize themselves in "a sock drawer for the anxious affects."[92] Still others just want to try something on, see what it looks or feels like to stand in someone else's place for a spell—to switch positions, even if only to switch quickly back.

The point bears out historically too. Women's sexualities, in the heady feminist moment of call-it-the-seventies, were defined and debated according to many competing terms, including whether and to what degree sexuality was erotic or social, collective or individual.[93] Shelves and shelves of books have been written on these subjects, but both the debates and the clarifications might be taken as indications of how, yes, we can fantasize about ourselves, but we can also fantasize about the world or the society or the context in which we find, or would like to find, ourselves. There doesn't need to be any precise biographical correlative—any lived or documented experience—for something to be worked out in fantasy. Senses, wishes, impulses; history, culture, structure; these things too hold us and are held by us.

Is Simone the subject of the songs she sings? The object? The narrator? Some combination? "All of the above" gives no clarity as an answer, but it also seems most likely to be correct. To try and pin down a more precise answer, in any case, risks imposing a logic on a fantasy expression whose purpose is the counterlogical work of holding together contradictory possibilities.

COVER SONGS OFFER GLIMPSES of the ways that artists can also be fans, but not all fandoms are the same. The one Simone kindled for Bob Dylan appears to be relatively special. Not only did she cover Dylan, but she kept covering him for thirty years, all the way through the recording sessions for her final studio album, *A Single Woman*, in 1993.[94] She explained some of her admiration to Phyl Garland around 1969: "Most of [rock music] is *junk*, but a lot of them are good and there's *one* guy I'd like to speak of who's not like us at all and doesn't try to sound colored. But he has his *own* thing, and I respect him and really admire him, and that's Bob Dylan. The man is his *own* man, has his own *statement* to make and makes it. He's a universal poet. He's not trying to be white *or* colored. The man is just a great *poet*. And I admire him very much."[95] If covering Dylan provided Simone with a chance to speak in the voice of a universal poet, this description suggests a slight shift away from what she was doing in, say, "Pirate Jenny." There, Simone used her body to occupy the space of a celebrated role and a high-culture text, and in so doing tilted its meaning, and its power, toward something more specific, something her own. Simone performing "Pirate Jenny" is very much the inverse of "not trying to be white *or* colored."[96]

Instead, Simone covering Dylan looks more like a negotiation, a trying on for size, a chance to look at one's self in the fitting room mirror and imagine who that person staring back might be or do if she were going to look like this. The chance to be the speaker of a Dylan song is less the chance for Simone to insert herself into a role she's not otherwise going to be offered than it is a chance to play someone she's not. Of course Simone was really "colored," black and proud. Of course she was really a woman, a musician, a wife, a daughter, and so many other things. But in the four minutes and forty-nine seconds of "Just Like Tom Thumb's Blues," Simone gets to be something else too, something she maybe otherwise wouldn't. The contradictions between being someone and being someone else do not cancel each other here.

Dylan matters to this fantasy as he was the one she drew toward, the one she worked through, the one she appears to have fantasized about. But for the success of Simone's performances, Dylan is beside the point. Credit for the transformations Simone accomplished by way of his songs goes to her, not Dylan. It's her work, her desire, her art that leads her to, as Frantz Fanon described such creativity, "introduc[e] invention into existence."[97] It was she who "perform[ed] with her whole self, albeit a self iterated to another power," in the kind of event that Tavia Nyong'o has recently dubbed "Afrofabulation."[98] Whatever we call Simone's imaginative work, however, I would stress that its purview included, at intervals, claiming space for herself and imagining herself otherwise. The result is a body of work that is both deeply black and also, at moments, staking out the utopian limits of such a project.[99]

The important, almost unbelievable thing about all this is how totally Simone succeeded in getting people to recognize and share in the fantasy, which is to say, succeeded in making it real. One review of a 1969 Berkeley performance found Simone's "I Shall Be Released" "one of the most memorable performances of a Dylan song by someone other than the author that I have ever heard."[100] Dylan numbered among the artists whose material she was seen to "zealously search[] out and bend[] . . . to her will."[101] Decades later, reviewing the memorial concert held the year after her death, Stephen Holden described Simone as "the ultimate pop diva, notoriously temperamental, musically beyond category and at one time the definitive interpreter of Bob Dylan."[102] I'd like to think, in that last particular especially, she would have felt seen. Regardless, it was Toni Morrison who, at the same event, made the point about Simone's expressions in the terms that actually matter: "She saved our lives."[103]

1972

1972 WAS THE YEAR Simone released *Emergency Ward*, a truly virtuosic partly live, partly studio album comprising only three tracks, two of which are an eighteen-minute medley that incorporates a version of George Harrison's "My Sweet Lord" and an eleven-minute interpretation of Harrison's "Isn't It a Pity." It was a year when Simone voiced not just a man, but a Beatle, claiming the power of that voice, but also reclaiming some of what she elsewhere said the Beatles took from black music.[1]

1972 WAS THE YEAR that kicked off with NBC television airing MGM's 1951 production of *Showboat*, the one that stripped the 1927 musical and 1936 film of nearly all its black actors.[2]

1972 WAS THE YEAR Simone appeared on *Sesame Street*, swaying and holding hands with four black children to the three-minute single version of "To Be Young, Gifted and Black." The episode aired on February 18, three days before her thirty-ninth birthday.[3]

||| ● |||| ● |||

1972 WAS THE YEAR Mahalia Jackson died in January (aged 60), Adam Clayton Powell Jr. died in April (aged 63), and Jackie Robinson died in October (aged 53).

||| ● |||| ● |||

1972 WAS THE YEAR the Black Liberation Army assassinated police officers Gregory Foster and Rocco Laurie at the corner of East Eleventh Street and Avenue B in New York City. After the killings, local authorities received a note describing the murders as a retaliation for prisoner deaths during the 1971 Attica prison rebellion.[4]

||| ● |||| ● |||

1972 WAS THE YEAR the white supremacist monument to the Confederacy was completed at Stone Mountain in Georgia, decisively rebranding literal treason as southern heritage.[5]

||| ● |||| ● |||

1972 WAS THE YEAR *The Harder They Come* was released. This first feature-length film from Jamaica, starring Jimmy Cliff, screened at the Venice Film Festival, where it was picked up for limited distribution in New York, shown to midnight audiences in April 1973.[6]

||| ● |||| ● |||

1972 WAS THE YEAR Angela Davis was acquitted by a Marin County, California, court on charges of kidnapping and first-degree murder. Despite the racially charged sensationalism surrounding it, the case was powerfully reframed in terms of a different kind of bias when Davis's opening statement argued that the prosecution's attempt to implicate her in a crime of passion was "clearly a symptom of the male chauvinism which prevails in our society."[7]

1972 WAS THE YEAR Shirley Chisholm, the first black woman elected to Congress, announced her campaign in the Democratic presidential primary, under the slogan "Unbought and Unbossed."[8] It was a year when black women, in particular, were claiming forms of public authority and respect that had not historically been on offer.[9]

1972 WAS THE YEAR James Baldwin published the teaser "Martin and Malcolm" in the April issue of *Esquire*, followed quickly by the book of essays into which it was collected, *No Name in the Street*. It was a year when black people were not only making history but also telling it.

"1972 WAS RIGHT ALL THE WAY," sang Nina Simone, in a cover of Exuma's "22nd Century."

> 1972 was right all the way
> Drums and bugles blasting all through the day
> Right wing, left wing, middle of the road
> Side winder, backswinger, backlash, whiplash
> Race stockings, red stockings
> Liberation of women, liberation of men
> Everybody carrying a heavy load[10]

The song was recorded in 1971. It was a fantasy about the future.

RCA promotional advertisement in the *Village Voice* (1972).

Obeah

Fantasy bespeaks something about who we are and how we work, but it can also answer the question of where we are or, more specifically, where we belong. The concept of belonging doesn't really separate out *who* from *how* from *where*, for belonging refers to place and placement, to be sure, but in the subjective terms of affinity, acceptance, fit. Our belonging may be legislated by facts or rules or laws or paperwork, but our sense of belonging just as often flouts legislation with feelings. At the juncture where the facts and the feelings of belonging contradict, fantasy can enter the picture.

Nina Simone belonged in Liberia. It was a point she made again and again. Recalling the beginning of her sojourn there, at the invitation of Miriam Makeba in 1974, Simone's autobiography records her hope that a visit to a place she'd never been before might "be like going home."[1] The same language shows up in "Liberian Calypso," her musical reflection on the period, in the refrain "You brought me home to Liberia / All other places are inferior."[2] Explaining her time off from performing while in Liberia, Simone told an audience in 1976, "I went home you see."[3] "This ain't my country," she said of the United

States in 1980. "I claim Africa."[4] In Liberia "I was at home!" she told Tim Sebastian in a 1999 BBC interview and many others over the years.[5]

The place where Simone belonged existed for her in specific terms. "My Africa had no countries," she recalled, "just hundreds of different peoples mixed through history into a rough cocktail and forced to seed an exiled nation in a far-off country: my great grandfather, Grandma, Daddy, Momma, me."[6] Her sense of belonging evoked an identity based in common history, taking Liberia as part of a more broadly African identity such as was emerging in the period of decolonization that began officially in 1957; at the same time, Simone's sense of belonging also evoked an identity based in difference, a rejection of the version of self bequeathed upon her by US history, a refusal, as she elsewhere put it, "to stay here and be Aunt Jemima."[7] This conjunction of commonality and difference is a potent route to a sense of identity, as Saidiya Hartman reminds us, for it "is only when you are stranded in a hostile country that you need a romance of origins."[8]

Simone's feelings of belonging in Liberia loom larger than the relatively small number of months between September 1974 and early 1977 when she lived in the capital city, Monrovia, in the heady days of the Tolbert regime, before the 1980 coup and the subsequent decades of political instability and civil war.[9] But feelings of belonging are not only allowed to be larger than the facts that support them; they are often encouraged to be. Such encouragement, at least, is a signature of modern nationalism. It fuels the kind of disciplining, ordering fantasies of belonging through which a national culture becomes local, through which something symbolizing the national structure—a flag, a pledge, a statue, a ritual, an idea, a way of life—is felt and often tested, measured, proven, as though it were primarily personal.[10] In the case of a diaspora and not a nation, of a Pan-Africanism and not a nationalism, the fantasy may be less disciplining, though it, and the identity it yields for us, can still certainly feel entirely, deeply ours, whatever the official paperwork may say.[11]

Nina Simone, studio shoot
for *Nina Simone and Piano*
(1969). Photo by Michael Ochs
Archives/Getty Images.

III ● IIIII ● III

BELONGING ISN'T STATIC, and our sense of belonging is often compatible with, perhaps even dependent on, a sense of our self that isn't static either. On the threshold of the 1970s, Simone was gravitating toward black. In early 1969, she and her musical director, Weldon Irvine Jr., cowrote "To Be Young, Gifted and Black," inspired by the title of Lorraine Hansberry's last, unfinished play.[12] Simone debuted the song that August at the Harlem Cultural Fair (aka "Black Woodstock"), showcased it in concerts through the rest of year, and released it as a single, all before a live recording appeared on *Black Gold* (1970).[13] The song charted in both the UK and the US Top 100, and *Black Gold* earned Simone her second and final Grammy nomination.[14] "To Be Young, Gifted and Black" was then covered by Donny Hathaway on his debut album *Everything Is Everything* (1970) and by Aretha Franklin on the album she named after it, *To Be Young, Gifted and Black* (1972). In October 1971, the Congress of Racial Equality (CORE) invited Simone to New York City on the pretense of a benefit, instead surprising her with a citation for her contributions to the movement.[15] This honor was overshadowed when "hundreds of delegates" to the CORE conference voted to adopt "To Be Young, Gifted and Black" as what was variously called the black national anthem or the national anthem of black America.[16] As far as Simone was concerned, the greatest of all the song's accolades was the last one.

In her autobiographical reminiscences, Simone waxes rhapsodic. It "really made me glow," she recalled. "I wasn't in the movement for personal glory, but this dedication made me very proud because it showed I was succeeding as a protest singer, that I was writing songs people remembered and were inspired by."[17] Indeed, *I Put a Spell on You* devotes nearly two of its fewer than two hundred pages to anecdotes about student activists, at CORE and the Student Nonviolent Coordinating Committee (SNCC), who loved her records, who listened to them at meetings, who rescheduled their conference dates so they could attend her concerts, and who "told me proudly that the only thing that ever got stolen from their offices—meaning the only thing SNCC workers stole from each other—were books and Nina Simone records, and that the only thing guaranteed to make members forget their non-violent training was for them to find out their Nina Simone records were missing."[18] This anecdote is clearly playful, good-humored, and yet Simone's repeated naming of herself in the third person also seems to align herself with these records as they move in a kind of perfect environment—one where they can be lost and found, stolen or replaced, all without forfeiting the context in which they belong.[19]

Protest music was a context in which Simone found a sense of belonging, but perhaps it is able to all come together at this moment in the early 1970s very much because that context itself was also changing. "Although gospel hymns were used in the marches and boycotts of the 1950s," writes Tammy L. Kernodle, "and the use of music as protest within the black community can be documented as far back as the seventeenth century, it was not viewed as an essential part of the early black freedom movement. . . . Through the Albany movement of 1961, SNCC redefined the public use of music."[20] The election by CORE of "To Be Young, Gifted and Black" as the black national anthem effectively displaced "Lift Ev'ry Voice and Sing," composed by J. Rosamond and James Weldon Johnson, the canonized "Negro national hymn" and the anthem of the National Association for the Advancement of Colored People (NAACP).[21] Moreover, this rapid terminological move between about 1955 and about 1970, from *negro* to *colored* to *black*, was a complex context too—on the one hand rejecting inclusion into white America in favor of creating a new black identity, and on the other distancing from America at all and setting sights on a more global, Africanist orientation to culture and history.[22] The "black" that Simone conjured in "To Be Young, Gifted and Black," then, wasn't precisely an existing part of herself, not something waiting there to be discovered or asserted, so much as something she was helping to create. Simone found belonging in music and identity at a moment when they coordinated in particular ways they hadn't previously. She belonged in order to be.

RACISM FANATICIZES ABOUT eternal contaminations.[23] Its proffered alternative to its own imagined fears is to insist on purity, which is also to insist that bodies and histories and identities are a whole lot simpler than they often tend to be. In this way, racism often imagines that all black people are black in the same ways, rather than extraordinarily heterogeneous in all the ways they actually are. There are no upshots to racism, though among its violent catalog of fantasies this one about simplicity can at least be bankable. And Jalacy "Screamin' Jay" Hawkins took it to the bank.

A failed opera singer with an outlandish but hard-to-verify life story, Hawkins is chiefly remembered for his 1956 song, "I Put a Spell on You," and even more so, since the song never charted, for the highly theatrical, often sensational, totally one-dimensional caricatures he evoked when performing it. Danielle C. Heard summarizes: "Hawkins became well known for playing up a stereotypical portrayal of a Haitian *ougan*, or vodun priest. Using props identifiable by US audiences as belonging to 'voodoo' practices—a smoking skull, a pair of tusks through his nasal septum, snakes, and fire displays—he spoke wildly in tongues, bugged his eyes, and generally performed as a charlatan *ougan*."[24] Another scholar refers to Hawkins as "a black Vincent Price."[25]

Vodun is a laden signifier. Often styled in English as *voodoo*, *vodun* broadly refers to a West African belief system that was transported to the Caribbean with the forced migration of its believers, where it developed in Haiti in particular. The term is often used interchangeably with *hoodoo* or *conjure*, a set of folk beliefs and practices developed among enslaved Africans in the US South, and with *obeah* or *obi*, a syncretic practice of (usually protective) magic developed by enslaved Africans in Jamaica possibly as early as the sixteenth century. Further confusion of these terms owes to imperfect accounts written by European colonists in the Caribbean—including Edward Long and Moreau de Saint Méry—and to the sensational repurposing of Afro-diasporic expressions as props for drama and horror in entertainments designed for white consumers—from William Earle's *Obi* (1800) to W. B. Seabrook's *The Magic Island* (1929) to George Romero's *Night of the Living Dead* (1968).[26] But it seems to be precisely this confusion among white audiences that Hawkins exploited, turning spell casting and literal black magic into a comedy act that secured bookings and sold records.[27]

Simone covered "I Put a Spell on You" for her album of the same name (1965), and it quickly became one of her charting hits. First reissued as early as 1969, Simone's version shows up frequently on her "best of" and greatest

Jalacy "Screamin' Jay" Hawkins
(1979). Wikimedia Commons.

hits compilations. Yet Simone's version, despite its opening strings and piano trills, largely follows the syncopations and bellowing vocals of the original, her contralto matching Hawkins's baritone. While not terribly different in terms of its sonic register, Simone's and Hawkins's performances of the song differ quite a bit in terms of their emotional deliveries. Simone sings "I Put a Spell on You" as a love song, in the persona of a lover who refuses to be scorned, while Hawkins sings his version with notably amplified menace, almost threateningly, as a man whose refusal is backed by force. The greater success of Simone's version may at least in part be credited to her alteration of the song's emotional landscape and what might be recognized as a simplification of the song's genre—making the song more legible, and even more palatable, to audiences whose chauvinisms might incline them to accept black women as desirous more readily than black men as willful.

Simone and Hawkins, in other words, work the song into different kinds of magic. Her performance signifies as a love song because it gives only the sound of her seductive voice as a referent for magic. Absent Hawkins's props and caricatures, Simone's performance, while powerful on its own terms, drops vodun from the story. She performs the spell but omits anything that would make its magic signal particularly black.

But that was 1965, and things change. Simone went on to correct her earlier omission at a 1968 concert in England where she performed a ninety-second version of "I Put a Spell on You," opening stiffly, her affect in the first verse flat and tight, until her animated, off-tempo delivery of improvised lyrics:

I can't stand it, you're running around, daddy
You know better now
I can't stand it when you put me down
So I went to Alabama and I got me some mojo dust
And I put a spell on you[28]

‖ ● ‖‖ ● ‖

BEFORE THE FANTASIES of Africa, there were fantasies of the Caribbean. Simone didn't have to travel anywhere as far as Liberia to dream of and alongside black diasporic cultures as they took shape in the decolonial era. For the whole of the twentieth century, New York City's neighborhoods—Harlem, Bedford-Stuyvesant, Crown Heights, San Juan Hill—had been points of contact and ports of call for Caribbean immigrants and the Pan-African thought they created.[29] Simone seems to have encountered it first in the Village.

Among its principle avatars for her was Macfarlane Mackey, known professionally as Tony McKay, who had been born on Cat Island in the Bahamas and came to New York City as a young man, on the pretense of studying architecture.[30] Nine years younger than Simone, almost to the day, he came up through Village clubs like Cafe Wha?, The Bitter End, and Cafe Bizarre—all at a slightly lower tier than the Village Gate or the Village Vanguard where Simone, when not touring the world, was already headlining.[31] By summer 1972, they would appear on the same bill at Lincoln Center's inaugural black music program "Soul at the Center," but not before McKay's act was rechristened as Exuma, a name he also took for himself and for their first album, released in 1970.[32]

Because Exuma has almost totally disappeared from histories and anthologies of the Village scene that he shared not only with Simone but also with the likes of Bob Dylan, Joan Baez, and Odetta, it's worth pausing to evoke his sounds. Exuma's was a repertoire that consisted of original, folklore-inspired songs played with traditional Bahamian and Caribbean instruments. The band inclined in the direction of faster, high-energy beats, often reminiscent of the Bahamian Junkanoo—a Caribbean festival sound much closer to Brazilian samba than to Jamaican reggae—and leaned heavily on harmonies. Recording with upward of eight musicians for a single song, the ensemble tended percussive, including multiple drums, rattles, and tambourine, as well as a bass and Exuma's lead guitar, but rarely if ever horns or other wind instruments—a further distinction from a Jamaican sounds like ska and rocksteady. Critics, even those becoming literate by the early 1970s in the idiom of reggae, couldn't locate the genre. They called Exuma's first album "a fascinating trip into African witchcraft and West Indian voodoo," or ascribed to him "a rare and unique experience of Caribbean music explosion and vibrations," or commended his "African-style."[33] However, Exuma's preferred term of art was obeah "because it evokes all the images of black

Village Vanguard, Greenwich
Village (1976). Photo by
Tom Marcello, Wikimedia
Commons.

III ● IIIII ● III

Soul at the Center street
advertisement, Lincoln Center
(1972). Lincoln Center for the
Performing Arts Archives.

magic—spirits, zombies, devils, ghosts and angels."[34] As late as 1988, he was appearing at music festivals as "the Obeah Man."[35]

When it came to lyrics, Exuma's imagery brought forward figures from obeah and vodun, but his imagination roved ecumenically in the direction of apocalyptic scenes. A largely favorable *New York Times* review of Exuma's 1977 off-Broadway musical *Junkanoo Drums* found the influence not only of "African belief systems" but of a Christianity that "seems to find the promises of Armageddon and the final judgment more interesting than anything else in the Bible."[36] One such song appeared on the band's third album, *Do Wah Nanny* (1971), and it became the first song of Exuma's that Simone would cover.

The song "22nd Century" is an eight-minute track that foils attempts at easy summary as it presents an apocalyptic catalog of bodily, political, philosophical, and technological change over the century-plus between 1971 and 2101. Its emphasis on transformation—for example, "Sex changing, changing, changing / Man is woman / Woman is man / Even your brain is not your brain"—undoubtedly accounts for its multiple subsequent covers by trans-identified artists including Mx Justin Vivian Bond and Rahne Alexander.[37] And while the song's vision of transformation may be part of Simone's attraction as well—uncharacteristically, her lyrics are unmodified from the original—she appears also to have been drawn to Exuma's Caribbean sound, his guitar backed by a percussion section made up of bells, foot drum, and cabasa, punctuated by hits on a triangle. At the very least, Simone's translation of Exuma's song into her own musical idiom shows less radical reimagining and more curious borrowing than many of her other covers.

Simone's cover was recorded in early 1971, in the sessions that produced *Here Comes the Sun*, though it didn't make the cut and was not released on that album or anywhere else until 1998.[38] Distinct from that album's other tracks, however, Simone's "22nd Century" is lushly orchestrated, layering piano and harp melodies onto swirling guitar sounds and keeping time with either a cabasa or something that rattles like it. Cymbals grandly substitute for the more modest triangle chimes of Exuma's original. Simone's vocals, meanwhile, perform their magic, attenuating vowels in the refrain "twenty-second century" and vocalizing across the bridge, before picking up tempo and scatting across the antepenultimate chorus, lending the song's climax a dramatic urgency that Exuma's version lacks. Compositionally intricate as it is, Simone's "22nd Century" is also experimental, trying new sounds, covering new artists, envisioning new worlds.[39]

As always, however, newness has precedents. Bongos and hand drums had sometimes accompanied Simone on concert stages since about 1968 or so, and among other places they can be heard clearly on her recording of "Just Like Tom Thumb's Blues" on *To Love Somebody* (1969), performed by now-legendary jazz percussionist Don Alias, who would record with Miles Davis the same year. By October 1969, during a live recording session at New York's Philharmonic Hall, Simone introduced her drummers as "the heartbeat of our organization," and she, one of the greatest pianists then alive, deferentially embellished the point: "The pulse of everything that we do centers around the drums, and of course if you think about that, really, seriously, you know that your entire life is centered around your heart*beat*. And that's rhythm, is it not?"[40] This midcareer overpronouncement notwithstanding, percussive sounds are arguably a part of Simone's repertoire even earlier than her more realized turn to Caribbean and Afro-diasporic inspiration around 1971, for example, in the ostinato pattern of "Four Women" on *Wild Is the Wind* (1966).[41] The presence of these earlier sounds can be explained as part of the sonic landscape of mainstream US music in the late 1950s, especially following the moment when Harry Belafonte's *Calypso* (1956) became the first LP to sell over a million copies, inaugurating what trade magazines of the day called a "calypso craze" that indiscriminately gathered all Caribbean sounds—and not just the rhythmic harmonies that originated in mid-nineteenth-century Trinidad and Tobago—under the sign of "calypso."[42] What's new with "22nd Century," in other words, isn't Simone's borrowings of Exuma's sounds themselves, so much as what, in retrospect, looks like the beginnings of her recognition of these sounds as expressing something that might be hers to explore in deliberate and specific ways.

COMPREHENSIVENESS IS A FANTASY of being able to do enough. It torments many researchers, sometimes leading us (me) to fixate on what we can't know, what wasn't documented, what cannot be archived in the first place. As it happens, the existing recordings and documents that capture Simone's life and career cluster heavily into the two or three years on either side of 1970. It's an issue of density: there is simply more available from this period than any other. The statisticians would call it "oversampling." Not coincidentally, the same period finds Simone at the peak of the international fame and public recognition she achieved in her lifetime, as well as at a period of significant personal loss and life-wide recalibrations. But if this archive can never be comprehensive enough—if some of whatever was going on in Simone's life will always remain in that life, will always only be hers, no matter what we may do to reconstruct it—perhaps the thing to consider is less Simone's life as such, and more the ways that whatever was going on in it may have found expression in some of the terms or idioms begotten by the history of that moment.[43] Perhaps the thing to consider is how the language we speak is always shared, even when the things we say to ourselves in it are not.

The sounds of the decolonial era vibrated with a language of invention.[44] Between 1962 and 1983, eleven Caribbean islands colonized by the British won their independence, joining neighbors Haiti (independent beginning in 1804) and Cuba (independent beginning in 1902). By the 1980s, as Kobena Mercer has influentially shown, a mature black diasporic aesthetic began to emerge, one that explored the dual cultural inheritances of Europe and Africa while at the same time taking on the full aesthetic complexities of the media (such as film, music, or visual art) in which its practitioners worked.[45] Prior to this emergence, however, and more contemporary with Simone's professional peak, was something equally potent yet more preliminary. Stuart Hall describes it thus: "The ambition to write, and to sing and make art, then, turned out to be itself subversive. It came, not just from the desire to construct an alternative culture out of more indigenous, vernacular or African sources—that came powerfully to the fore later—but from the drive to subvert from within the very colonial cultural inheritance which had shaped and misshaped us; and in a way to lay claim as fully modern black subjects to a future which we were coming to regard as rightfully our own."[46] What Hall describes is less the formation of a distinct aesthetic and more the creation of a distinct sense of identity, one whose edge was whetted against European colonialism and its racist logics.

Diasporic identity interweaves cultural, ethnic, and national identifications into histories of displacement, resettlement, reconnection. Based on what we have listened to Simone say so far, it should be no surprise that she might have been drawn toward the aesthetic and identity emerging out of the Caribbean at about the turn of 1970. Certainly, its sense of invention, of claiming one's self, resonated with an orientation to which her 1960s activism and consciousness-raising was already leading. Moreover, "certain moves, certain arguments and epiphanies," writes Brent Hayes Edwards, "can only be staged beyond the confines of the United States, and even sometimes in languages other than English."[47] It doesn't seem to have especially mattered that Simone "wasn't" herself Caribbean—something that was happening in diaspora claimed a part of her, and so she claimed it. Simone may have been trying to figure out if and to what extent it was where she belonged, or to what extent diaspora's complex and difficult representations worked for her, or she for them.[48] She certainly wasn't alone in doing so at exactly this moment in time.[49]

But if the historical circumstances of emergent Caribbean and more broadly Afro-diasporic aesthetics and identity were part of what made Simone's explorations in this period possible, these historical circumstances are necessary but not sufficient if we're trying to hear and understand how someone "at the time" took something in. Simultaneity is a weak measure of connection: How many things are happening around us that we're not part of, not aware of, don't find out about until later?[50] The material reality of those things arguably bears on what we take in, yet doesn't determine it. Plus, we often absorb more than one thing at the same time. The period in the early 1970s wherein Simone is most obviously exploring black identity through Caribbean, African, and Afro-diasporic cultures stacks neatly on the period at the end of the 1960s in which she is exploring voice and authority in her covers of the likes of Bob Dylan. The 1971 sessions where she records both "22nd Century" and "Just Like a Woman" indicate that these periods overlapped. But viewed with enough distance, 1971 arguably also looks like a transitional moment, a point where one set of fantasies yields to another.

Diaspora is fantasy of belonging, but one that—at this historical juncture of the 1970s anyway—was fueled by creativity, invention. Such a fantasy is quite a bit different than the fantasy of comprehensiveness with which we began. The circumstances under which one frets about doing enough may be quite discrepant from the circumstances under which one more assertively gets to be and do. Diasporic strategy is a fantasy that works to the side of the fantasy of comprehensiveness. Both build archives, though differently designed ones, with diasporic archives perhaps more willing to tolerate what's not there, to imagine that absence isn't necessarily loss because negation can itself be meaningful, can be what Stefano Harney and Fred Moten call "this being together in homelessness, this interplay of the refusal of what has been refused."[51]

‖ ● ‖‖ ● ‖

REFUSAL CAN MAKE WORLDS. Some identities emerge from fantasies of refusal, fantasies of not being something else, fantasies of defense against something we imagine to be worse. Some identities are constructed out of double negatives, as in Hazel Carby's reflections on the condition of being black British in which there was "no flexibility or malleability to her unbelonging," or Saidiya Hartman's astonishingly generative account of the afterlife of slavery, founded on a violence "it is not possible to undo."[52] The double negative cancels itself, leaving the promise of some positive meaning in its place. But in the moment of its articulation, all we know is what that something isn't, not what will happen if, eventually, its promise is kept.

Double negatives belong to the grammar of language, not music. Yet Simone's music gets close to conjuring something that sounds like it could be one, as her piano alternates between spare quarter notes and the cross-talking flurry of a descending tremolo in her cover of Exuma's "Dambala." Named for Damballah Ouedo (variously Damballa or Dambala), a prominent creator god in Haitian vodun, Exuma's chanting and percussion-forward evocation of the god's power transforms, at Simone's precise and dexterous piano-playing hands, into an exquisite incantation that solicits the god's powers for revenge. Despite her significant rearrangement of the song's music, Simone's lyrics are once again unchanged from Exuma's:

Oh Dambala come Dambala
Oh Dambala come Dambala
Think of the wings of a three-toed frog
Eat weeds from the deepest part of sea
Oh Dambala come Dambala
Oh Dambala come Dambala

On the seventh day, God will be there
On the seventh night, Satan will be there
On the seventh day, God will be there
On the seventh night, Satan will be there

You slavers will know
What it's like to be a slave
Slave to your heart
Slave to your soul
Oh Dambala come Dambala
Oh Dambala come Dambala

You slavers will know
What it's like to be a slave
Slave to your mind
Slave to your race
You won't go to heaven
You won't go to hell
You remain in your graves
With the stench and the smell
Oh Dambala come Dambala
Oh Dambala come Dambala[53]

Simone's Dambala is not Exuma's, but, consequentially, neither is he Zora Neale Hurston's. The anthropologist, writing of Haitian belief systems in 1938, concluded that "Damballa and his suite are high and pure. They do only good things for people, but they are slow and lacking in power."[54] Whether or not Simone's Dambala is slow, the court he holds with God and Satan, like his promise to turn slavers into slaves or his threat to banish the dead from the afterlife and to their earthly graves, suggests power enough to upend the world.[55]

"Dambala" is not the first time Simone sang a fantasy of vengeance. One might even imagine her version of the song as a kind of reprise of her earlier "Pirate Jenny." In both cases, the degradations wrought by white supremacy are what need to be avenged—though, given the lifetime Simone lived through between the latter recording in 1963 and the former in 1973, the violence in each case may be the same kind but may perhaps have been legible to her in a far greater degree. More to the point, however, while the same theme animates both songs, the idiom is quite distinct. In "Dambala" vengeance no longer speaks between the lines of a high-culture object that Simone's elite audience will recognize, but instead in the emergent parameters of a vernacular aesthetic. Undoubtedly this change is political, as any such aesthetic change is. But it may also be a shift that doesn't—can't—entirely know what it's shifting toward, not a turn so much as a step. It may be a refinement, a way of repeating oneself in order to be heard better, or perhaps because one has a better sense of what one wanted to say. Saying something one way is, inevitably, also not saying it any other way. In this case, Simone perhaps says something one way in order to refuse to have to be heard in another.

As Hurston observed, "Gods always behave like the people who make them."[56]

III ● IIII ● III

WHAT BELONGING DO we fantasize when we know we can't go home again? Between 1980 and her death in 2003, Simone often shuttled between Amsterdam and Los Angeles, though her permanent addresses were primarily in France—first in Paris and then in the small commune of Bouc-Bel-Air, just south of Aix-en-Provence, and later in the beach town Carry-le-Rouet, west of Marseille. This more than two-decade French sojourn was longer than she'd lived in North Carolina, which she left at age eighteen, and longer than the stretch (roughly 1955 to 1974) when she was based in and around New York City. But France was arguably there in the offing all along—for instance, when Simone recorded Jacques Brel's "Ne Me Quitte Pas" in 1965, or even when she took her name from Simone Signoret in 1954.[57]

If Simone harbored fantasies about France, it seems they took the form of France fantasizing about her. As she tells the story in *I Put a Spell on You*, arriving in Paris in 1980, Simone rented a modest apartment and tried to play a small, "seedy" club in Pigalle called Les Trois Mallets, "not much bigger inside than the old Midtown Bar in Atlantic City."[58] Despite Simone's popularity in France, despite the rare chance to see a big star at the height of her game play to café tables in an intimate venue, no one bought tickets. "It was only later that I understood," she wrote.

> The French admired me not only as a musician but as a star, in the same way that they loved Edith Piaf, and they didn't separate the life from the music. Most audiences expect a performer to go on stage, to play the songs they like and maybe a couple of new ones; then they go home content, thinking their ticket money well spent. The French, especially Parisians, aren't like that at all; they demand that a star lives the life of a star every minute of the day. So they expected me to be staying in a luxury suite at the Georges Cinq Hotel and to be seen at celebrity parties, and they wanted to read about me in society pages. If I didn't do that, then in their eyes I wasn't the same person—I wasn't Nina Simone the star, the person they would queue for hours to see. Many of my French fans—and I know this because they told me—simply didn't believe it was me playing in that little club in Pigalle.... Later, when I did go back to the Georges Cinq and I did play the Olympia Theatre, they lined up around the block to buy tickets and gave me a ten-minute ovation the moment I walked on stage.[59]

Simone's words stop short of saying that the person the French needed her to be was the person she went to France in order to get back to being, though that suggestion hovers over this passage and elsewhere in *I Put a Spell on You*—for example, in the second insert section of photographs, the penultimate of which documents her in fact playing at the Olympia in Paris, before the final portrait whose caption announces its subject *"Enjoying life back at the top."*[60] *Back* would seem to be the operative word: it is the way she went to the Georges Cinq, it is the way she enjoyed her late-career success. Though her life in Paris was arguably a new life—postdivorce, post-Liberia, post-RCA—it nonetheless appears to have been one that reunited her with a part of herself she'd lost in the places she was used to living that life. Such are the things places can sometimes do for us.

I think too about the photograph of a twelve-year-old girl that, we have seen, a thirty-seven-year-old woman put on the back of *Here Comes the Sun*. Sometimes we go backward to go forward. Sometimes what might seem from the outside to be a dislocation is simply the map we have plotted in order to find ourselves wherever we happen to have ended up.

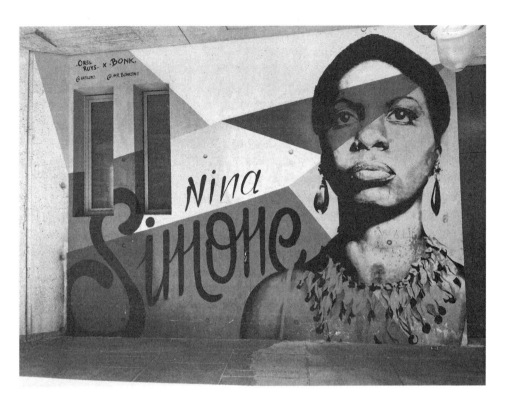

‖ ● ‖‖‖ ● ‖

Nina Simone mural by Orel
Ruys and Mr. Bonkone,
Paris (2022).

REVISION IS A FANTASY that difference and continuity can coexist. Shortly after metastatic brain cancer claimed Bob Marley at the age of thirty-six, in May 1981, Simone paid her first homage. Reaching for some of Marley's capacity to overlay biblical images and Jamaican cultural references into popular music that sounds like prophecy, Simone wrote and recorded "I Was Just a Stupid Dog to Them" on *Fodder on My Wings* (1982), a song that repeats the following lines:

> I was just a dog to them
> They didn't want to change
> Just a stupid dog to them
> With a funny sounding name
>
> Bob Marley had died a week before
> Bratislava was a place to go
> Just a stupid dog to them
> Now everything will change[61]

Despite its debased title and morbid lyrics, the song delivers an upbeat percussive rhythm, alongside Simone's piano and a jazzy, almost ska-like trumpet. The tempo slows slightly, almost to a pause, before the portentous final (and, in later verses, repeated) line "Now everything will change." While that musical change anticipates the change announced in this line, the stolid observations contained in the prior lyrics meaningfully don't. What the song gives us, then, is a twist, a moment that shifts expectations and invites surprise. The overall effect is less dramatic than simply poetic, and this lyrical twist can accordingly be read as an apt tribute to the man who wove the government yards of Trenchtown into the center of a creative cultural universe.

But Simone didn't leave things there. *Fodder on My Wings* ends with a second, unusually short (thirty-three-second) tribute to Marley called "They Took My Hand," the entire lyrics to which are:

> You took my teeth
> You took my brains
> You tried to drive me so insane
> And now you're trying to take my eyes
> But it is finished
> Because I'm too wise
> And that is why Bob Marley died

And that is why Bob Marley died
And that is why Bob Marley died
You took his eyes

The reversal in these lyrics echoes the poetic mode of "I Was Just a Stupid Dog to Them," but with the more surprising twist by which taking "my hand" is not the expected metaphor for accepting help so much as a synecdochical butchering, dismembering a body for its parts. The song is angry, and, coming at the end of the album, the anger feels like a revision of the earlier, more meditative position of "I Was Just a Stupid Dog to Them." What had in the first instance been a matter of prophetic change becomes in the second instance a scene of outrageous theft. Yet the tune of "They Took My Hand" is effervescently jazzy, so tonally out of sync with the violence of its lyrics that the song as a whole lands somewhere shockingly on the emotional spectrum between ironic and deranged.

Simone didn't leave things there, either. She would not only speak about Marley, but also speak through him. In 1990 at Montreux, she performed "No Woman, No Cry," introducing the song as "in honor of Bob Marley."[62] Three years later in Los Angeles, Simone recorded that song in the sessions that produced A Single Woman, though it was cut from the album, released only on its expanded version in 2008. On a California concert tour late in 2000, Simone wove a righteous harangue against the presidential election stolen by George W. Bush together with a cover of Marley's "Get Up, Stand Up" and left the stage with an exhortation to the crowd, "Now you hear me. So you go and do something about that man."[63]

It's clear that Marley casts a long shadow across Simone's last two decades, numbering her among the black women intellectuals he influenced, from Lauryn Hill to Saidiya Hartman.[64] What's less clear is precisely what she uses him to evoke. Simone's imagination during the 1970s seems to have been fired by Caribbean, African, and Afro-diasporic art, sound, and imagery, and the stature Marley began to assume late in that decade as a spokesperson for a kind of emergent Pan-African postcolonialism makes him an understandable candidate for her attention.[65] It's also possible that her tributes and evocations of Marley were less specifically about Marley himself than about some of the other black political leaders with whom she may have associated him, other lives brutally extinguished before their time, such as those of Medgar Evers, Malcolm X, and Martin Luther King Jr.

This last possibility may be a stretch, and it comes forward only by implication. In her final years, Simone often compared and conflated among black male leaders she had known, for instance, speaking ruefully in 1999 on the possibility of a black president in the United States despite her sense of Jesse Jackson's inadequacies: "There's not been a man since [King]. His dream came true with Nelson Mandela, because Nelson got it done in South Africa."[66] In 1998, she performed at the New Jersey Performing Arts Center in Newark, where her requiem for King, "Why? (The King of Love Is Dead)," likewise mentioned Mandela.[67] In a late interview, she spoke more generally, "They kill all of the black leaders. How can anyone expect me to live in a country where, bang-bang, our leaders are shot dead."[68] We unconsciously make such substitutions all the time, transferring the intensity of our attention and investment in one person to another person, plotting people into the patterns of our own attachments, turning one love object effectively into another.[69] But because Marley was not an explicit part of these associations, perhaps he wasn't on Simone's mind here at all. Perhaps her interest in Marley was, genuinely and specifically, an interest in Bob Marley and not in anything or anyone he could be made to substitute for.

Even if Marley didn't stand in anyone's place, though, Simone did appear to stand in his. She covered his songs, but even before she did so, the ones she wrote about him use a grammar that articulates ambiguous and multivalent referents for the "I" and "my" positions. Only a poetic logic would allow for "you" taking "my" teeth, brains, and eyes to be the "that is why" which explains someone else's death. Taking from one body isn't typically assumed to harm another. Whatever connections, whatever kind of symbiosis, is being conjured here, substitution or trading places or being someone else seems to be a part of the scene.

Perhaps it matters, too, that before Simone stood in Marley's place, he had stood in hers. In 1966, Bob Marley and the Wailers recorded a cover of Simone's "Sinnerman," off *Pastel Blues* (1965), as "Sinner Man."[70] If Simone knew about this cover, she never, to my knowledge, spoke of it anywhere, at least anywhere that was recorded or written down. Maybe this is a lacuna in the record, or maybe it genuinely reflects something that never happened. In either case, the lack of any record perhaps has to do with the likelihood that in 1966 Simone's words and sounds floating as far south as Jamaica— where upstart musicians reworked them among eclectic covers of black US-American music that were being synthesized in studios and dance halls into the distinctive Jamaican sound that, as reggae, would filter into the diaspora and then the world—may not have meant anything in particular to her.[71] Whereas, Marley's cover, if she knew about it, may have meant more by the time of his death in 1981, on the other side of Simone's initial explorations of

Caribbean, African, and Afro-diasporic aesthetics, perhaps from the vantage of the small Paris apartment three thousand miles and a continent away from the Liberia she told people, again and again, was her home.

Or perhaps the fantasy tugs in yet a different direction, away from both Marley himself and Marley-as-someone else, away from any history or pre-history of borrowed words, and instead toward that complicated voicing through which Simone made songs her own. The titular lyric of Marley's "No Woman, No Cry" allowed Simone to speak in the syntax of Jamaican English, where the sequential negative produces emphasis rather than cause and effect—semantically closer to "woman, don't you cry" than the often mistakenly presumed Anglicization "without a woman, you won't cry."[72] Marley's song, then, enacts a gendered performance of reassurance, consistent with his career-long displays of masculine and often sexualized bravado. When Simone sings these words, it's far less obvious what her relationship might be to the "little darlin'" on whom the song bequeaths that reassurance. Yet as with many of Simone's other covers, the gendered voice she ventriloquizes here doesn't seem merely incidental to her performance. It registers, clearly though not transparently, in the only lyric she changes—at least in the 1990 Montreux version—such that Marley's pal Georgic, the friend who "would make the fire lights" "in the government yard in Trenchtown," becomes Simone's gal Georgia. Such a small change feels like an insistent one—something asserted, something that means something. Perhaps here again is a fantasy in which Simone has the chance to change or move among positions. Perhaps it's a chance to offer herself the reassurance she might have wanted from any number of men who, by 1990, were not around to speak these words to her themselves.

All of these possibilities are guesses, though. The pieces are unmistakably here, but what they add up to isn't.

"EXUMA, YOU HERE?" Simone can be heard to say at the top of her only extant recording of "Obeah Woman," on *It Is Finished*.[73] Her third cover of an Exuma song—and the last track on Simone's final RCA record—comes from the title track and opening song on Exuma's first, self-titled album. This chiasmatic movement across their two recording careers is perhaps emphasized by the fact that Simone's performance is less a cover and closer to something like a riff. Departing from her habit of covering Exuma without changing his lyrics, Simone's "Obeah Woman" changes *all* of them—even the title, which, in the original, had been "Exuma, the Obeah Man." That the song is a cover at all is only evident from her gestures toward Exuma, such as Simone performed when evoking him at the song's opening, or on the album's liner notes where she gave him a writing credit.

Unlike "22nd Century" or "Dambala," or indeed many other of the songs Simone covered, "Exuma, the Obeah Man" is on its own terms almost uncoverable because it serves as a musical introduction by and about Tony McKay. "Exuma, the Obeah Man," draws eclectically on imagery from traditions of Caribbean folklore and obeah and makes reference to entirely specific locations like Gumelemi Cay in the Bahamas, in order to describe phenomena including the mystical conditions of his birth ("Tony McKay was my given name," goes one line) and his relationships to gods and planets. About as far as is possible to be from a kind of poetry or sentiment with a broad potential for identification—from the kind of "universal poet[ry]" with which Simone credited Bob Dylan, for example—the lyrics to "Exuma, the Obeah Man," are replete with details that simply wouldn't make sense if voiced by someone else.[74]

What Simone retains from Exuma's version is music. She employs the original tune's polyphonic rhythm but translates it to many fewer instruments than Exuma's ensemble sound and, notably, eschews the backing vocals on which his version relies. The only voice in "Obeah Woman" is Simone's, though it alternates meaningfully between speaking and singing. The spoken lines are articulated to the beat of the drums, and in a few cases Simone attenuates the vowels in her words, infusing the speech with melody. Yet these spoken parts are generally asides, and in them Simone seems to be talking about herself. For example, "You know about the holy roller church?" she asks the audience.

Ain't that where I started?
Ha I know

We've outgrown it now
And I'm proud
That I did it
That I came through

I like money, yeah
I like fine clothes
I like all of it
But I know where my roots are, you hear me?

Sometimes my daughter says
"Mama I don't understand them people"
I don't either, but I'm born of 'em!
Hear me?
[laughter] And I like it[75]

What these spoken verses have in common is a concern for history—where she started, where her roots are, of whom she was born. The tense of Simone's speech alternates between the present and the past, and her glance is directed unmistakably backward. Meanwhile, the origins described here line up pretty indisputably with Simone's own life story.

As the beat behind her words stays constant, Simone's performance shifts into proper singing, and the song's perspective changes:

Obeah woman
Yes, I'm the Obeah woman
Do you know what one is?
Do you know what an Obeah woman is?

I'm the Obeah woman
From beneath the sea
To get to Satan
You gotta pass through me
'Cause I know the angels
Name by name
I can eat thunder
And drink the rain

[spoken aside:] Been through enough

Yeah they call me Nina
And Pisces too

There ain't nothing
That I can't do
If I choose to
If you let me

I'm the Obeah woman
Above the pain
I can eat thunder
And drink the rain
I kiss the moon
And hug the sun
And call the spirits
And make 'em run
You hear me?
You hear me?
'Cause I ain't playing
Never was
Just waiting for my time
Waiting for my time
Have to learn patience
Have to learn patience

Here, the enumerated details no longer check out against the more objective parts of Simone's life story. She ascribes to herself fantastic powers to communicate with spirits, angels, and devils, to be in intimate contact with celestial bodies. In addition to Simone's persona changing in this shift from speech to song, the tense in which she expresses herself does as well. Descriptions of the Obeah woman's powers and bearing consistently use the present imperfect and the future tenses. The only use of the past tense in the preceding lyrics comes in the spoken aside "Been through enough." The shifts from speaking to singing, from past to future, from Nina Simone to Obeah woman, line up rather neatly, a duality in clear and symmetrical parts.

Until the very end, that is. If these formal elements of "Obeah Woman" present a study in contrast, what reconciles them appears to be a fantasy of refusal. As the song closes, Simone sings:

Obeah woman
You people from the islands
Know about the Obeah woman
I didn't put the name on myself

And I don't like it sometimes
The weight is too heavy
The weight is too heavy
[Spoken:] Let's finish it

What had been an act of claiming power ("I'm the Obeah woman") and identity ("They call me Nina / And Pisces too") resolves into a burden ("I didn't put the name on myself / And I don't like it sometimes"). Here the tense evoked is the imperfect, and the burden would seem accordingly to be historical, a weight that accumulated over time and is still accumulating. The way the song imagines that burden might be put down is through refusal or, more specifically, a refusal to continue, an interruption of song by speech, and so in the voice and mode the song associates with Simone herself: "Let's finish it."[76]

"Obeah Woman" displays a maximal version of Simone's borrowing and elaborating the creative resources that Exuma seems to have represented to her, and that, by extension, she drew from the period's emergent Caribbean and Afro-diasporic aesthetics and identity. At the same time, Simone retains masterful control of the adaptations, adoptions, and transformations these aesthetics may have wrought on her own sense of self, such that she is able to both command them and limit them—to say where and how they come in and when they stop. At the culmination of a period of learning about herself through sounds and cultures foreign to herself, Simone ceases to "hand over omnipotence" and instead insists on the need to face the self that remains.[77] That cessation could happen for any number of reasons. Maybe the fantasy trails off, or maybe what it offers is exhausted. Maybe it's not the fantasy so much as one's self who reaches the limit of how excited one can bear to be. Or perhaps something that had promised to reconcile a contradiction becomes something that catches a person in a new contradiction. At any of these moments, it would not be at all surprising if something one had been excited to carry around suddenly started to feel like something we didn't put on ourselves, a weight that was too heavy. What's more surprising, or at least more significant, is that Simone seems able to put it down.

Audience

Fantasies are ours, but that doesn't mean we're all alone in them. They involve ourselves without being purely self-involved. Erotic fantasies, for example, express an attachment, a way that the self reaches out to something beyond itself. Even though the erotic fantasy and the object that excites us in it are generated in our body-minds, its situation is distinct from more properly narcissistic attachments, which, writes Freud, tend not to be erotic at all.[1] It's the difference between being excited about something we've created for ourselves and being alone with ourselves.[2] The English term for that fantastic excitement is Greek to us: *cathexis* is how James Strachey translated the name for this investment or allocation of psychic energy to an object, person, or idea. Freud's own German term, *Besetzung*, has more spatial connotations, of occupation, allocation, filling up, taking over. All this can be said fairly simply: being overtaken can feel exciting, even if we're doing it to ourselves.

Philosophers have spent a lot of time debating whether other people exist or whether, in the terms just mentioned, there's ultimately anything other than ourselves to excite ourselves. Depending on whom you ask, fantasy in this mode can look variously like a stopgap or a totality, a supplement to reality or reality itself. Jacques Lacan, for instance, dryly defined love as giving something you don't have to someone who doesn't want it; and, with such a definition in place, it should be no surprise Lacan's thinking spared little positive regard for fantasy, valuing more often the Real that he said could be found beyond it.[3] On the other hand, Melanie Klein took a more holistic approach, positing an unconscious process of "splitting" wherein we project parts of ourselves outward, allowing ourselves to insist that what is outside ourselves is not ourselves and, sometimes, thereby to bring it safely back in.[4] No matter which side of the debate you land on, however, what these theories of fantasy cannot wholly explain is the way some people or objects or ideas solicit our cathexes more consistently, more intensely than others.

Indisputably, Nina Simone was—and remains—a magnet for such intensity. Accounts from those who witnessed her performances ring together in their sense of the alteration brought on by the experience, the sense of her leaving an audience involuntarily changed, different than she found it. Concert reviews praise the general effect: "Miss Simone is a mood-setter rather than a singer of songs"; "she is building a mood and drawing her audience into that mood"; "she communicated instantly and drew a tumultuous response"; "She has no trouble pulling her audience with her while singing"; "She is like a sorceress whose performances are like communal acts between herself and her audience."[5]

Individual reminiscences evoke something more potent still. Sam Shepard, a busboy at the Village Gate in the summer of 1964, recalled Simone's performances as "absolutely devastating to watch. It was a real performance as well as just being something heard."[6] Charles Aznavour, meeting Simone around the same time and in the same place, later recalled, "Nina Simone didn't make a conscious effort to get a hold on the audience; they were captivated anyhow. There was this magic when she played on stage."[7] Raymond Robinson reported from a 1966 concert at Philharmonic Hall that "the feeling one gets watching Nina Simone can't be expressed in words, it can only be felt."[8] Linda Yablonsky saw Simone perform at the Village Gate in about 1969 or 1970 and "remember[ed] her face, mostly her eyes, and the way they took us all in, first with suspicion, then welcome, then they seemed to scan some inner landscape that had the power to alter the outer one."[9] Maya Angelou saw her "plunge beneath the wood and ivory of the piano to reach and manipulate the raw nerve ends of her audience. The response is instant and automatic."[10] Sylvia Hampton, who maintained a lifelong friendship with Simone, testified, "Listening to her album was truly amazing but to see her perform transformed your very being," and again, "No matter what, she was always able to tap into her audiences and even the most reserved would have no choice but to be moved by her."[11] Nick Cave recalled Simone's last London concert, as late in her career as 1999, as "the greatest show of my life" in the wake of which "we too were changed and would never be the same."[12]

The transformative excitement of Simone's audiences was, notably, not mirrored in her own accounts of her performances, which instead emphasize the work that went into constructing them. As she related in an interview with Arthur Taylor in 1970:

> At each concert, each television show, each performance, I psych out the situation. Every room is different. The people in it are different, their mood is different, the time of day is different; all that goes through me before I perform. That determines what I'm going to sing and what mood I'm going to try to develop.
>
> Sometimes I go to the concert hall earlier than usual, and I've done things like count the seats, try to get into the mood of the place. I'll know what kind of people come here if the seats are very lush; I'll check the position of the stage, the intelligence and education of the light and sound men, the mood I'm in, the mood my musicians are in and what I want to say. And that is influential and will certainly determine what I'm going to play.
>
> I never make up a set or a concert until thirty minutes before I go onstage, sometimes less than that. The musicians working with me know they must come to get the list of songs or the order of the concert; they sometimes cannot get it until five minutes before we're going onstage, because everything until that moment has influenced my selections. By that time I'm feeling completely different from the way I felt when I first entered the place.[13]

The account she gave in *I Put a Spell on You* is yet more modest: "I never felt proud of being a performer or got vain about it, because it mostly came naturally and I didn't feel that I completely understood or controlled what happened on stage anyhow. I did my preparations as carefully as possible in order to set the scene, but having done that the rest was difficult to predict. I knew the songs to play, and in what order, but the difference between a good professional performance and a great show, one where I would get lost in the music, was impossible to know. It just happened."[14]

Downplayed by this mild frustration with the unpredictability of her shows is the incredible and consistent hard work that Simone put in, and kept putting in, even offstage. As late as her last RCA album, *It Is Finished* (1974), whose title bespeaks some of Simone's eagerness to be done with her contractual obligations there, friends nonetheless witnessed her "daily practice of Rachmaninoff and Bach and other intricate pieces from the classical repertoire on her baby grand piano and how she later transformed the seemingly effortless trills and flourishes into the introductions of various songs on the album."[15] This combination of diligent practice and "It just happened" may be what gives her work the quality that Richard Elliott recalls, listening to *Emergency Ward* (1972), of a "performance that feels simultaneously improvised and carefully worked-out."[16]

Such tensions, anyway, seem to be part of who Simone was, what she brought with her, what her genius looked like. And across her performing career these tensions intensify to such an extent that they can look like discrepancies—with her owning some part of what happened and projecting the rest onto an audience whose members reciprocate with projections of their own.[17] For example, on the one hand, when Simone was performing "Pirate Jenny" around 1963, according to her longtime guitarist Al Schackman, "She'd get to a certain part—'Kill them now or kill them later?'—and people, families who brought their children, you'd see them leave. Kids were crying. Oh, they couldn't take it."[18] On the other hand, after the 1964 Carnegie Hall concert where it was recorded, Simone didn't often sing "Pirate Jenny" in concert, on the grounds that it was emotionally draining for her.[19] What's on these two hands doesn't contradict but also isn't the same. More than one thing can be true at once, of course, though it's often the privilege of audiences to get to see just one thing and the burden of the performer who commands those audiences to wrangle all the other things.

The commanding part is what matters, though—to the fantasies of everyone involved.

Nina Simone at Carnegie
Hall (April 12, 1963). Photo
by Alfred Wertheimer/MUUS
Collection via Getty Images.

COMMON SENSE HOLDS that it's a bad thing when our moods or feelings are overridden by someone else. However, research in neuropsychology increasingly points to the ineluctability of such a circumstance: body and environment interact to create physiological responses that register emotions in our conscious minds as second-order experiences. The difference, in other words, is whether we're sad so we cry, or whether crying makes us sad, with the latter perhaps being the case more often than we assume. But while this question of priority, of what's "really" happening, matters hugely in the clinical context where effective treatments must be identified, it matters quite a bit less in everyday life. Whether or not, physiologically speaking, we generate our own moods or feelings, it remains important to social life that we maintain a sense of our own agency, that we imagine we're involved in a way of being together that allows us to also retain a sense of our individuality, our psychic integrity.

Except of course in the few cases where it doesn't. Socially sanctioned exceptions to the priority of individual responsibility for moods and feelings include being in an audience or a crowd, rooting for a team, or being part of what social theorists call "a public"—especially when the experience overtakes us, shows us that the emotions generated together by, say, two people are not simply equal to the added-up emotions of one plus one.[20] To be a fan of something is often to idealize it, and while not all members of an audience will be fans, idealization isn't a bad name for the responses Simone's performances seem to have drawn out of the audiences she constituted.

It had an antagonistic side as well. Simone could demand things from audiences that they didn't have to give, sometimes raging against the ways the raucous energy of a festival or a club failed to live up to the silent and attentive composure of a classical recital. Documentaries and biographies abound with stories of times when Simone stopped playing and stormed offstage or else told audience members to sit down. This kind of behavior seems to have become much more common for her in the 1970s, though as early as 1961 she lectured a "boisterous" audience at the Apollo Theater on manners, later defending her actions to an interviewer by saying, "If you can't [get an audience to like you], then you must get them to respect you."[21] "Respect" here means something less like admiration and more like deference, which Simone sometimes managed with aggression. At the Montreux Jazz Festival in 1976, she informed her audience that she'd begun writing a new song for the occasion of the concert, "But I decided you weren't worth it, because I figured that most of you were just here for the festival."[22] In a late interview,

Simone reiterated, "I demand perfection from myself and the audience. . . . If you don't want to listen, stay the hell home."[23] But even earlier, in 1967, one longtime reviewer asserted that "any performance by Nina Simone is essentially a battle of wills—hers against the audience's."[24] That such "battle" so often resulted in the transformative, involuntary harmonies the likes of which we have seen fans attest reminds us that antagonism and aggression too are ways of making a demand, of reaching out, of being in relation.

No wonder, then, there are so many fantasies of Nina Simone: she solicited them.

WHILE THERE'S EVIDENCE to point to the likelihood that Simone's sense of herself was shifting through the 1960s and after, other evidence points to the likelihood that her sense of her audience was as well. While Simone had always—since childhood—performed for mixed-race audiences, she began somewhere around the late 1960s to name her audiences as black. It seems so obvious that Nina Simone made music for black people that the shift I'm identifying has rarely been anything anyone has said out loud. Yet the phenomenon seems to pick up through the 1960s, as, for example, when performing "To Be Young, Gifted and Black" at the University of California, Berkeley, in October, 1969, Simone punctuated the second verse with the aside, "This is addressed to the black students at Berkeley, of course."[25] It's that "of course" that fascinates, for all the ways it suggests the need to say the thing that shouldn't need to be said.

Perhaps this articulation of a specifically black audience had something to do with the fact that, while Simone's concert audiences were mixed-race, they still often tended white. When she performed "Mississippi Goddam" and "Pirate Jenny," Sylvia Hampton recalled, Simone sometimes emphasized that these songs in particular "'were for all you black folks out there'"; often, Simone "called for all the black people in the audience to stand up— sometimes it was as few as two—and said, 'I'm singing only to you. I don't care about the others.' Curiously her white audience would often clap madly."[26] A fairly exact instance of this dynamic was recorded as Simone spoke before a performance of "To Be Young, Gifted and Black" ("our latest song") live at Philharmonic Hall in October 1969: "Now it is not addressed primarily to white people, though it does not put you down in any way. It simply ignores you [audience laughter and applause]. For my people need all the inspiration and love that they can get, so [audience applause]. So, since this house is full, and there are 22 million blacks in this country, I only want one million to buy this record, you understand? [audience applause]."[27]

Whatever else is going on here, Simone's identifications with and demands on her audience rhyme with the transformative quality we have already seen

RCA promotional advertisement
in the *Village Voice* (1970).

attributed to her live performances. The impersonal, general "you" of her address speaks in turn to black and white audience members, assigning meaning and consequence to black and white identities, yet leaves it entirely up to individuals to decide which category to sort themselves into. One result, as the advertising copy for *Black Gold* (1970) put it in a full-page *Village Voice* ad, is a white audience left to "listen to what you miss out on by not being black."[28] At least one reviewer, of Simone's 1968 concert at the Montreux Jazz Festival, admitted her effect on the audience left him feeling "indecently white."[29] No wonder, then, about the laughter and the applause. That's the sound of white audiences refusing to believe in their own specificity, refusing to believe that not everything is for them. Most things we laugh at aren't funny, and indeed this audience laughs not because what Simone says is a punch line, but because sometimes you have to turn something into a joke in order to be able to be in on it.[30]

The audience's work, however defensive, is part of what Simone made happen. She didn't allow her concert attendees to sit back and simply enjoy a performance. Rather, Simone's performances elicited reactions that were both cerebral and visceral.[31] They were performances that transform you, if you let them, or that require a defense like laughter if you're not letting them.[32] It seems that Simone had a habit of accusing her audiences of the truth.

"NINA SIMONE REPRESENTS the eternal artistic enigma," wrote Maya Angelou in a 1970 profile for *Redbook*. "Her personality contains contradictions of gigantic proportions."[33] Such contradictions, or what I've been calling tensions, register in Simone's oeuvre, and if you want to put your finger on a place where the tensions between the improvised and the worked-out, between transformation and defense, between the attachment of cathexis and the ambivalence of genius all come into "gigantic proportions," try "Ain't Got No/I Got Life." Simone composed this song as a medley of two numbers from the first act of *Hair*, Gerome Ragni, James Rado, and Galt MacDermot's hippie rock musical that more or less flopped off-Broadway in its six-week, October–November 1967 run at the brand-new Public Theater in New York's East Village.[34] Simone may have seen it there, or heard the cast album released in December, or caught its almost immediate revival in a December–January run at the midtown Manhattan discotheque The Cheetah; but in any case, just fifteen days after the Broadway version of the show opened at the Biltmore Theatre on April 29, 1968, Simone recorded her own version of "Ain't Got No/I Got Life."[35] "I thought a lot of the songs [from *Hair*] were cool," Simone is reported to have said, a rather sotto voce assessment of her alchemical union of two of this musical's numbers, creating a song that moves between privation and possession, quite literally between nothing and something.[36]

Listen to the things that, in different versions of the song, she "ain't got":

home
shoes
money
class
skirts
sweater(s)
perfume
bed
mind
mother
culture
friends
schoolin'
love

name
ticket
token
god
work
job
father
sisters
brothers
cousins
aunts
uncles
clothes
food
wine
country
faith
children
lovin'
water
air
smokes
place to stay
earth
church
cigarettes
no nothing
long to live
family
words
hope
change
TV
man
liquor
woman
parents
anybody
pot

face
freedom
hamburgers
responsibility
piano
songs
husband
relatives[37]

And listen to what she's got:

hair
head
brains
ears
eyes
nose
mouth
smile
tongue
chin
neck
boobies
heart
soul
back
sex
arms
hands
fingers
legs
feet
toes
liver
blood
freedom
freedom in my heart
smile (and it's my smile)
laughs (sometimes)
headaches

toothaches

bad times too, like you

soul (though it's been strained a little lately)

life (and I'm gonna keep it)

Simone released different recordings of the song on at least five albums, and it became so much of a concert staple in the last years of the 1960s that at least six more live recordings exist. Across these many performances, Simone frequently spun the lyrics, sometimes drawing from the *Hair* version, though often enumerating items in a different order than they appear there, and many times adding her own. On occasion subsequent verses in the same performance repeat some of what we might call the bigger items on the list: schoolin,' god, faith, love, home, mind, money, country. Her tendency to spin, however, was almost totally restricted to the "Ain't Got No" list of privations, which is why that list is considerably longer than the other. The catalog of "I Got Life" was performed almost exactly each time, with only minor variations toward its end, and even these variations were rarely one-offs and instead tended to be repeated across subsequent performances. "I Got Life" not only says something different than "Ain't Got No" but also says it in a different way, with a different performance style. Simone's renditions of the song would seem deliberately to alternate between sections that were improvised and those that were carefully worked-out. Such alternation, reiterated across dozens of performances, might express any number of things, though the one that speaks loudest to me is a sense of irresolution.

However, the song's two parts have been uniformly interpreted by critics as resolving into a progress, a narrative of movement from nothing to something, from negation to assumption. What's incredibly appealing about these interpretations is how they center Simone's power to claim space, often pointing to this performance as an exemplary instance. For example, Daphne Brooks sees Simone building "a new black anthem," in a performance that "encompasses a full range of emotions and sociopolitical messages, the emotions and messages she so masterfully translated into a vast repertoire of recordings and live performances, spanning a career of more than four decades."[38] Kara Keeling proposes that "what [Simone]'s got are the fundamental elements over which Black feminists continue to struggle—our minds, our bodies, our souls, and our brains—our life energy."[39] Emily J. Lordi argues that "Simone transforms expressive deprivation into sensual survivorship by performing an extravagant, virtuosic seizure of multiple expressive modes."[40] Amber Jamilla Musser maintains that "Simone reterritorializes her flesh. She takes back her body from a landscape of lack and flatness."[41] Joshua Chambers-Letson, watching a performance in London during the summer of 1968 when Simone's brother and bandmate Samuel Waymon joins her vocals for the second half of the song, writes, "They stand in the flesh together. She's got her brother. He's got his sister."[42] And Katherine McKittrick, in a chapter called "I Got Life/Rebellion Invention Groove," contends more generally but no less urgently that "music, music-making, and music-listening, together, demonstrate the subversive potential of shared stories, communal activities, and collaborative possibilities."[43]

These are powerful arguments, eloquent words, worthy conclusions. Yet they point directionally to a place of statements and anthems and principles and standing, a place where things are and can be more or less worked-out. They invite us to see how the tensions Simone carries and expresses find resolution, and to accept this invitation, we should regard "Ain't Got No/I Got Life" as the proposition it is, and not, or less, as something Simone kept performing, a song that ended only to begin again at the next concert, as a series of performances rather than a singular performance. In this way, critics' interpretations perhaps make matters neater than Simone herself precisely left them. At minimum, it seems to me that one can take decisive action   one can build, or struggle, or transform, or seize, or take a stand, or reterritorialize, or make, or collaborate—and not actually feel all that more resolved than one was before taking such action. Yes, indisputably, in these performances Simone claims space in a way that is both feminist and affirmative of black life. She's doing something. My hesitation stems from my wishing, but not really believing, that something done is something finished.

SCHOLARLY AS WELL as vernacular traditions identify Simone, as Daphne Brooks writes in the finest synthesis to date, as a pioneer in the project of how black women "redefine what we think modernity is and does."[44] My honest response, written in the margin of my copy of Brooks's book the first time I read these lines, was "FUCK YEAH," and my enthusiasm for her study persists despite the fact that the project of the present study is different. My pages have been thinking about Simone as a person, at a relatively individual scale. At that more personal or individual scale, Simone becomes maybe more complicated, but certainly less abstract, more part of her own story and less part of modernity as such. Listening to Simone so closely, her ordinary contradictions inevitably appear. The push and pull and ambivalence and self-difference of psychic life by design all begin to show up and take over. These complexities can be heard in Simone's words and her actions and her art, just as they probably would for most of us if we were ever listened to at this level of detail. None of this makes Simone less black, or less feminist, or less of a pioneer, or less herself. Rather, it tries to create some room to see more parts of her at once, to take account of the nonsingular relations she may have had to her blackness or her feminism or her pioneering.

A writerly fantasy enters the picture here, and it leads me to believe that trying generously to see or understand or find the language to describe what I hear in someone as they happen to be audible—intimately, individually, as well as socially—is a way of treating them with dignity. It's a self-justifying fantasy, given the probability that Simone doesn't need me to confer dignity on her, given the likelihood that she's doing just fine, thank you very much. And it's a fantasy that defends itself with recourse to that last refuge of any scoundrel, method—a fantasy that claims that if critics are going to undertake the awesome task of enlisting Simone's contributions in some necessary revisions to the world as we know it, what remains to be done is to follow with a push broom, sweep up some of the more granular details, and sprinkle them back over the conversation we share: to say it's not just that Simone's "got life," but also that she has the more particular life she happens to have lived.

Why must the reader put up with the writer's fantasies? What choice do any of us have, short of putting down the book? Writing is always a fantasy of a kind, a working through of all manner of ambivalences, an expression of the wish that putting pen to paper or fingers to keyboard is sufficient to make something else happen too.[45] Due to the accidents that make up my own life, paying careful analytic attention is how I know how to show that I love something. It's arguably not the most satisfying way to do so, and there's certainly no claim here that anyone else ought to do the same, nor that I'm in any way uniquely qualified for the task, however much I do try to do my homework. To the extent that there's a claim here at all, it's something like: my fantasy that I could adequately express my love for Nina Simone sustains this writing, even if she isn't here to love me back. That fantasy holds together the very one-sidedness whereby the person I'm trying so hard to listen to is necessarily oblivious to me, and it holds together the contradiction between my desire to do something to and for someone and the impossible satisfaction that comes with the likelihood that they need nothing done, at least nothing that I could possibly do.

Does that mean all critical writing is merely a fantasy? No, I don't think so. But it does mean that fantasy will almost always be at least one part of most critical writing, even though different writing will express very different fantasies.

FANTASY IS WHERE we can at once be both lost and found. By all accounts, Simone's breakout performance was a September 15, 1959, concert at New York's Town Hall theater, recorded and released the same year as *Nina Simone at Town Hall*. But breaking out meant no one knew quite where she fit in. Simone recalled, "After Town Hall critics started to talk about what sort of music I was playing and tried to find a neat slot to file it away in. It was difficult for them because I was playing popular songs in a classical style with a classical piano technique influenced by cocktail jazz. . . . They finally ended up describing me as a 'jazz-and-something-else singer.'"[46] Why did the emphasis fall on jazz and not classical? For the same bad reasons emphasis often falls where it does: "Calling me a jazz singer was a way of ignoring my musical background because I didn't fit into white ideas of what a black performer should be."[47] (In 1984, Simone told the BBC's Mavis Nicholson that her very first good review had come only the year before, when the *New York Times* compared her to Maria Callas as a diva. "Before that, I'd been labeled a jazz singer, a blues singer, a high priestess of soul, which, I'm not sure what that is.")[48] Outrageous as racism's banalities always are, Simone was not the first either to experience them or to balk at the fact that the definitions belong to the definers, not the defined.[49]

It's worth noting, however, that though Simone's account offers a credible explanation of her work musically, and rightly refuses the categories that misdescribe it, it nonetheless stops short of acting like "what sort of music I was playing" is a bad question. Instead, Simone seems to hold on to that question—for more than forty years. In 1968, she somewhat generously offered that "it is as difficult for me to describe myself as it is for writers to describe me."[50] But more often frustrations came across. In a late 1970 conversation with Arthur Taylor, Simone notes, "Some critics say I'm a jazz singer, others say I'm not. Still others will say I'm a jazz singer plus another kind of singer. The truth is that they don't know what I am, and I'm glad."[51] She is aware of the difficulties

Nina Simone and the Vogues
concert poster (1968). Collection
of the Smithsonian National
Museum of African American
History and Culture.

Presents IN-PERSON

NINA SIMONE
& THE VOGUES

Sunday, Nov. 3rd, 8:30 p.m.

BUSHNELL MEMORIAL ⬩ Hartford

Tickets at Bushnell Box Office & Leading Record Shops ⬩ $3.00, $4.25, $5.50

of being categorized, aware as well of being miscategorized, and yet refuses to set the record straight. She's "glad" critics don't get it. "It's always been my aim to stay outside any category. That's my freedom," she told one reporter in 1967, refusing the question even as she then gave an answer in double negatives: "However, freedom, to me, is the definition of what jazz is, so I can't say I'm not a jazz performer."[52] In the 1980s, Simone began teasing, or perhaps taunting, critics and journalists, offering up categories like "African-rooted classical music," or "African classical music," or sometimes "black classical music," specific enough that her oeuvre would likely be the only instance, a genre of one.[53] The question of category starts to seem, in its perpetual nonresolution, like an antagonism on both sides, even if she's not the one who started it.

Genre problems concern the scholarship as well, both because Simone, as we've seen, set them up and because scholars studying her have some responsibility to explain their findings. A sample of the best attempts to acknowledge Simone's methods and summarize her approach includes descriptions of Simone's work as "an eclectic repertoire that blended jazz with blues, gospel, and classical music," a "crossing the lines of musical genres," "an eclectic, one-woman summation of musical confluence," a "trademark eclecticism . . . [that] explore[d] the dismantling of musical boundaries," an "expansive musical style and desire not to be categorized as an artist," a "jazz-turned-folk-turned-pop-turned-who-knew-what-she-might-do-on-any-given-night diva," "radical unclassifiability," or simply "unclassifiable."[54] (A 1970 FBI memo, less beholden to scholarly responsibility than to its own terms of art, referred to her as "Nina Simone, Negro female vocalist.")[55]

It can be so challenging to fairly describe the ways Simone worked in more than one genre at once that the question of why she did so can feel secondary. The obscurity of that "why" question comes not just from the ways that Simone talked, or refused to talk, about her genre categories but also from the ways she doubled down, early on in her career, in creating music that was generically difficult to classify. Other musicians whom critics find generically frustrating might choose to regroup and try to capture the success that can come with being more immediately legible. Such, arguably, was Beyoncé's trajectory from *I Am . . . Sasha Fierce* (2008) to *4* (2011), or, more contemporary with Simone, Van Morrison's from *Astral Weeks* (1968) to *Moondance* (1970). But it wasn't Simone's move at all. Instead, she committed to showcasing her mastery of piano across a range of genres, despite the fact that this instrument, prominent in classical music, features often in jazz but only sometimes in blues and not usually in folk.[56] Meanwhile, Simone's extraordinary voice was never professionally trained and derived not at all from the classical training she brought to bear on musical styles more anemic to the piano, including "quoting" or working classical measures into jazz standards.[57] She regularly chose as well to cover songs and instrumental pieces from films, shows, and operas—locations where some amount of musical fusion is already common.[58] It begins to seem plausible that this endless question of the musical genre to which Simone's performances belonged was one way that she expressed her commitments to opacity—to a fantasy of not being, or not having to be, wholly legible.

A curiosity among Simone's remarks that supports this possibility comes from an interview with Phyl Garland published in 1969, wherein Simone muses, "I hope the day comes when I'll be able to sing more *love* songs, when the *need* is not quite so urgent to sing protest songs. But, for now, I don't mind."[59] The same sentiment also shows up in the 1970 interview with Arthur Taylor: "I want to go back to love songs someday. I don't get a kick out of going onstage everyday and singing protest songs; I love love, but I'm a voice and I influence millions and I know exactly what we want to do. I know a good protest song will make a man or a woman feel, I could be doing a little bit better every day. Music is one of the strongest elements we have."[60] Much later, in 1988, Simone told a BBC journalist that she was "stuck" with protest music because "people don't think about the fact that I'm a woman and sing as much [*sic*] love songs as I do."[61] Her words in all three interviews also call to mind a line from "Go Limp," performed on *Nina Simone in Concert* (1964), a verse that's almost an aside and in any case not really part of that song's story, wherein she sings:

> For meeting is pleasure
> And parting is pain
> And if I have a great concert
> Maybe I won't have to sing those folk songs again[62]

Singing a song about not wanting to sing these kinds of songs looks congruent to naming a genre category that refuses genre categories. In both cases, we're being told that what we're beholding isn't right, without being told what the right answer is.

One way of describing such behavior might be as insulating, self-protecting; to allow one's self to be recognized as "a voice" even if it means not getting to voice the love you want more of. The former child prodigy was likely aware, as Tavia Nyong'o reminds us, that "the virtuoso always risks being scapegoated as a freak of nature, even as they exemplify a potential that is immanent to the human."[63] Meanwhile, the practicing artist almost certainly knew, as Fred Moten contends, that "art is the transmission of the secret, but the secret is transmuted in every moment of its transmission. I think that transmutation must show up as obscurity; but such obscurity must also be recognizable; an obscurity that people can feel and know, but not necessarily by way of supposedly simple and supposedly direct declarative statements."[64] Who wouldn't want to hide a little? Who wouldn't want to do so by taking advantage of the ways they have practiced being seen?

III ● IIIII ● III

"YOU'VE GONE ON RECORD recently as saying you're lonely where you lived, or did live, in Switzerland," a British journalist pointed out to Simone in a 1988 interview for the BBC show *The Wire*. "Do you think it's because people are frightened of the Nina Simone legend?"

She barely let him finish before replying, "Yes, I certainly do. They think I'm bigger than life. And, I suppose—I know the music is."[65]

III ● IIIII ● III

Nina Simone (1986). Wikimedia
Commons.

|||●|||||●|||

OPACITY IS NOT a problem to be solved. Édouard Glissant famously intro-duced this concept in 1990 as a "subsistence within an irreducible singular-ity," a real and total truth whose form is not "the preconceived transparency of universal models."[66] Opacity names at once an alterity, a mode of relation, an ethical demand, a form of political legitimation, and a poetics.[67] More practically speaking, one major point of the concept of opacity is to remind us that we can recognize the existence of something that isn't transparent to us. Such a recognition based in nontransparency has been developed by many subsequent commentators, though there are good reasons to admire the spin given by C. Riley Snorton, for whom opacity becomes a way to perceive how difference can take a transitive form—how the part of someone that is opaque to us may, indeed, be one way we *come to know* their humanity, based not in its similitude to ourselves but in its own irreducibility.[68] In any case, opacity insists that clear resemblance isn't the precondition for one person to relate to another. Come as you are, and in that way we begin to sort something out.

The needfulness of opacity as a concept derives from the fact that we too often do the opposite and treat the irreducibilities of other people as though they are symptoms of a problem. "A symptom is both an expres-sion of a process and a blockage against accessing what's causing it," writes Lauren Berlant. "A cough could mean so many things; an addiction can have many motives; in both cases the very disorganization of the symptomatic subject makes people want to over-organize causality."[69] Ironically, people are often vexed by the disorderliness of symptoms—the symptoms that are taken to be a problem in their own right—and not as much by the under-lying problem.

The point becomes particularly evident in the cases where one in fact en-courages or enables symptoms in other people because one likes their effects. For example, some symptoms look in their expression like social graces, a reason perhaps that some heterosexual men report being attracted to the "charm" of women suffering from the deficient self-esteem, extreme consci-entiousness, and low expectations that stem from depression.[70] For example, stoicism in the face of bad news is commonly regarded as resilience or brav-ery, despite the fact that an inability to frankly express emotion is among the key indicators of poor mental health.[71] For example, a teacher might ask an underperforming student whether everything is all right at home but rarely asks the same question of a consistently high-achieving student, even though productivity-perfectionism is often a way of coping with trauma.[72]

Simone's symptoms were understood to be a problem. She was called moody and diva-like, mercurial and depressed. Simone was called angry, though she said she didn't mind.[73] Like almost all talented black women, she was called difficult.[74] In the index of nearly all the major biographies, one finds these adjectives, or synonyms for them, beneath her name as subheadings. Many of these same biographies agree that Simone received a mental health diagnosis for which she began medical treatment at least by the 1980s, though accounts differ as to the diagnosis, which is variously referred to as depression, schizophrenia, multiple personality disorder, chemical imbalance, and bipolar disorder.[75] This inability to name the problem reinforces the possibility that its symptoms were, for many, the real issue.[76]

Never, so far as I am aware, did Simone publicly discuss her mental health, apart from the episode on the 1966 Cosby tour, nor any diagnosis or treatment. The latter don't register in *I Put a Spell on You*, nor in the biopics in which she participated, nor in the many interviews she gave to journalists. By contrast, diagnosis looms large in the posthumous biographies, films, and journalistic appraisals. Diagnosis is used to explain Simone's behavior when it's erratic; medication is used to explain her behavior when it's more predictable.[77] Diagnostic tools are of course descriptive, not explanatory, though it's hardly Simone's interpreters who are the worst offenders in the widespread misapprehension to the contrary. Nevertheless, among the drawbacks with mistaking a description for an explanation is the way it can lead to writing sentences that read as though what we do when we're living with mental illness is done by the illness.[78] The result, grammatically anyway, is a confounded representation of agency, which further obscures the fact that, phenomenologically speaking, you don't *have* an illness so much, as it were, as you *are* it—the illness you manifest does not exist apart from your manifestation of it.

What we see in the commitment to diagnose Simone is an attempt not only to explain her in terms to which she never appears to have consented but also to attribute her agency to a part of her that is described as less a part of her than of some outside influence.[79] Think about it this way: when someone is hiding, we often act like they're absent and need to be found. In fact, they're hiding, and our ability to say so suggests that we know that they are. We may not know exactly where or why, but "what are you doing?" and "where or why are you doing it?" are not the same questions. The latter may be opaque to our reasoning. The former isn't—you're hiding, we get it. But if we act like we don't, if we conflate the questions, if we confuse the description and the explanation, we risk mixing up the things we can easily know and the things we can't. Simone's experience of mental illness offers an exemplary instance of how her life is taken as a problem that interpretation can solve, not an opacity but a transparency that we can't see through but, with enough work, imagine that we will.

PEOPLE DON'T NEED us to unravel them; more often, they need to be given the room to do it safely for themselves. According to one story, sometime in the mid-1980s, Simone showed up for an interview with a journalist at a London hotel, wearing a gorgeous fur coat under which, it gradually became apparent, she was wearing nothing else.[80] I enjoy this moment for its mischievousness, for what strikes me as its hilariously 1980s, Bob Guccione aesthetic. But Simone's friends, and perhaps the unnamed journalist, experienced her as acting unstable in public. We have seen that our clothes, as a genre of self-expression, can be one way that we engage the psychic work of fantasy; yet whatever tensions or contradictions Simone's gesture was meant to hold together didn't achieve their aim, and they became legible instead as an instance where psychic contradictions overwhelmed her ability to hold them. Psychology reserves an extraordinary word for this phenomenon: *decompensation*.

When we decompensate, we haven't necessarily stopped fantasizing or given up on fantasy, but the part of fantasy work that's understood as a successful adaptation has begun to falter. The parts of our self that we're using fantasy to hold or protect become undefended, at least partly, and their consequent exposure can sometimes change them—as when an old newspaper is suddenly exposed to air and becomes brittle all at once.[81] Brittleness, of course, is not the inevitable fate of the exposed self, but in many cases such episodes can nonetheless be something like terrifying on their way to being transformative. For that reason, these episodes earn negatively connoted names like "break" or "collapse." We who have them sometimes insist, especially toward the beginning of such an episode, that the breach in our defenses was the problem. Doing so is an easy way to avoid the fact that our defenses often began as responses to deficit, crisis, or even trauma—as efforts to save our own life.[82] In any case, we tend not to act like it was the circumstances in which we attempted to go on being that were the problem that, eventually, they became.[83] Sometimes we hesitate to recognize how we may be facing payment on a debt we ran up with ourselves—we may turn the problem inward or perhaps flavor it with guilt, and act instead like we never should have gone into debt in the first place, like we should simply have had enough to cover our psychic expenses, like we did something wrong when we didn't spend what we didn't have. We act, in other words, like the problem is the symptom, our decompensation, and not the part where we don't, and maybe never did, have the room to do it safely.

When the person who breaks down has fans, she may find fandom particularly fickle. As a kind of idealization, fandom demands the appearance of the version of the person who is a star, not the version of the person who is a person. Meanwhile, the person, if she can't bear to be a star in the ways that sacrificed her person, but she still wants to be a star, has to figure out how to inhabit both roles, or to what extent it's possible to synthesize them. The records of Simone's experiences alternate between worry about her decompensation, as described earlier regarding the fur coat, and protective silence from friends and family. Joe Hagan is one of the few commentators to give her credit, though in the progressive, optimistic idiom of recovery: "For every battle Simone waged with her depression, however, a rawer, freer personality emerged."[84] It's nice to think that it gets better, and sometimes it does. But mostly it's just difficult "to dissolve the defenses that accommodate the world and protect the aesthetic pattern we call our personality."[85] Or, as Simone herself put it to a journalist in 1969, "You don't basically change your character. You grow, but you don't change your character. When a circle gets wider, it's still a circle. It's just gotten wider, maybe a different color. But it's still a circle. What I always was is being affirmed in a deeper sense."[86]

That's the easy part, though. It gets much more difficult when what we always were is being disaffirmed, yet we still are it. In that deeper sense Simone spoke of, we have no choice but to be ourselves, even when there's no applause.

Fantasies

Remembering always requires a bit of forgetting. Any legacy is a curation, an interpretation, a choice of where to place the emphasis. Such choices are no more free of desires or unconscious wishes than forgetting is. The stories we tell as we build Nina Simone's legacy are, accordingly, fantasies—they suspend and relax the tension between what we want to know about her and all things we can't, or won't. Knowledge, here as always, is never innocent of desire.

As before, saying that something is a fantasy doesn't make it not real, and one way we know that fantasies of Nina Simone are indisputably real is that they are consequential. The intangible dreams of people have a tangible effect on the world.[1] What we desire from Simone shapes what we will know about her, and what we know about her shapes her legacy. Our fantasizing about Nina Simone becomes part of the foundation on which we collect and collate and juxtapose her—it fuels the assumptions that launch an inquiry or imitation or homage. Fantasy helps determine what is or isn't part of a Nina Simone archive.

Further accounting is therefore necessary to understand how our collective fantasies affect how we classify Simone, how we understand her, and which other stories come to bear on hers. Our fantasies of Simone may resolve our own tensions, but we often take a further step and articulate our fantasies into propositions about her, not us. We often treat the fantasy—what had been a synthesis between contradictory elements—as a new thesis to be debated, a position to be taken. So, for example, to emphasize Simone's legacy as a black woman pioneer may entail a shift away from her feeling that color and sex "fucked [her] up in the first place."[2] Or to emphasize Simone's legacy as an iconic musician can allow us to forget the ways she felt so marginalized in her career, the ways she wanted to sing love songs, the ways she meant to become a classical pianist. There's no perfect place to lay emphasis, however; any position we take is, necessarily, a defense against every other one. So, the one we take, the fantasies with which we invest Simone, should ideally be the ones that help create the future we want her—as well as us—to have.

The future always has a history. The world we live in is one Simone helped create, but it is in many ways not the world she lived in. At the least, she came before us, is a part of our past, which is not something she, or anyone, manages in the same way to be for themselves. We live in her "after," and my wondering is about how from that vantage to honor her place in our "before."[3] I imagine that what it means to treat Simone with dignity is not just to honor what we need from her but also to honor something about how much it may have cost her to become the person we are able to need.

‖ ● ‖‖ ● ‖

THERE ARE, FIRST and foremost, the things we hear in her voice. In the mid-1980s, "My Baby Just Cares for Me" became a theme song for the famous eau de parfum Chanel No. 5. The company's artistic director, Jacques Helleu, chose the French actress Carole Bouquet as the new face of an enormously successful rebranding campaign, and it was Bouquet's chic moves and looks that were captioned by Simone's early recording in one of the perfume's high-production commercials directed by Ridley Scott.[4] Following up on the exposure this advertisement provided, the British reissue label Charly Records rereleased "My Baby Just Cares for Me" as a single in late 1987, which then peaked, rather poetically, at number five on the UK Singles Chart in November.[5] More than three decades after Simone recorded an album to which she had signed away all rights at age twenty-four, it had yielded a hit song.[6] (She would later sue, successfully, to recover both rights and royalties.)[7]

Almost the same week as the single dropped, the Bristol-based firm Aardman Animations released a Claymation video for "My Baby Just Cares for Me."[8] Here, a humanoid feline, smoky gray and feminine, standing upright and elegantly dressed, ventriloquizes Simone's lyrics while a trio of other animated cats backs her up on the piano, drums, and bass cello. Scenes with the band playing a tiny club are interspersed with those of the singer's "baby," an all-white cat in a bowtie who arrives late to the show, gets turned away at the door, sneaks in, gets thrown out, and sneaks back through the roof, landing onstage and in the singer's arms. Visuals for the song's instrumental middle incorporate film images of actual instruments, especially the piano, being played by unseen hands.

There is no question that the animated video, as much as the Chanel commercial, propelled "My Baby Just Cares for Me" to its second life as a late-1980s hit. Simone herself told the BBC in 1999, "It started out as a piece of Play-Doh, for children, in England. It started out as a video, for children, and then it got bigger and bigger, and everybody started to hear it. And it became very famous. And it's the most famous song I have recorded."[9] There is also no question that Simone took some genuine pleasure in this unexpected reversal of fortune. Yet that pleasure appears to cling to the presumption that the hit was something she did—that it was "the most famous song I have recorded"—and not something that was done with her song by someone else, or, what's more, something done without her.

Chanel's commercial and Aardman's animation were neither the first nor the last times Simone's music would be played without her body being visible.

||| ● ||||| ● |||

From "My Baby Just Cares for
Me," Aardman Animations
(1987).

A career-long tension existed between the ways that Simone's voice, heard on a recording, tends deep and in that sense masculine, while her body, seen in a performance, was styled conventionally feminine.[10] In the age of radio play especially, Simone's audiences likely experienced her sound differently in recording and in live performance.[11] Her concerts not only included her body, of course, but also deliberately drew attention to it—for example, in Simone's tendency across decades of existing performance footage to spend one early number (often somewhere around the third) away from her piano and dancing onstage, something she can be seen to do in Rome, Antibes, Harlem, Montreux, and even Hamburg in 1989, where the self-consciously exaggerated shaking of her fifty-six-year-old ass earns cheers from the crowd.

But while the gap between Simone's masculine-ish sound and her feminine look is plainly a gendered one, both the Chanel commercial and the Aardman animation instead divide Simone's sound from its singer's black body. In both cases, the conventionally high femme avatars Simone is given signify as something other than black—whether through Bouquet's fair complexion and windswept brown hair, or the gray cat's sloping nose and hapless white boyfriend. The Aardman animation seems cautiously aware of the erasure, opting to visualize no one playing a piano rather than materialize a pair of hands with any racial markers at all.[12]

There's no doubt that Simone's availability to the kind of appropriation that retains her sound and ignores where it comes from—and indeed the fact that she is available to it decades before her death, while her career is still active—stems from the pernicious logics of racial capitalism. Accordingly, it does not seem incidental that her black body is what gets omitted while leaving her gender and her voice behind, as though these weren't connected parts of the same instrument. The ad and the animation demonstrate how a regime of racial capitalism can turn any performance—even a performance of self, an iteration of individual talent—into something fungible, something whose integrity can be dismantled, something that can be stripped for parts.

It would, however, be inaccurate to say that this wanting of Simone's song without Simone's body primarily represents a desire to harm Simone, to vanquish her, or in some violent way pare her down. That would be a fantasy of domination, not one of appropriation, and domination is not in any straightforward sense what these texts accomplish. Instead, these texts seem to be animated by an ambivalence about their object, a kind of desire that leads toward something undesirable. That desire for what Simone offers, and that simultaneous violence toward she who offers it, results in a tension that calls out for a fantastic resolution. The fantasy that ensues, I think, is one reason it can be so hard to get white people to acknowledge the appropriations of those whom they racialize: because that racism isn't committed to the hatred of another so much as it's often based in some kind of much more terrible love.[13]

The fantasy that Simone's voice could come from somewhere other than her particular body, already set in motion during her lifetime, structures a large part of the legacy of Nina Simone. I doubt Simone would have put the matter quite this way, but I also suspect she nonetheless understood the issues. If she did, she perhaps would have registered some of the irony in the injunction to "Share the Fantasy," the tagline in which the Chanel ad culminated. And, speculating further, some amount of all this might have been on Simone's mind the day in Vienna in the late 1980s, when she showed off her new jacket to her friend Hannibal Means, telling him, "I walked into Chanel in Paris and took it and told them, 'You people owe me millions of dollars!'"[14] This "sharing" was less a fantasy than a protest.

THE MOST FATAL of all tensions is between life and death, and one kind of fantastic object that exists to resolve that tension is the relic.[15] In Latin Christendom, from which the term *relic* derives, the object's denotation is specifically corporeal: a bodily fragment—bone, tooth, blood, sweat—that lives beyond the body. In this sense, however, there could be no relics of Nina Simone because she left no body behind. After Simone's death in 2003, her body was cremated, and her ashes were scattered across "several African countries."[16] By all accounts, these arrangements were in accordance with Simone's wishes.[17] But those wishes implicitly repudiate pilgrims, for no one site has been or could ever be designated as Nina Simone's grave.

Miraculously, however, relics emerge. Angela Davis summons one in the story of the time Simone visited the Marin County, California, jail where Davis awaited trial in 1971: "When [Simone] finally appeared, she was holding a beautiful red helium-filled balloon. I learned that she had engaged in an extended verbal battle with the guards, whose evocation of the rules was no match for Nina Simone's tenacity. Over the next period, as it gradually lost its buoyancy, this balloon remained one of the few permanent fixtures in my cell. Even when it was entirely deflated, I preserved it as a treasured artefact of my time with the amazing Nina Simone."[18] Like the body of a saint, the balloon may deteriorate, yet something of it can be preserved. In fact, relics get restored and rehabilitated all the time—their preservation is an active process, and the reliquary that frames and presents a bodily relic often comes to matter just as much as the relic does.[19] In Davis's case, narrative preserves the balloon Simone gave her, and elsewhere imagery does. As Davis tells the story of Simone's visit in Shola Lynch's documentary *Free Angela and All Political Prisoners* (2012), the camera tracks a red balloon in soft focus against a background of overexposed light. The balloon is also made to live again as it is stylized next to a silhouette of Simone in the artwork for the multiartist tribute album *Nina Revisited: A Tribute to Nina Simone* (2015).

Astonishingly, another, yet more bodily Nina Simone relic survives in *Stranger Than Kindness*, the Royal Danish Library's 2020 collaboration with Nick Cave. This immersive multimedia installation reflects Cave's body of work, including influences, and one item exhibited is a masticated piece of Simone's gum. Its story goes like this. In 1999, Cave invited Simone to play at the Meltdown Festival in London. She came onstage chewing a piece of gum that she took out of her mouth and stuck on the piano as her set began. When it had ended, Cave's longtime collaborator Warren Ellis snatched the gum off the piano, placed it inside a towel Simone had used during the set to mop her brow, and placed it all in a yellow plastic Tower Records bag, where it remained for twenty years, a sacred relic kept out of sight. In preparation for exhibition in Copenhagen, the gum was removed, copied via a wax mold, and cast in silver and later gold, in collaboration with an artisan jeweler in London named Hannah Upritchard. One silver cast was shared with the Belgian designer Ann Demeulemeester, who in turn collaborated with a jeweler in Munich named Klaus Lohmeyer to transform the piece into a ring and a sculpture. Meanwhile, the original piece of gum went on exhibition at the Royal Danish Library, presented on a marble pedestal in a showcase box lined with gold velvet.

These events are lovingly detailed in Ellis's memoir *Nina Simone's Gum* (2021). His story's drama centers on the transformation of a personal object into a public monument. "I no longer had control over the gum," he writes near the conclusion. "From the moment it had left my drawer, in fact, it was taking the reins. It was creating its own life, like an album, or film, or painting once it has been let go."[20] Ellis's love and reverence for Simone set the plot in motion, but once it's moving, the collaborations and connections that Simone's gum inspires are what begin to matter: "The gum was the relic laid in the foundations of a monument being built through love and care, with Nina Simone as the goddess over all."[21] Like all monumental stories, this one is ultimately not about the rock on which the church is built so much as it's about the church.

III ● IIIII ● III

SOME FANTASIES CONGEAL into deliberately monumental forms. In those forms, fantasies can become fixed, sometimes literally concrete. That monumentality or concreteness, I think, represents the working through of the kind of desires that biographers often also have—desires to fit the complex contingencies of history and the contradictory pattern we call a personality into something comfortably narrative or sculptural or modeled. These fantasies subtend the possibility that something can best be defined by the clarity of its boundaries rather than the mess of its contents.

We could begin with the concrete expanses of streets named for Simone in Heidelberg; Paris; Nijmegen, the Netherlands; or Belval, Luxembourg; or with the I. M. Pei–designed geometric edifice of the Rock & Roll Hall of Fame into which she was posthumously inducted in 2018. But let's instead go back to Tryon, North Carolina, where, the town's self-promotions will cheerfully to tell you, it all began. Never mind that there isn't much evidence that the place where Simone was from numbered among the places that mattered to her. *I Put a Spell on You* spends no time registering any particular pleasure or hometown pride, though its narrative does acknowledge efficiently how growing up in a segregated small town in the 1930s and 1940s left its mark on Simone. It is therefore more than a bit ironic that the same small town in North Carolina in the first two decades of the twenty-first century has now sought to imprint Simone's mark on it.

It's not precisely the town itself, however, that makes these decisions. In Simone's case, the agents behind Tryon's monuments to her were individual entrepreneurs. Two years after her death, in 2005, Simone's childhood home at 30 East Livingston Street was purchased by a businessman and former economic development director for Polk County, Kevin McIntyre, with the intention of turning it into a museum.[22] Shortly thereafter, Crys Ambrust, a retired University of South Carolina professor, private collector of Simone memorabilia, and founder of the nonprofit Nina Simone Project, spearheaded the sculpture of Simone dedicated in 2010 in a park on Trade Street in downtown Tryon, which for the occasion was christened Nina Simone Plaza.[23] Meanwhile, when McIntyre was ultimately unable to bring to fruition his house museum project, 30 East Livingston Street sold in 2017 for $95,000 to an LLC created by four New York City–based artists: conceptual artist Adam Pendleton, sculptor and painter Rashid Johnson, collagist and filmmaker Ellen Gallagher, and abstract artist Julie Mehretu.[24] In 2018, the National Trust for Historic Preservation (NTHP) conferred "national treasure" status on the house, officially the "Eunice Waymon Birthplace," and as of 2024 the NTHP website includes proposals for "reuse concepts" that will turn the house into more than a landmark.[25] The NTHP's work also aims to create long-term plans for the ownership and stewardship of the site. While the future of memorializing Nina Simone in Tryon is therefore likely to end up more collaborative than it began, nonetheless it was a small number of individuals who set into motion something that, at the most foundational level of conception, probably won't change.

That is to say, the framing terms of these memorial projects conjure for Simone a legacy of birth and home and place and placement. They name Simone as one of Tryon's proudest children, and they brook no alternatives. Ambrust explained his motive for creating the Nina Simone Project as astonishment at a missed opportunity: "Any other town in the world that could claim Nina Simone as a local daughter would have it plastered on every building, on every street, in order to build the reputation of that community."[26] Zenos Frudakis, the sculptor of the statue erected on Tryon's Nina Simone Plaza, envisioned his work as extending from birth to death, describing his likeness of Simone as "a grave, in a sense, a bronze casket. So if anybody ever says they want to move it, you can say, 'If you move it, you're moving her grave.'"[27]

The reliance in these explanations on material metaphors is perhaps not incidental. Things like buildings and streets and caskets are physical objects, undeniably tangible in their size and substance. The use of such metaphors in the preceding explanations lends heft to the far more abstract concept of belonging, with its epiphenomenal history of being *from*. The largeness evoked by these metaphors perhaps aims to outbalance how easily the fact that Eunice Waymon was born in Tryon could be incidental—a lot of people, after all, are born in places to which they have no relationship. Buildings, streets, and caskets, museums and sculptures, go a long way toward making what could be incidental into something more weighty and therefore more indisputable. However, this sense of belonging's concreteness, such as could motivate a person to presume that it matters that Nina Simone was from Tryon, is a fantasy too. Its content is not at all identical to the fantasy Simone expressed when she insisted in a slew of interviews after 1970 that she was at home in Liberia, but its operation is much the same.[28]

Of course, when museums and sculptures emphasize the places people come from, they contribute to a much larger social ecology. Tryon's monuments to Simone create cultural pilgrimage sites designed to attract out-of-town visitors and thus comply with national templates for the revitalization, through cultural tourism, of nonurban, often deindustrialized areas.[29] These

Nina Simone statue, Tryon,
North Carolina (2018).
Wikimedia Commons.

sites also fit more specifically with the long-standing commercial logic of a town whose economy since the late nineteenth century centered on forms of cultural tourism—inns, arts, local viticulture—including the proximity tourism that comes with being within an hour's drive of both Ashville, North Carolina, and Spartanburg, South Carolina—and, in Simone's youth, along a railroad line that stopped six times a day to and from Charleston.[30] The idea of making something out of a birthplace, in other words, was hardly something invented with, by, or for Nina Simone's birthplace. It's a common currency in the kinds of monumental history where *something* is exchanged for coherence. But that doesn't make it inevitable, either.

MATERIAL OBJECTS AREN'T the only things that build monuments; the fantastic ways that art envisions the world can feed into legacies as well. Nikki Giovanni's 2007 collection *Acolytes* features two poems about Simone. The first, "A Prayer for Nina," reads:

Nina Simone:
Was a beacon against the stormy sea of bigotry and hatred
Was a quilt against the cold of indifference
Was courage to the cowardly
Was boldness to the timid
Was love to the lonely
Was Home to the lost
Is ours for now
And evermore
Amen[31]

The poem begins in the past tense of "was" and visually funnels down to the present tense of "is" before announcing the messianic time of "evermore" and closing with a final affirmative interjection of prayer, "Amen."[32] It envisions a past that lays the groundwork for a sustained, elongated present. The poem shares in the temporality to which monuments aspire.

The subsequent poem in Giovanni's collection, "Howl (for Nina Simone)," pushes more evidently in a monumental direction. Its lines begin with interjections like "Yes" or "Sure" and imperatives like "Call them out, Girl" or "Don't stop just because it hurts."[33]

In the final three stanzas, these imperatives shift to descriptions:

You were singing
For a higher power
To a higher power
Needing a higher power
To sing you home

You are forever Young
Gifted and Black
You are forever with the righteous
You are forever Nina

Howl, Baby
Call down the sun

To scorch the lies
Call down the stars to write the truth
Call down Call down Call down
And we will worship
At the altar[34]

The implied "you should" of the imperative mood becomes the descriptive "You were" and "You are forever," assertions to be made rather than possibilities to be encouraged. The poem's final image resolves from the epiphenomenal actions of singing or worship to a more concrete object, the altar, where those actions "will" happen. At the altar is where Giovanni's vision for (and to, and of) Simone lands.

The form that vision takes matters too. A poem may contain the image of a monument, but a poem is not usually considered one. And yet it seems meaningful that in making "Howl (for Nina Simone)," Giovanni's enjambed sentences and paratactic grammar, as well as her title, signal a remaking of one of the twentieth century's most undeniably monumental poems, the one by Allen Ginsberg that appears on its title page as "Howl, for Carl Solomon."[35] Ginsberg's poem, famously daring, famously banned—and, now that you mention it, a poetic debut almost exactly contemporary with Simone's musical debut, and yet one typically lauded with far more fanfare than hers—metonymically stands among US-Americans of Giovanni's generation as a self-evident statement about the power of art to live in infamy.[36] Remaking this statement about Simone enables Giovanni to claim power in much the same ways as Simone did through her myriad acts of covering, and thereby owning something of, her white male contemporaries beginning at the end of the 1960s. Giovanni's poems thus enact what they envision for Simone, a pair of "forever" monuments that link her past to and beyond our present.

IT'S OFTEN VISITORS who give monuments their gravity. If Giovanni's "Howl (for Nina Simone)" wants to build Simone an altar, it also wants to find her a chorus:

Call them out, Girl
Tell them they have to sing with you
Have to sing with Lorraine
Have to sing with Langston
Have to sing for Schwerner, Chaney, and Goodman[37]

We find a similar impulse in Monica A. Hand's *me and Nina*, whose poems frequently juxtapose Simone's words or perspectives with those of other kindred artists, including Gil Scott-Heron, Bob Marley, Lorraine Hansberry, Langston Hughes, Lucille Clifton, and the poet herself.[38] These poems unmistakably locate Simone in dialogues, as does Randy DuBurke's beautiful illustration sequence "Nina Simone: CIVIL JAZZ!," which allegorically juxtaposes Simone singing or playing the piano with scenes populated by contemporary civil rights and antiwar protests.[39] Across these various works, the common fantasy of Nina Simone, and what indeed turns out to be one of the more common fantasies of Nina Simone, is this one that surrounds her with people she can talk to.

Simone herself knew how to have a conversation. The ways she did so could be informal and sometimes quite improvisational. Sylvia Hampton recalled that Simone was "a terrible flirt, and loved to 'play' with the various suitors that tried to get close to her."[40] *I Put a Spell on You* corroborates Hampton's observation in a story about the time Simone met Louis Farrakhan in the early 1960s and tried to fend off boredom in his company: "Minister Farrakhan talked on into the small hours and I sat there staring at his shoes, sipping my gin and wondering what he'd say if I invited him upstairs. He kept giving me these looks as if he knew what I was thinking. At last I couldn't stand it any longer and came out and asked him. It was more out of mischief than anything else, but he spoilt the fun by turning me down."[41] Simone's flirtatiousness in this story shows itself as a kind of spontaneity or playfulness, an inclination to use sex and intimacy not only to seek pleasure but also to shift the tone, the direction, and maybe also the stakes of a social scene. It seems too that these kinds of flirtatious expressions weren't restricted to men in whom Simone held sexual interest, and indeed could be extended to friends. Michael Alago tells one of the best such stories, about the time in 1999 Simone asked him to join her in the tub. They met at her hotel in London before a show that night, and "Nina shouted: 'Everybody out, except Michael!' and suddenly we were alone. 'Sugar lips,' she said, 'I know you're gay, but I think it's time for a bubble bath!' So the next thing I knew, she'd stripped down, I was in my boxer shorts, and we were in a tub full of bubbles drinking champagne and laughing like teenagers. And that's how I will always remember her."[42]

Flirtation is often a way of approaching or experimenting with an emotional connection. Whether we're flirting with a person, an idea, or an interest, we usually flirt with serious things, and yet to take flirtation seriously almost invariably puts a stop to it.[43] Flirtations are thus not easy to sustain, yet in many of the stories Simone tells or that are told about her, she comes across as someone who's fairly accomplished at relating to others in this more improvisational way. It's not difficult to imagine that such an openness to attachment—to say nothing of her musical fluency, her technical mastery—is part of what gave Simone's performances their undeniable charisma.

This same charisma, this demonstrated ability to be in conversation, very likely clarifies why Simone has so often been a magnet for playwrights. She was the inspiration for the character Malika in Sonia Sanchez's *I'm Black When I'm Singing, I'm Blue When I Ain't* (1982) and was among the inspirations for Edith Hemings in James Baldwin's final play and last completed work, *The Welcome Table* (1985).[44] In her own guise, Simone shows up as a character in the Broadway jukebox musical *A Night with Janis Joplin* (2014) and in Shlomo Carlebach's off-Broadway *Soul Doctor* (2010), where what begins as a chance meeting with Simone in the Village sets the "rock- and-roll rabbi" on the path to his life's work. Meanwhile, Simone's own story gets told through ballet in *Nina: By Whatever Means*, choreographed by Mthuthuzeli November (2023), and in stage performances of her own music in Laiona Michelle's *Little Girl Blue* (2019) and in Christina Ham's *Nina Simone: Four Women* (2016). This last play in particular determinedly sets Simone within a conversation and does so by turning her into a character who sifts through the aftermath of the 16th Street Baptist Church bombing alongside dramatically realized versions of the characters she sings about in "Four Women": Aunt Sarah, Saffronia, Sweet Thing, and Peaches. The play uses dialogue to create contrasts among the characters and from there to arrive at a sense of what black women may have in common once they admit some of their differences from one another.

In interviews, Ham speaks movingly about what her play tries to accomplish, for example, when she told Sarah Scafidi in 2017: "For women, no matter our color, our self-esteem is always kind of shaky. You know? But I think when you layer on color, and then you layer on socio-economics and all this other stuff, it goes into a deeper place. So, I tried to explore that more. I also tried to explore Nina's own self-esteem issues, because while she was pro-Black, pro the people, pro the Movement, basically writing the soundtrack for the Movement, she also had her own issues with self-esteem."[45] Ham's explanation draws a line between the past and the present, acknowledging the things Simone's accomplishments still could not resolve and the things, therefore, that we live with just as much as she did. *Nina Simone: Four Women* would seem to be written as what's sometimes called "a history of the present," at least inasmuch as the play uses the past not for its own sake and not as an object of revision but instead as a way to make sense out of how our present came to be.[46] And, indeed, for those of us who lived through 2017, with its multiplying public allegations of sexual harassment and cascading failures of accountability, women's "shaky" self-esteem would inevitably stand forward as one of the present's prominently unresolved historical conditions.

We've come a very long way from flirtation, however. Perhaps that distance has to do with the history of the present that Ham's play engages, which, like the dialogues into which dramatists and poets and illustrators set Simone, conjures for her a kind of social connection that in the end isn't quite like the ones she created for herself. Or, said more simply, perhaps it is because what the past contains could have led to any number of presents besides this one. The differences between Simone's conversations and the ones artists have created for her after the fact register as the differences between being flirtatious with an intimate and being in conversation with a peer, and those sound like differences of emphasis rather than differences of kind. The more contemporary texts, in other words, evoke a Simone who talked to People in History about Things That Mattered not so much to her (in the most irreducible sense) *personally* as to her (in that same irreducible sense) *historically*. These contemporary texts register the fantasy of a Simone whose existence in the past cleared the way for us to exist in the present. That fantasy is one where Simone helps us tell our own origin story, and in that fantasy, we get to be the road taken, not the flirtation that succeeded by never turning into something serious. This fantasy is understandable, even desirable; but it's also different than the ones it seems Simone engaged in.

This fantasy where we surround Simone with history and peers and conversation only becomes harsh in moments when that dialogue proves to be beside the point. Consider the video for Beyoncé's "Sandcastles" (2016), which briefly visualizes the LP cover of *Silk and Soul* (1967) and samples Simone's cover of Dusty Springfield's "The Look of Love" off it.[47] This moment, like the poem by Warsan Shire that Beyoncé reads over the soundtrack that Simone's sample provides, layers black women's art into a story about a kind of restorative assertion of self-worth that the video's chapter title calls "Forgiveness."[48] Yet these layers, all this artistic copresence, doesn't necessarily engender conversation—and in this case, despite the many very contested interpretations of Beyoncé's *Lemonade*, it doesn't feel hugely controversial to say conversation is being aestheticized without actually being attempted.[49] "Sandcastles" cites Simone much as it reads Shire's poems: monologically, as part of a sovereign performance that may not entirely be about Beyoncé but that is in every way utterly about her.[50] Like Hand's poems or Ham's play this citation to Simone expresses a fantasy about origins, though a more prescribed one, a genealogy of Beyoncé's artistic lineage. Citing Simone here is less a matter of history and more a matter of inheritance. It is, maybe, in that sense, less generous than what Ham and others are doing, though of course there's still no wrong way to fantasize. And certainly any of us is capable of pretending at conversation, of borrowing its appearance, in order to claim to be of something but not in it.

THE FANTASY OF SIMONE as our origin is close kin with the body of work that translates Simone into other artistic media. While plays and poems and illustrations such as we've seen surely participate in this kinship, another set of Simone-inspired texts works more explicitly through ekphrasis. Rather than stage a conversation or dialogue in which Simone might participate, these texts treat her music as something that can be transmuted into another artistic form.[51] For example, lyrics from "Four Women" appear early in Paule Marshall's novel *Praisesong for the Widow* (1983) when protagonist Avey Johnson tries to establish for herself something about her friend Thomasina Moore's skin tone.[52] This medium-to-medium translation, by which the novel renders sound in the nonauditory verbal form of written words, understands Simone's text as both fluid (translatable) and fixed (citable), and so while "Four Women" may be a point of origin or inspiration for *Praisesong for the Widow*, it is also employed as a collaborator.

Something related happens in *Four Women* (1975), a short experimental film directed by Julie Dash that showcases a dance piece choreographed and performed by Linda Young.[53] The film opens with nearly two minutes of dance by a figure draped in a transparent, chrysalis-like shawl. Her motions evoke struggle, pitted against a sonic landscape of tribal chanting that's then interrupted by cracks from a whip, the gurgling of water, and the wailing of anguished voices. As a studio recording of Simone's "Four Women" begins, the scene dissolves into one of Young, face now visible, costumed in turn as each of the four. The film's final shot focuses not on the body's movements but in extreme close-up on the face of Peaches, confronting the viewer with the same body part that the opening movements occluded. The film uses Simone's song but also embellishes around its edges. Simone's "Four Women" does not concentrate on the violence of enslavement or the trauma of the Middle Passage, but Dash's *Four Women* makes these latent elements manifest. *Four Women* makes "Four Women" into a testament to the afterlife of slavery, presenting the viewer with sound and motion to substantiate Peaches's penultimate lyrics "I'm awfully bitter these days / 'Cause my parents were slaves."[54] The result, again, feels collaborative, preserving Simone's text whole while making something new, not out of it so much as together with it.

The cover version of "Four Women" featured in the ending credits of Tyler Perry's *For Colored Girls* (2010) could be considered an honorary member of this set. Still collaborative, though a song-to-song translation and so not ekphrastic, this recording aims to preserve something of Simone's original

||| ● |||| ● |||

From *Four Women*, dir. Julie
Dash (1975).

by sampling her vocals for the entire first verse about Aunt Sarah. Newly re-recorded vocals follow, performed by Lisa Simone as Saffronia, Laura Izibor as Sweet Thing, and Ledisi as Peaches.[55] Less honorary and more officially in line is the video released in June 2020 by drag superstar Latrice Royale, whose lip sync to an adapted live version of this four-part "Four Women" draws on theatrical performance and two-dimensional art, with its character-specific costume changes and title cards depicting historical black women, running the gamut from Harriet Tubman to Oprah Winfrey.[56]

Perhaps all of these ekphrastic uses of Simone home in on "Four Women" because that song's lineup of different women, with different origins and self-expressions, thematizes something that ekphrasis materializes. To say this another way, whatever else it does, "Four Women" envisions a possibility of copresence for its characters. Narratively speaking, they do appear in sequence, but historically speaking they are coeval with one another. And it's that temporality that the Simone-inspired ekphrastic texts so consistently envision, whether through the ongoingness of slavery's afterlife or the over-dubbed duet between a mother and daughter, recorded more than a half century apart so each woman sings from her prime. The desire to make something out of Simone's text, while still preserving it, is a desire to keep something going without ever being able to exhaust it.

An inverted version of this fantasy of intermedial collaboration comes beautifully to the fore as Adepero Oduye plays Simone in her self-directed short film *To Be Free* (2017). The film opens with Oduye assuming the stage in a small club, silhouetted by stage lights that point into the camera, singing "My Way" and then dancing to a Simone-inspired drum-and-piano instrumental called "No Fear."[57] It's a studied imitation, a performance that works not only through its well-appointed visuals but also in terms of Oduye's carefully articulated vocal elongations that very precisely capture the movements and visual elements of Simone's own performance style. As the song is sung, however, her elongations get longer and become exaggerated, as the sweeping, almost flapping movements of the final dance surely do. The film's final two shots, lasting just seconds each, show Oduye-as-Simone sitting silently at her greenroom vanity, an undrunk whiskey in front of her, head in her hands, unreflected in her own mirror. Exaggeration yields to exhaustion, a sonic multitude contracting to a quiet solitude. It's a story of sacrifice, of having given too much. It shows us something not just about what collaborations can create but about the artistic energy and the present tense that, in doing so, they can consume.

▌▌▌ ● ▌▌▌▌ ● ▌▌▌

From *To Be Free*, dir. Adepero
Oduye (2017).

||| ● |||| ● |||

From *To Be Free*, dir. Adepero
Oduye (2017).

THE PRAISE OFTEN lavished on Simone toggles between recognizing her as singular and celebrating her as summative. Variations show up in the vocabulary of both critical and vernacular assessments, which use words, on the one hand, like *prodigy, virtuoso, genius*, and, on the other, like *eclectic, expansive, convergent*. It's all correct, but it's not all the same. This perception of Simone's different successes in multiple directions perhaps begins to explain the many fantasies of imitation that have inspired younger generations of musical artists. They seek to be like Nina Simone precisely because there is no one like Nina Simone.

One genre of imitation is the cover album. These began to appear immediately after Simone's death, with The Walkabouts' *Slow Days with Nina* in the summer of 2003, followed by Barb Jungr's *Hymn to Nina* in 2008. That same year, Lisa Simone released *Simone on Simone*, covering thirteen of her mother's hits, the first of which, "Music for Lovers," features a concert recording where Lisa sings and Nina accompanies her on piano.[58] An incomplete list of the many subsequent cover albums includes Kellylee Evans's neo-soul *Nina* (2010); Meshell Ndegeocello's pop-rock *Pour une Âme Souveraine: A Dedication to Nina Simone* (2012); the experimental group Xiu Xiu's electronic/avant-jazz *Nina* (2013); and Ledisi's R&B reimagining, *Ledisi Sings Nina* (2021). Meanwhile, RCA commissioned an official tribute album, released in 2015 as the hip-hop-heavy *Nina Revisited: A Tribute to Nina Simone*, with six tracks by Lauryn Hill, two by Lisa Simone, and others by the likes of Mary J. Blige, Usher, and Common.

These covers make a fitting tribute to the artist who so definitively covered others. The challenge, of course, is just how definitively Simone did so, and the relative impossibility her success thereby creates for those who would attempt to reproduce it. While all of the aforementioned albums include covers that are excellent in their own right, their overall relation to Simone can at moments feel comparatively meek or, worse, simply derivative, especially in instances where the songs covered—like "Angel of the Morning," "Just Like a Woman," or "Ne Me Quitte Pas"—already circulate in well-known versions by artists other than Simone.[59]

This problem gets partly solved by the very many genres these cover albums express. Working in genres Simone never touched, like neo-soul, electronic, or hip-hop, offers a way of following her that in the very same gesture departs from her. The point holds not only for the albums full of covers but also for the too-many-to-count one-off covers by a huge number of artists over the past thirty years. In all cases, the more successful versions ultimately feel less like covers and more like homages—hat tips to Simone that are nonetheless clearly grounded in the covering artist's musical idiom rather than hers—such as Jeff Buckley's electric guitar riff on "Lilac Wine," Kimbra's jazzy crooning through "Plain Gold Ring," or John Legend's bedroomy ballad version of "Please Don't Let Me Be Misunderstood." Simone here serves not only as inspiration but more immediately as occasion for these artists to be versions of themselves that would never be mistaken for versions of her.

The fantasy of singing Simone's songs twins with the fantasy of accompanying her. We see the latter most clearly in the remix albums that isolate Simone's vocal tracks and layer new music underneath. Many fewer of these exist than do cover albums, which perhaps says something about something, but like cover albums these remix albums began to appear immediately after her death. In 2003, Chicago-based DJ Felix Da Housecat released three versions of his "Heavenly House" remix of Simone's "Sinnerman." Soon after, in 2006, Sony/BMG, at the time the rights holder for Simone's RCA catalog, brought in more than a dozen other DJs to set Simone's vocals to techno beats in the popular but critically panned *Nina Simone: Remixed and Reimagined*; and in 2021 Verve updated the effort with seven remixes alongside other remastered tracks on *Feeling Good: Her Greatest Hits and Remixes*.[60] In 2018, remix artist Amerigo Gazaway, as part of his Soul Mates project, released "The Miseducation of Eunice Waymon," which reimagines Lauryn Hill's acclaimed solo album as a series of duets between her and Simone.[61]

More abundant than either the cover or the remix, however, is the Nina Simone sample. Simone's vocal and piano tracks have been variously used by rappers and hip-hop artists, including Cassidy, Common, Fashawn, 50 Cent, Flo Rider, Flying Lotus, Jay-Z, Kanye West, Lauryn Hill, Lil Wayne, Mos Def, Talib Kweli, Timbaland, and the Roots. Simone's musical appeal for hip-hop artists in particular likely has to do with the genre's simultaneous formal commitment to aesthetic experimentation and political commitment to social critique—two commitments that, without question, Simone's career uniquely exemplified.[62] While sampling, much like covering and remixing, can be, in Tricia Rose's succinct phrase, "an invocation of another's voice to help you say what you want to say," hip-hop samples of Nina Simone appear to push the point further.[63] As Salamishah Tillet has argued, sampling Simone "aurally ties the hip-hop generation to the black freedom struggle" and thus creates for many artists a way of living through a history that they would otherwise only be living with.[64] Sampling is indeed a way of speaking through someone, but unlike covering, it is also a way of speaking alongside them—less ventriloquism and more copresentation.

But the history evoked in gestures like these is never simply history as it was. The importance granted to Simone through imitation and homage isn't the praise she said she wanted. "All these rappers think they're doing something," she told an audience at Carnegie Hall in 1992. "All they're doing is imitating me 30 years ago."[65] In the last decade of her life, however, as she began to be credited as an inspiration—for example, in 1996 when Lauryn Hill topped charts singing "So while you imitating Al Capone / I'll be Nina Simone and defecating on your microphone"—the mainstay of Simone's objections shifted to artistry.[66] In a late interview, she told LaShonda Katrice Barnett, "What [hip-hop artists] are doing is not musical. Yes, they are protesting against racism in this country, but it's just a beat and some talk. . . . Who is getting the message from protest rap? Hardly anyone, it's just something to shake your ass to. If the message of the music was taken seriously, there would be more noticeable black political leaders."[67] Asked about Lauryn Hill specifically, Simone repeated the point, "I've heard of her. If they are going to call my name and emulate me, they should acknowledge that I am a perfectionist. I work very hard to create music."[68] The point echoes one she had made about Hill in 1997: "I just wish she had sung one of my songs."[69]

It's honestly difficult to imagine that Lauryn Hill didn't work hard. But the force of Simone's assessment doesn't belong to fact so much as it belongs to time. One of the genuine luxuries of the future is its ability to choose things about what counts as its past, and so it is for Hill, as well as any number of other artists subsequent to Simone, to locate themselves in relation to her, to claim to be like Nina Simone precisely because there is no one like Nina Simone. It may not be generous, though it is certainly human, that Simone may have disdained this order of operations—to have wanted something like that last point, that there is no one like Nina Simone, to come first.

‖ ● ‖‖‖ ● ‖

CONCERT REVIEWS OFTEN praised Simone for setting a mood.[70] In this context, *mood* generally connotes the creation of something like an atmosphere or environment, one that affects our state of mind or feeling, often temporarily. Simone's music and performances, we have elsewhere seen, regularly achieved this effect, expressing emotions that torque or adjust, or maybe reflect or amplify, the audience's own. For very likely the same reasons, her songs have in the past few decades become soundtrack go-tos for prestige television and Hollywood alike.[71]

Consider the mood Simone is used to set in the third season finale of *Bojack Horseman*.[72] Driving his yellow convertible along a particularly straight stretch of two-lane highway through the desert, in a direction that points away from his most recent, astounding personal failures, Bojack pushes his foot on the accelerator and takes his eyes off the road and his hands off the wheel. The scene, framed to this point mostly by symmetrical shots, yields to a slow areal pan that moves the viewer's gaze counterclockwise just as the car drifts across the yellow lines and into the oncoming lane. As Bojack turns his head to the right and then swerves into a screeching stop back in the proper lane, the scene's images fail to be not only symmetrical but also, in every sense, straightforward. This series of actions is scored by Simone's 1976 recording of "Stars."

This soundtrack could tend a bit literal, just a simple captioning, as Bojack's life experiences—far more than Simone's own—mirror this saddest version of this saddest song about the professional experience of personal failure. But this episode knows that a state of mind is hardly a stable or self-consistent thing, and that a mood therefore often expresses more, or differently, than the person experiencing it may consciously intend. Accordingly, the show scores "Stars" across a three-scene stretch, beginning extradiagetically at the end of the prior scene and continuing through the end-title credits that follow this one. To get Simone to evoke a mood, *Bojack Horseman* makes sure to extend her song in time.

It makes a lot of sense to do it this way. Moods are very much about this kind of temporal connection, even though there is some disagreement about what kind of time we're talking about. For one, Martin Heidegger thought a mood (*Stimmung*) to be proleptic, anticipatory, a condition that makes it possible to orient one's self toward something.[73] For another, Christopher Bollas argued a related point from the opposite temporal orientation, suggesting that moods may be recursions to prior self-states or attempts to reexperience or re-create something, "acts of conservation and protest."[74] Meanwhile,

||| ● |||| ● |||

From *Bojack Horseman* (2016).

III ● IIIII ● III

From *Bojack Horseman* (2016).

Jonathan Flatley splits the difference, reminding us how moods are points of entry into structures of feeling, though when the right mood does not seem available, a new, sometimes revolutionary mood must be found or invented.[75] *Bojack Horseman* doesn't quite know where it lands in this debate, as the title character's forward propulsion across the landscape is countered, in the scene we're discussing, by his inability not to feel the tug of the very things he's running from. All we viewers are left with is a sense that the melancholy mood evoked by Simone's "Stars" takes up more time than the moment it might otherwise be said to caption, that the mood lingers on either side of the moment of crisis itself.

Is the melancholy mood evoked by Simone singing "Stars" in this episode conjured by the song or by the show's use of the song? Even if the likely answer is *both*, that answer is not the same as the one we might give about the mood evoked by Simone singing "Stars" at the Montreux Jazz Festival where it was recorded. Thus, the tricky thing about using Simone's music to set a mood in this way is that whatever fantasies Simone was working through when she sang and recorded "Stars" are almost certainly not the same as the fantasies that *Bojack Horseman*, or anyone else, scores the song in order to resolve. There is, necessarily, a difference between evoking a mood oneself, as Simone did, and borrowing a mood someone else evokes, as *Bojack Horseman* here does. Inevitability, we cannot transport the song whole into a new context because any new context will make the song feel different, even if the track itself hasn't otherwise been altered.

The issue isn't just about context but also about agency. That is, the mood someone has or sets can't wholly be borrowed and transposed into a context where *they* are not. Our moods, after all, are not only ephemeral but also always at some level irreducibly personal—few people doubt that they are ours.[76] Precisely because moods are temporary, their perdurance, their insistence or rigidity, has been theorized by psychologists as defensive postures. That classification holds even in the case of a good mood, which harbors the potential to become a screen behind which a person hides in order to negate or deny the things that would, under ordinary circumstances, bring anyone's mood down.[77] Understood as a defense, in other words, our moods exist first and foremost to shore up we who are having them. Though we can come into contact with, or be affected by, someone else's mood, that doesn't exactly make it ours.

Part of what's behind the use of Simone's songs to set a mood, then, may be the wish that one *could* use another person in this way, that we could take what the person creates without taking the person in toto. There's nothing desultory, perhaps, that such a fantasy would arise around Simone, whose ability to create a mood is something people admire about her, whereas they tended not to admire it when she was, as she was so often called, moody. While the noun, *mood*, describes a state of mind we can all get into, the adjective, *moody*, tends to refer instead to a state of mind that, in this moment anyway, is more obviously individual. To be moody is not to create an atmosphere or environment so much as a storm brewing in the distance, from which the rest of us may want to seek shelter. To get to experience the mood Simone creates without the moody Simone herself is equally an attempt at destruction (get rid of Simone) and preservation (have Simone in another form).[78] The fantasy animating soundtracks is that we could borrow one and leave the other behind.

SOMETIMES AN OBJECT—A TEXT, a song—doesn't set a mood so much as it triggers one. It evokes in our present a prior sense of our self, and it becomes a way of psychically returning to something. That something can be a subjective thing, something internal to our minds or our experience, but, more intriguingly, it can also be the affective (bodily, felt) sense of something beyond one's self, something that reaches variously toward another person or perhaps instead toward something impersonal, large, and social. Such evocations are possible when, for example, an object (a song) becomes hyperidentified with a product or scene—as, say, Céline Dion's "My Heart Will Go On" has indelibly with the blockbuster film *Titanic*—and when encountering the object (hearing the song anywhere) therefore invites us to connect with the social context of its use (the film).[79] But such evocations can register in a more individual way too, such as when hearing "My Heart Will Go On" invites you to recall not only *Titanic* but also the person you watched it with, where you were, how it all felt. It's this kind of affective conjunction of the personal and the social that Lauren Berlant calls "inhabiting the zone of lived structure" and Kara Keeling refers to as "the rhythms of the poetry from the future."[80]

One fantasy of Nina Simone allows her to be conjunctive in this particular sense—to be both a person and a structure, to move somehow seamlessly between these positions. In this fantasy, Simone's person is evoked or the personality behind her music is summoned, and yet in the end it never matters that what appears is instead ultimately inside the experience of the person who called. This use of Simone, this fantasy of conjunction, is notably common in fantasy expressions marshaled by and around white women.

The sound of Simone singing "Either Way I Lose" lures Reno, the twenty-three-year-old white female protagonist of Rachel Kushner's *The Flamethrowers*, into a bar, setting the novel's plot in motion.[81] Why Nina Simone? Within the narrative, her sounds evoke something personal as they call to mind how a college classmate of Reno's, one Chris Kelly, had tried to make a documentary about Simone in the 1970s during which the novel is set:

> He tracked her down to the South of France. Nina Simone opened the door in a bathrobe, saw that the visitor was holding a camera, lifted a gun from the pocket of her robe and shot at him. She wasn't a good shot. Chris Kelly, who had turned and run, was only hit once, a graze to the shoulder, as he tore through the high, wet grass beyond her farmhouse. He got no footage of Nina Simone but I somehow saw this robe

from which she had produced her gun. Flowy and feminine, pink and yellow flowers with greenish flourishes, semi-abstract leaves. Nina Simone's brown legs. Her flat, calloused feet in a pair of those unisex leather slippers.[82]

The episode loosely adapts one from the summer of 1995, when Simone was throwing a party at her home in Bouc-Bel-Air and experienced what she identified as racist harassment from two teenage boys on the adjacent property. She fired buckshot over the hedge, striking one boy in the leg; the neighbors pressed charges.[83] "I was shocked that I did it," she told the *Guardian* in 2001, "but not sorry."[84]

This kernel of antagonism—the racism that Simone's neighbors apparently flung at her, or maybe the lifetime of experiences with racism that disposed her to take notice of whatever it was they said—means, among very many other things, that Simone's body mattered to that nonfictional scene. In Kushner's fictional translation, Simone's body also matters, though in an entirely different way. The blackness that Simone embodied and that she fired shots to protect becomes a pair of "brown legs" that support some "feminine" costume. In fact, Simone defended a body marked by history, while in fiction Simone succumbs to a body exhibited aesthetically. *The Flamethrowers* does more than the prestige television soundtracks that evoke Simone's music to set a mood, using its pages instead to conjure her bodily, and yet it does so in a way that does not make substantial the person who lives in that body. Simone appears here as Reno's prop.

There would be no point in belaboring this one example were it not the recent culmination of a well-worn pattern. Inaugurating that pattern is unquestionably the blockbuster *Point of No Return* (1993), starring Bridget Fonda as assassin Maggie Hayward, code name Nina. Her love of Simone's music is established early on and repeated through the film all the way to the denouement, at which point her field mentor (Gabriel Byrne) takes her copy of *Nina Simone at Town Hall* to remember her by. Five of Simone's songs feature in the movie's soundtrack, four of them as part of an extradiagetic score that shows us something about Maggie's state of mind. Yet this too is more than setting a mood. The film eschews Simone's body yet repeatedly evokes her character, pairing instead the largeness and richness of Simone's sound with the emotionally withholding performance and petite stature of Fonda's body. In the central such scene, as a lover (Dermot Mulroney) expresses frustration that he can't get closer to this secretive woman, Maggie uses Simone's music to stand in the place of her own interior experience, a kind of emotional prosthesis: "My mother loved Nina Simone. She used to play her records all the time. I grew up listening to this music that . . . sounded so . . . passionate, so savage. All about love and loss. I play Nina Simone when I think about my mother."[85] Here, Simone marks an inheritance, an Oedipal scenario, a scene of attachment. Any real details of who or what is being attached don't come forward in Maggie's speech, so much as the fact of her desire for, and feelings about, the possibility of an attachment. She offers up a promise of disclosure that doesn't much deliver, but its abstraction satisfies the lover who simply wanted something. Simone provides Maggie with a passable cover for the vulnerability she can't otherwise bear.

A similar use of Simone's voice in the service of enabling white womanhood takes place in the final scene of Richard Linklater's *Before Sunset* (2004), as Jesse (Ethan Hawke) puts on a CD of the 1968 Montreux Jazz Festival recording of "Just in Time" and sits down on the couch belonging to Céline (Julie Delpy), with whom he'd fallen in love nine years before but not seen again until today. "Did you ever see Nina Simone in concert?" asks Céline, who at first talks over the music, reporting that she's seen Simone twice.[86] She begins to sing along with Simone's words "Now I know where I'm going / No more doubt or fear," then laughs and resolves into a thoughtful silence with reflective, downcast eyes, leaving Simone to supply the words that aren't otherwise being said. From here, the black woman's words and the white woman's body continue to merge, as Céline imitates Simone's gait and gestures from a performance she'd attended, and the camera cuts to Jesse as the sole audience member of Céline's reenactment. Elements that have so often been called distinctive about Simone's performance style instead become something that can be imitated, borrowed, claimed in the privacy of one's home as one's own movements. This scene is one of mutual seduction between Céline and Jesse, and yet her desires are negotiated more indirectly, using Simone as a proxy.

It's notable that all these scenes distinguish Simone as someone so special that she can even make you special by virtue of having been in proximity to her, and yet that specialness is up for grabs, not something that Simone herself gets to dispense. These are scenes where a black woman has been hollowed out so that white women get to wear her desire, her beauty, her power as their own armor. *Point of No Return* and *Before Sunrise* make male lovers the occasion that requires this armor, the costume one wears into a battle of the sexes. Accordingly, the stories these scenes tell are not about femininity per se but about its operations within heterosexuality. Disguising one's self behind Nina Simone becomes for these women a way to get a man to love them without demanding of them the self-exposure that love can bring, without requiring that they be entirely themselves and instead allowing them to claim some more idealized qualities as their own. While one may doubt that a young Julie Delpy had to do much to get a man to notice her, in fact the wish here isn't about who gets to be beautiful so much as about who gets to have control over how one is being noticed, and what one is being noticed for. Reinforcing the point is the independent fantasy/horror film *Witch Hunt* (1994), in which the brothel madam Vivian Dart (played, not incidentally, by veteran drag performer Lypsinka) first appears on-screen lip syncing to Simone's "I Put a Spell on You," before using supernatural powers to transmogrify the face and physique of one of her employees to a john's specifications.[87]

There is no question whatsoever that Simone is not the only black woman used by white heterofemininity in this way, and in a sense, the operative fantasy in these scenes may not be precisely a fantasy of Nina Simone so much as a fantasy about white heterofemininity.[88] Nonetheless, what matters for present purposes is how this process, by which the preceding examples make Simone substitute for emotions or desires that white women don't wish to disclose, doesn't preserve Simone as herself. Rather, it preserves a caricature of her, one that is inconsiderate of any gap between her aesthetic effects and what she, intentionally or unintentionally, may have been expressing. As these white women hold Simone forward like a shield in front of their own vulnerabilities, Simone herself gets hidden. In the tangled ways that white womanhood finds to speak in heteropatriarchy, black women are often the collateral damage.[89]

EARLY IN THE FILM *Black Panther: Wakanda Forever* (2022), Princess Shuri (Letitia Wright) conveys her esteem for the gadgets littered around the MIT dorm room belonging to the scrappy prodigy-inventor Riri Williams (Dominique Thorne). "To be young, gifted, and black, right?" offers Williams, intimating knowingly toward shared experience. Then, registering with some disappointment that the princess has failed to recognize the deficits a South Side girl had to overcome in order to be standing here, Williams says, mostly to herself, "I guess you don't say that in Wakanda."[90]

POLITICS IS CONTESTATION, though political fantasies are often ones in which that contestation adds up to something. For all the ways that Simone was socially marked—by race, by gender, by national history—she could still be hard to place. During the 1960s, Simone found favorable reception in Europe, where she built one of her most devoted fan bases. Many European countries, especially France, and some African nations, especially Algeria, received her politically, a kind of a black ambassador from the United States, reporting on race relations back home.[91] Those politics, like all politics, are scenes of contestation, of irresolution and mess; in conveying them, Simone, like any messenger, risked becoming a kind of shorthand for the political itself—never mind the particulars of the politics in which she engaged or her own positions within them.

Simone's political significance at this much more general level comes to the fore in Darina Al-Joundi's one-woman play and accompanying memoir, both titled *Le jour où Nina Simone a cessé de chanter* (*The Day Nina Simone Stopped Singing*). The daughter of an atheist and cosmopolitan father, raised in Beirut in the decade preceding the onset of the Lebanese civil war (1975–90), Al-Joundi uses Simone's music to signify a set of sexual possibilities and Western values threatened by the political gains of fundamentalist Shiite Muslims. She recalls, at her father's funeral, "My father never had a God. He made me swear, 'Daughter of mine, watch out that these dogs don't use the Koran the day I die. Daughter of mine, I beg you, I would like some jazz at my death, and even some hip-hop, but definitely no Koran,'" and, as the thing he feared very much comes to pass, his dutiful daughter "took out the cassette of the Koran and replaced it with Nina Simone's 'Save Me.'"[92]

That song is a canny choice. Simone recorded "Save Me" for the 1967 RCA sessions that led to *Silk and Soul*, though the song was only released later, as a single (a B-side to "To Be Young, Gifted and Black"), and not included on *Silk and Soul* until its "expanded edition" in 2006. The better-known version of "Save Me," accordingly, was its author's, released on Aretha Franklin's *I Never Loved a Man the Way I Loved You* earlier in 1967. True to Franklin's style, "Save Me" evokes church, transposing the desire for divine love and eternal salvation into a desire for romantic love and an end to heartbreak. Simone's cover follows suit, and while she had a practiced ability to turn a romantic song into a protest song—as she had with "Tomorrow Is My Turn" or "Please Don't Let Me Be Misunderstood"—"Save Me" comes a few years later in her career, by which point Simone had been singing protest songs openly and such a maneuver was less required. To make Simone's "Save Me" feel really political, in other words, Al-Joundi has to contrast it with the Koran.

The fantasy here seems to be one where Simone's politics feed into ours, but the consequence is to use Simone politically, for what she signifies, without exactly engaging in the political arguments about which she cared, and for which she fought. In making such moves, Al-Joundi is not alone.[93] Consider the widespread reproductions of Simone's image from the 1969 Jack Robinson photo shoot, taken in the short number of months between late 1969 and early 1970 when she sported an Afro.[94] The images unmistakably signify Black Power, and their circulation on coffee mugs and throw pillows reevokes that signification without any more precise engagement with Simone's politics or their nuances, without any reckoning that what wearing an Afro meant in 1969 is not what it means in 2024, if for no other reason than that the 2024 moment has the 1969 moment behind it in a way that the 1969 moment, by definition, cannot. None of this is to say that any of us should get rid of our Nina Simone coffee mug. But it may be worth admitting that the mug's image, however clearly historical, is there chiefly to evoke something about the present.

Assuming a connection between 1969 and 2024 based in general sameness, rather than irreducible difference, creates a sense of continuity, and such a sense can obscure that the present's relation to the past is always motivated, never neutral. Obscuring this point can be good for politics but obstructing for fantasy. The past is the condition of the present, but acting like it's more of the same—in other words, confusing the two—can create an obstacle to a version of the present we might urgently need, or simply want.[95] Political fantasies try to push past that obstacle, even though, with enough time or entrenchment, one political fantasy will often, itself, become the obstacle to a new one.[96]

THE OTHER SIDE of continuity is haunting. The reality show *We're Here* sends a team of drag queens to support queer and gender-variant people living in small-town America, and the episode in which cohost Bob the Drag Queen (Caldwell Tidicue) dresses like Nina Simone takes place in Selma, Alabama. Simone had joined Martin Luther King Jr. in Montgomery, Alabama, on March, 25 1965, where, at the conclusion of the third and largest march between these cities, she performed "Mississippi Goddam" outdoors, in a sweater vest and plaid skirt.[97] Fifty-five years later, a different, more iconic Simone look seems to have inspired Bob the Drag Queen, and his appearance in Selma evokes the much-photographed prints Simone wore in London on BBC television in 1966. We have elsewhere seen that Simone's clothes, as well as her sense of herself as expressed through them, were shifting in the mid-1960s. Bob the Drag Queen's evocation of Simone pulls that later sense back across the cusp of 1965, to make it present at the moment before it took place. Costuming is not, however, the only thing here that makes time collapse.

Midepisode, the queens meet with JoAnne Bland, Lynda Blackmon Lowery, and Joyce Parrish O'Neil, three living witnesses to Selma's "Bloody Sunday," whose conversation draws a line from police violence against civil rights protesters in 1965 to police killings of unarmed black men in 2021. It's not this repetition that becomes overwhelming for Bob, so much as the possibility of its disruption. "Knowing what my ancestors processed, so I could sit here," he begins, dissolving into sobs. Then, speaking much faster, "I'm from Alabama, Mississippi, and Georgia, so I'm the direct descent of slaves. My grandma's grandma was a slave. So what they had to process so I could sit here [sobbing] . . . on this couch. [sobbing] And you feel . . . and you feel bad because it didn't happen to you."[98]

The space between past and present can be measured in many ways, and one of them is grief. Because both the present and the past shape the present, our ability to distinguish between them often accords with some personal or collective desire for the thing designated as "past" to shape the present less, and in that sense to be over.[99] When the past does not feel like it is over—when, as in the conversation just described, the violence is recognized as continuous—the present becomes haunted. The past ceases to be a tomb where the dead are buried, becoming animated instead as the site where they died, an unmarked grave where history and the present meet.[100]

Unbearable history must still be borne, and the strain of that necessity can find support from fantasy's power to help you occupy a position that

III ● IIIII ● III

From *We're Here* (2021).

Nina Simone at the BBC,
London (1966). Photo by
David Redfern/Redferns—
Getty Images.

isn't your own. For Bob in this moment, however, the blurring of subjective boundaries doesn't defend against the pain of history so much as it lets that pain in, affording him a way to acknowledge his distance from it. This scene from *We're Here* resolves with a conversation about survival and struggle, fantastic motifs of acknowledgment that aim to designate the past as over without making it go away. Arguably, Bob the Drag Queen's Nina Simone look anticipated this resolution. His evocation of Simone as an influence, an antecedent, makes her related to his present, marks the succession of her timeline with his without letting them collapse. A sense of succession allows something to be over and also to be held close. Those tensions, which the fantasy of succession resolves, clear psychic, social, and also political space. That, almost invariably, is the space in which any forward movement takes place.

WE CAN RETIRE monuments without wanting to retire monumentality. That desire, I think, registers in the backhanded language of a 2001 concert review in which Gene Santoro sighs that watching a sixty-eight-year-old Simone perform "was a little like trying to glean the glory of Rome from its ruins. But the fact is, they don't make Nina Simones anymore."[101] It's never easy to find ways to compliment great people whose best work is behind them, and I don't envy Santoro the task. At the same time, seeing someone for who they were, as he tries however generously to do, gestures inevitably in the direction of refusing to accept who they are capable of becoming.

James Baldwin knew this. He comes out against both monuments and monumentality in the short essay "Faulkner and Desegregation" (1956), in which he examines how the recent Nobel Prize–winning author charismatically mythologizes racist and violent aspects of southern history. Baldwin insists that the result is dishonest, even and perhaps especially when Faulkner presents that history in ruins. So compelling, writes Baldwin, "is the image of ruin, gallantry, and death thus evoked that it demands a positive effort of the imagination" to recall some of history's other, more noncontroversial facts, such as "Southern slaveholders were not the only people who perished."[102] The first problem is that ruins focus our gaze on particular points from the past, points whose particularity can be so distorting that we miss the second problem, which is that we're looking backward at all. Destruction will bind us to the thing that has been destroyed, whereas real change, Baldwin argues, instead "implies the breakup of the world as one has always known it, the loss of all that gave one an identity, the end of safety."[103] The ruins of one world stop being ruins when they transform into the foundation for the next world, when they cease to hold us back and become instead a resource for building forward.

To put this point in other terms, we might say that in a ruined world, they do not make Nina Simones anymore; while in a truly changed world, they might not even know how. It's true that neither world has a Nina Simone in it. But it matters to what I'm trying to say here that the ruined world is the one we live in, every day, while that truly changed world is the one Simone tried, so many days, to play for.

III ● IIIII ● III

THE EMPHASIS SO FAR has been on the distance between our fantasies of Nina Simone and Nina Simone's fantasies of Nina Simone. But of course the very reason we engage Nina Simone in the act of making our world stems from a wish to echo some of her own world-making gestures. One of the things for which she is most celebrated is making people feel free.

Asked point-blank what freedom meant to her, in Peter Rodis's documentary *Nina Simone—A Historical Perspective* (1970), Simone answers with a clearly unrehearsed but sincerely delivered line than has earned this interview viral status in the age of streaming video: "No fear."[104] Though phrased in the negative, this answer has a more rhetorically positive preface: "I've had a couple of times on stage when I really felt *free*," she says, "and that's something *else*. That's really something else." The "No" in "No fear," accordingly, isn't exactly Simone saying no.[105] Instead, Simone suggests here that her performances and songs aren't purely defiant, not, in any absolute sense, an antithesis, or a negative liberty, or a freedom from. Rather, this freedom is "something else," holding the place we move toward without knowing precisely what it contains.

Simone had meditated on freedom before. One notable instance is her recording of "I Wish I Knew How It Would Feel to Be Free" on *Silk and Soul* (1967), the most legendary performance of which took place at the Montreux Jazz Festival in 1976. There, she opens with an extended piano intro lasting more than a minute, followed by vocals that begin melodious and mellow, though by the second verse something has slowly but unmistakably shifted, and the ends of both piano and vocal bars are punctuated by notes in a lower key. The effect of this progression is awesome, as it seems to build the song's delivery toward an incredible fury—one that feels right and yet seems to emerge from nowhere. As if to reinforce the mood, Simone follows the conclusion of the second verse with the spoken aside, "Cuz if we ain't we're murderers." Yet into the third verse the mood shifts again, decisively away from the prophesied anger and toward something more joyous, delivered with elongated vocals in a higher key, with verses fastened together by Simone's now smiling spoken aside, "Aw yeah, the spirit's moving now" and her improvised lyrics "Jonathan Livingston Seagull ain't got nothing on me / I'm free . . . and I know it!"[106]

Freedom emerges from Simone's performance as a state one can "be" in, and yet a state that comes into being through significant emotional shifts in her delivery, leading some observers to suggest that Simone equates freedom with improvisation.[107] Such a suggestion is not at all wrongheaded, but it makes freedom sound as though it was spontaneous, accidental, unplanned, and, whatever else can be said about this or indeed any Simone performance, it took root in profound and disciplined practice. Moreover, the freedom she evokes in this performance isn't, or isn't just, her individual freedom.[108] As with "No fear," feeling free isn't a cancellation, wiping the slate clear in order to bring something wholly new into being. Rather, feeling free looks like a process of trying to bring forward "something," a potential as yet undeveloped that, nonetheless, the world already contains. In both the 1970 interview and the 1976 performance, freedom is *something*, reminiscent of what Fred Moten has called "the freedom drive that animates black performances," or what Robin D. G. Kelley identifies as the "freedom dreams" that animate black radical imaginations.[109] Simone imagines how an old world isn't simply negated but also transforms into a resource for building a new one.[110]

Something marches dialectically forward, and we can follow Simone's lead. Within a year of the Montreux performance, the Combahee River Collective Statement will argue, "If black women were free, it would mean that everyone else would have to be free since our freedom would necessitate the destruction of all the systems of oppression."[111] Later, Assata Shakur will describe her coming to revolutionary consciousness: "One day i was happy just to be alive and young and moving. The next day i felt like the world was coming to an end."[112] Later, Audre Lorde will tell an audience of historians, "Recognizing the power of the erotic within our lives can give us the energy to pursue genuine change within our world."[113] Later, Toni Morrison will write, "Nina Simone helped delay the beginning of the end. So when the end arrived, it was unrecognizable as such."[114] Later, Denise Ferreira da Silva will write that "the radical force of Blackness lies at the turn of thought—that is, Blackness knowing and studying announces the End of the World as we know it," and Alexander Weheliye will ask, "It's the end of the world—don't you know that yet?"[115] Later, Saidiya Hartman will observe, "Black feminism is the desire for the end of the world as we know it."[116] Later, Angela Davis will draw a line from Ferguson to Palestine and name it after a song sung during the Mississippi Summer, *Freedom Is a Constant Struggle*.[117] Later, Achille Mbembe will insist that "for a large share of humanity, the end of the world has already occurred."[118] Later, Tourmaline will write, "I'm not satisfied with Black trans lives mattering; I want Black trans lives to be easy, to be pleasurable, and to be filled with lush opportunities. I want the abundance we've gifted the world—the art, the care, the knowledge, and the beauty—to be offered back to us tenfold."[119]

Later, freedom was and will be *something*, and the only way out of this world will still be through it.

Something

(Reprise)

"Every song that I sing—to me, it is important that it communicates something to someone," Simone told an interviewer sometime in the late 1960s. "It is not just a song," she repeated. "It is something that says something to someone."[1]

IT TURNS OUT I was someone. The first time I ever remember hearing a Nina Simone song I was twenty. It was about a third of the way through Marlon Riggs's experimental documentary *Tongues Untied*, as a femme-of-center person walks "the waterfront curbside" along Oakland's Lake Merritt, smoking and reflecting.[2] The voice-over tells a story of loneliness and social isolation, of sex work and hope, as this person waits for a man "who in my fantasies comes for me, in a silver, six-cylinder chariot." These words are set against the faded sounds of Simone singing "Black Is the Color of My True Love's Hair."

Watching Riggs and listening to Simone, I recognized a part of myself in a story that wasn't about me. The blackness of which Simone sings, and on which her luxurious notes place indelible emphasis, anticipates the film's radical conclusion, that black men loving black men is *the* revolutionary act, and this is a conclusion whose most immediate addressee I am not. Yet I watched *Tongues United* over and over during my twenties and many times since. I cannot say what this moment spoke to me, even though I will tell you with conviction how inestimably much it did.[3]

This first encounter of mine with Nina Simone belonged to the realm of the aesthetic. The blackness of which she sang, from which she sang, was something whose beauty called out to me. It was something that I related to. It sparked desire, and as in so many moments when one aches to possess a *something*—to fold it into one's sense of self, the better to become oneself—it didn't matter to my desire that its object was black and I wasn't. And, hey, maybe that desire for beauty wasn't in and of itself violent, though the world in which I would set out to pursue it sure is. There's a part of what I wanted from Simone that I recognized isn't for me, and that part stood in tension with the fact that I wanted it still.

Writing this book became a scene of fantasy, an attempt both to adapt my desire and to adapt to my desire, to experience it differently, as something more obviously benign like fandom, or maybe bland like expertise. Writing became an exercise in cultivating the creative part of myself to contain some more ruthless parts of myself, an exercise I'd wager all writers use writing to do at least sometimes. The fantasy was that by writing about Nina Simone, I could shift the ratio, make my desire more about her and less about me. The fantasy was that by listening seriously to Nina Simone, whatever I desired from her came within bounds, became harmless. And maybe my desire mostly is, and also maybe no one's ever is. Maybe that's one reason why reconciling desire's contradictions should not just be fantasy's work, but all of ours.

ONE NINA SIMONE cover stands out above the others. In February 2016, at Joe's Pub in New York, the performance artist and chanteuse Lady Rizo arranged her annual birthday show for Simone, a night of tributes and invocation and homage. This year she gathered an ensemble, with different artists coming onstage for a number or a duet. Somewhere in the middle of the set Mikal Kilgore emerged wearing an ampersand shirt listing what were instantly and horribly recognizable as the names of young black men murdered by agents of white supremacy: Michael & Trayvon & Tamir & Laquan. Bearing witness with these names printed across his chest, Kilgore opened his mouth and sang a low, attenuated, unmistakably Simone-inspired cover of "My Man's Gone Now."

Taking cues from Simone's famous one-off performance that expresses so much more than it says, that night's performance too tended minimal. Yet the simplicity of its elements—a song, a shirt—came together in juxtaposition as something greater than the sum of their parts. It was immediately clear what we were listening to even as there was something delayed about the expression's unfolding, some kind of statement that exceeded this moment of its iteration. The crowd's attention needed to focus if we were going to hear the emotional force of the understated cross talk between the shirt and the song, if we were going to be able to listen to this protest that harnessed a voice so feelingful and rare and a violence so unforgivable and unrelenting. Kilgore performed a set of stunning tensions held together, beheld together, by people who in this moment, if we listened right, could at least not fail to honor the terrible beauty that follows when a meaning is artfully shifted.

It said something about something to someone.

ACKNOWLEDGMENTS

Fantasies of Nina Simone was mostly written between March 2020 and February 2022, plus or minus a lifetime on either side. In that long stretch of making and unmaking, I have learned so much from so many people, and I am grateful for a life that is larger than I can take in or hold at once. Still, to those whom I have neglected to name, the omission is not intentional, and my gratitude, however ill-represented, is sincere and real.

Endless appreciation goes to audiences and colleagues and collaborators who allowed me to share this work and to make it better: at Dartmouth College (Don Pease, Kyla Schuller, Christian Haines, Eng-Beng Lim, Kate Nicholson); at the Columbia University American Studies Seminar (James Kim, Peter Murray, Matt Sandler, Cristobal Silva); at meetings of the American Studies Association (Daphne Brooks, Joshua Chambers-Letson, Eddie Hill, Salamishah Tillet; Danielle Davis, Elliott Powell, Karen Tongson); at the Gender Studies Program at St. Michael's University (Maura D'Amore, Tim Mackin, Crystal L'Hote); and at the Department of English at Bates College (Eden Osucha).

Some preliminary but essential thinking about affect happened for me at the "Queer and Now: New Directions in Queer Theory" conference at the University of Wisconsin, with the Sexual Politics/Sexual Poetics collective (Kadji Amin, Katie Brewer Ball, Ramzi Fawaz, Zakiyyah Jackson, Uri McMillan, Amber Musser, Roy Pérez, Jennifer Row, Shanté Paradigm Smalls, and Damon Young).

Fordham colleagues in the Race, Empire, and Colonialism area group (Cathy Chaput, Diane Detourney, Chris GoGwilt, Glenn Hendler, Robb Hernández, Julie Kim, Fawzia Mustafa, Sasha Panaram, Stephen Sohn, and Suzanne Yeager) read versions of two different sections and made important interventions. In and for that group, I'm grateful to James Kim, who offered me the phrase "an ethics of listening."

Fordham's Comparative Literature Program (and its erstwhile program directors James Kim, Shonni Enelow, and Tom O'Donnell) hosted colloquia with Christina Sharpe in 2018 and Fred Moten in 2019, which opened up space.

For other things at Fordham in the past few years, thanks also to Andrew Albin, Laura Auricchio, Andrew Clark, Crystal Columbini, Bob Davis, Karina Hogan, Yiju Huang, Laurie Lambert, Corey McEleny, Yuko Miki, Kathryn Reklis, Dave Swinarski, Dennis Tyler, Vlasta Vranjes, Sarah Zimmerman, and the much-missed Eva Badowska, Ben Dunning, Scott Poulson-Bryant, Kris Trujillo, and Rafael Zapata. The Ladies of English, Carole Alvino, MonaLisa Torres-Bates, and Labelle De La Rosa, as well as Kerri Maguire and Annmarie O'Connor, put the "support" in support work and accordingly have my hugest thanks.

Ian Balfour and Ben Wurgaft checked my German, *wie es gute Freunde tun.*

Michael Gillespie took me for ramen and shared his insights and his enthusiasms, which were more buoying that he probably knows.

Janet Neary gets a special shout-out for six years in a row affording me the privilege of guest teaching a unit on Nina Simone to her amazing honors students at Hunter College.

Phil Blumenshine dropped the phrase "accuracy without precision" into conversation over dogs and coffee one Hartford morning, and I have been carrying it around ever since.

Raúl Coronado, Jennifer Doyle, Greta LaFleur, Eng-Beng Lim, Dana Luciano, Tavia Nyong'o, Kyla Schuller, and Kyla Wazana Tompkins, members of my 2020 COVID-summer writing group, aka the morning posse, are the people I spent the best writing days with in years.

Thanks, too, to the members of various reading groups: Phil Blumenshine, Rachel Buurma, Will Clark, Marcy Dinius, Adam Fales, Laura Heffernan, Dana Luciano, Sasha Panaram, Joshua Trannen, and Omari Weekes.

Patrick Blanchfield and Abby Kluchin have long been some of my favorite people to talk with about psychoanalysis. Their *Ordinary Unhappiness* podcast showed up late in this writing and helped me rethink some details from the ground up.

Sarah Blackwood and Sarah Mesle first invited me to write about music. This book would not exist, and certainly not in this form, without the conversations and voices they fostered with *Avidly.* Max Cavitch deserves similar praise for his incredible work at *Psyche on Campus.* Lindsey Andrews and Night School Bar are inspirations.

Dalila Scruggs and her colleagues at the New York Public Library, keepers of the flame, have my gratitude.

Stephen Fragano offered extraordinary, careful, and detailed research assistance, often finding things I didn't know to look for.

Research-based writing in pandemic times has been possible thanks to Fordham's indefatigable interlibrary loan and document delivery services, Z Library, and friends with institutional access who traded pdfs and responded to my frantic requests, very much including the greater academic Twittersphere and all the people there who were extremely online with me in 2020. Even though I often needed materials immediately, I made a point to purchase and/or order through my university library a hard copy of every single digital scan I consulted. I wouldn't be here without books and libraries, and I want there to be more of them in circulation.

Courtney Berger at Duke University Press has been a great friend as well as a patient and fantastic editor. Two anonymous readers responded judiciously to the manuscript twice each, and the final version is unmistakably improved for their attention to it. Thanks to Laura Jaramillo for guidance getting the manuscript into production, to Susan Ecklund for meticulous copyediting, to Courtney Leigh Richardson for amazing design work (I mean, *look* at this), and to Ihsan Taylor for helping things assume their final form. Thanks, also, to Ken Wissoker for the early intervention by which, when I described plans for an entirely different book, with kindness and impeccable tact he asked what else I was thinking about.

For the many images that grace these pages, I express appreciation for a Manuscript and Book Publication Award from Fordham's Office of Research and to the Leonard Hastings Schoff and Suzanne Levick Schoff Memorial Fund at the University Seminars at Columbia University for their help in publication. Material in this work was presented to the University Seminar in American Studies (number 429). My thanks to Arthur Nager for permission to include one of his original images.

Other conditions of possibility include discogs.com, the Nina Simone Database maintained by Mauro Boscarol, Academy Records in the East Village, Rough Trade Records in Williamsburg, Café Loup (RIP), and Three Lives & Company Bookstore, plus apartment 15Q and everyone who ever came to a party there, smoked out the window, or chose a record.

Geoffrey Heron's conversation contained early glimmers of this thinking, and I regret that he isn't here to see where it all went.

Mandy Berry shared the story of the time she didn't see Nina Simone because "being gay ruined my life" (ask her to tell it; it's really good). Ian Balfour, Sarah Cefai, Adam Fales, Jason Fitzgerald, Jason Fleetwood-Bolt, Matt Haugen, Mark Horn, Lynn Horridge, Jeff Insko, Jamie Jones, Raleigh Martin, Meredith McGill, Atiba Pertilla, Jason Potts, Scott Poulson-Bryant, Andy Rotman, Daniel Spector, Ben Steverman, and Sharif Youssef sent me clippings. Kyle Turner sent films. Kwame Holmes sent texts. Leigh Claire La Berge sent encouragement, as did Colin Dayan. Jean-Thomas Trembley gave notes on style. Emma Bianchi cut an adverb. Chip Badley traded drafts. Chris Mitchell listened to *Wild Is the Wind*. Elliott Powell, thank you for being a friend. Tim Stewart-Winter, back in the day, alerted me to the existence of Nina Simone studies. Hugh Ryan kindly answered my questions and furnished me with sources. Robert Reid-Pharr said things a long time ago that ended up mattering now. Greg Seigworth encouraged my affective response. Stephen Best gave me things to think about. Kandice Chuh contributed to my aesthetic education. Jonathan Flatley set a mood. Elizabeth Maddock Dillion knows about the obeah woman. Geoff Gilbert walked me along the Canal Saint Martin and told me about the time he saw Nina in Paris. Paul Conrad fangirled with me at a gay bar in Atlanta. Roxanne Panchasi mailed me a hat. Robert Chang gifted me a giant MP3 library of Nina Simone albums one day around 2004 or so, and, as with so many things he gave me, it changed my life.

Some new friends who hung out as I worked: Farah Bakaari, Peter Boudreau, Peter Brown, Samuel Catlin, Nathan Douglas, Jason Farr, Jess Goldberg, Aston Gonzalez, Stephen Guy-Bray, Brad Harmon, Travis Chi Wing Lau, Cody Madsen, Patrick Nathan, Jay Shelat, Connor Spencer, James Zarsadiaz, Brendon Zatirka. And not new, but so wonderfully present: Kirsten Gruesz, Francine Housier, Virginia Jackson, Anna Kornbluh, Deidre Lynch, Meredith McGill, Andy Parker, Stephen Vider, and Kalima Young.

Some of the usual suspects: Elan Abrell, Tara Bynum, Amanda Claybaugh, Lara Cohen, Brian Connolly, Pete Coviello, Hilary Emmett, Jonathan Beecher Field, Jody Greene, Claire Jarvis, Dana Luciano, Justine Murison, Meredith Neuman, Janet Neary, Sianne Ngai, Julie Orlemanski, Jasbir Puar, Joe Rezek, Jordy Rosenberg, Dana Seitler, Caleb Smith, Gus Stadler, Jill Stauffer, Kathryn Bond Stockton, Rei Terada, Pam Thurschwell, Teresa Toulouse, Rafael Walker, Delci Winders, Nate Wolff, Daniel Worden, Ben Wurgaft. I really wish I could hand copies of this book to Corey Capers, Beth Freeman, and Danny Thompson.

Some of the other people without whom this book and its author would not have been the same: Frank Caruso, Ray Cha, Frank Cheers, Chris Comerford, Adrian Dimanlig, Greg Edwards, Spencer Everett, Christian Gullette, Byron Harrison, Peter Hill, Jon Kay, Virginia Kim, Brian Klinksiek, Victor Ng,

Frank Pasquale, Ian Shin, Mikey Stevens, Morgan Tingley, BG Wright, and the lads of Hell's Quarantine (Brad Anderson, Seth Carlson, John Havard, Patrick Kwan, Mike Moore, Davis Nguyen, David Polk, Koichi Eric Sakamoto, Liam Stack, Ben Steverman, Tim Stewart-Winter).

Sam Draxler knows what he did—and hopefully how much I love him for it.

Rahne Alexander is as incredible a guide to the twenty-second century as she has been through the late twentieth and early twenty-first.

Adam Fales offered his talent for listening to the places where the harmonies could come in. He's a beloved collaborator, a wealth of information, and an accomplished practitioner of friendship as a way of life. I'm lucky to have been his student.

Noah Glassman modeled how to listen and taught me how much can be said as a result. Thanks for staying and seeing me through.

Aufie listened to "Pirate Jenny" studiously and, for that among many other things, I will never stop loving him. Zekie doesn't care, but his puppyishness and his capacity for joy surely pick up on something that reverberates in Nina's oeuvre, and I'm grateful for his attempts to alert me to it. Thanks, too, to Hussham, Hina, and Kiki, to Robin, Tim, and Lupo, and to the queer canine kinship of chosen family.

Edward Hui hunted through bargain bins, schlepped records in suitcases, fixed the needle on the turntable, somehow never tired of talking about this work over dinner, and was otherwise a greater friend to this project and its author than either could have dreamed. He found me just in time and changed my lonely nights that lucky day.

LAUREN BERLANT POSSESSED the rare and magical gift of writing show tunes for shows that hadn't been written yet.

I tried my hardest to write this book for Lauren, even though I had begun writing it before the coffee date in January 2019 when Lauren told me about her cancer, which (who knew?) was just a month before I found out about mine. But mine got better and Lauren's didn't, and those circumstances never seemed remotely fair, even in the frenzied midst of the too many things I took on that next year to prove to myself that I deserved to be alive. Then came March 2020 and COVID and lockdown and despair. I began writing in earnest, trying now to prove to the world I knew it was there, that I hadn't abandoned it and that, maybe, therefore, it hadn't abandoned us all. I tried to say, and for a while believed, that I was writing this book to save Lauren's life rather than my own.

We visited twice after that, first in July 2020, over noshes from the vegan Jewish deli in Sheridan Park, which we ate in the garden as the lake breeze blew across the humid afternoon, and we took pictures and talked about how our pets take sides when we argue with our intimates. And Lauren asked me what this book was really about, and I said, but I didn't know.

Then it was May 2021, and we were vaxxed and Lauren was in a wheelchair, and we drank fancy seltzers and gossiped about our friends, and she showed me the cover of her next book and said she didn't know if she'd be around to see it published but "I hope I am," and I hoped too. And Lauren asked me again what this book was really about, and I said, but I still didn't know.

Then—it felt suddenly—Lauren died. And that turned out to be even harder than I could have guessed, and it gets harder all the time, not least because Lauren isn't here to ask me what this book is really about, and therefore I'm not able to say what I finally know: Lauren, it's about how much I love you.

SOMETHING

1 Coates, "Nina Simone's Face"; Brooks, "'Ain't Got No/I Got Life.'"
2 Here and throughout I have learned from Vaillant, *Adaptation to Life*.
3 Brown, "'What Has Happened Here,'" 297.
4 On the longer history, see, for starters, Davis, *Women, Race, and Class*; Carby, *Reconstructing Womanhood*; Wright, *Black Girlhood in the Nineteenth Century*; Field and Simmons, *Global History of Black Girlhood*.
5 *We* is meant as a figure, not an assertion. *We* is used here and in what follows to evoke patterns and behaviors that are associated with or resulting from unconscious process, as broadly construed within psychoanalytic theories. It seemed meaningful to build in a rhetorical *we* because identification is a big part of the story that follows. At the same time that *we* presumes shared aspects of human consciousness, it is my view that there is no such thing as a universal subject, and so *we* will not be used to describe what I am able to recognize as historically contingent or culturally specific positions.
6 E.g., Brun-Lambert, *Nina Simone*, 87; Hagan, "I Wish I Knew How It Felt to Be Free," 11.
7 My sense that fantasy happens at the unconscious level is consistent with canonical psychoanalytic understandings, from Freud to Laplanche, as elaborated later in this section. However, my sense that unconscious fantasy is expressive—that its expression is not just mental or affective but also expressive in social action, including creativity—is informed by the account put forth by Michael Balint, who posits the existence of a "creative" area of the mind, in which mental constructs he designates as "pre-objects" become the mental constructs more conventionally designated as objects. The dynamics of the creative area are distinct from that of the Oedipal (where three figures compete) and the transferential (where two figures engage) but are also not precisely the place where one is alone. This study shares in Balint's assumption that "it is probable that more primitive interactions—congenial to the level of the basic fault and of creation—take place all the time" (Balint, *Basic Fault*, 25).

8   Lauren Berlant: "Statements are fantasy in drag" ("Poisonality," 451).

9   Nina Simone, "Please Read Me," *'Nuff Said!* (RCA, 1968).

10 It's perhaps worth noting, though, that fantasy has rarely commanded an entire volume in the psychoanalytic literature, perhaps because the kinds of problems that send patients into therapy are almost always ones for which fantasy isn't a strong enough solution. One major exception is Hanna Segal's attempt to supplement Freudian metapsychology with a Kleinian-inflected account of unconscious fantasy that "Freud never worked out in full" (*Dream, Phantasy, and Art*, 16). Many of Segal's examples are drawn from her own clinical practice, though, again, fantasy is not for these patients the presenting symptom.

11 Most of this psychoanalytic scaffolding will happen in this book's endnotes, however, in an effort to keep the focus on Simone. In these notes there will be a lot of Freud, plus some of the British post-Freudians who pull in the direction of what became object relations and attachment theory, some nods to the twentieth-century French "linguistic" tradition, as well as psychoanalytically inflected scholars of other things, like Frantz Fanon and Hortense Spillers. The range of reference, in other words, is eclectic, a nonsystematicity that I justify with the fact that eclecticism is a much vaunted orientation within clinical psychoanalytic practice. For a particularly lucid testament to this effect, see McWilliams, *Psychoanalytic Psychotherapy*, 20–23. I've also learned a lot from Luepnitz, "Thinking in the Space between Winnicott and Lacan."

12 Freud, "Negation." One way to understand the difference here is as between an unknown (a negative, something that was never there) and something forgotten (a positive, an absent presence).

13 There are many reasons, however, why the latter fantasies can be difficult to pin down, and I can tell you right now that I do not know and won't try to guess at the truth of who Simone was. This study instead falls back on the assumption that the person who called herself Nina Simone carried through her days that mess of only partially expressible processes, memories, interests, and motivations that Freud taught us to call the unconscious. Presumably, like that of all people, Simone's psychic life was animated by the ruthless, unfiltered, and ambidextrous force called desire, and, also like those of all people, her desires were hewn by the mechanism called fantasy. I'll elaborate a method for interpretation later, but no matter the methods in play, I want these interpretations to be ethically sound. For any claims I make about what Simone may have thought or felt or fantasized, I'll offer evidence and approach it with care. When it comes to the unconscious, nobody gets the last word, least of all me.

14 "Fresh-like," episode 3.4 of *Insecure* (dir. Stella Meghie, 2018, HBO).

15 The precise definitions of *emotion* and *affect* are matters of some ongoing debate, but within modern psychology the latter term at least broadly refers to a postcognitive but largely involuntary somatic response; affects register in the body, in response to stimuli, but they are not necessarily expressive or social. Anger, for example, might be my affective response to, say, a frustration. My body might register anger through a clenched jaw, a frown, a reddening of

the face, an increase in blood pressure. I can have an anger response without being conscious of it or without being able to communicate it to another person with any self-awareness. The ability on my part to recognize, identify, interpret, communicate, or perhaps disguise my affect would belong to the realm of emotion. Rei Terada provides an elegant summary of this distinction: "By *emotion* we usually mean a psychological, at least minimally interpretive experience whose physiological aspect is *affect*. *Feeling* is a capacious term that connotes both physiological sensations (affects) and psychological states (emotions)" (*Feeling in Theory*, 4). More expansively, Jonathan Flatley writes, "Where *emotion* suggest something that happens inside and tends toward outward expression, *affect* indicates something relational and transformative. One *has* emotions; one is affected *by* people or things" (*Affective Mapping*, 12 [all emphases in original]).

The confusion of terms is at least in part a problem of inheritance. The Latin noun *affectus* can be translated as "affect," but also "emotion," "passion," or less exactly "mood." It can also be translated as "affection" or "fondness" or even "goodwill," suggesting a generally positive connotation that makes it an inappropriate descriptor for the parts of contemporary affect theory that now go by the names "negative affects" or "ugly feelings." Meanwhile, the Latin verb form *afficere*, legible in the French *affecter* and the English verb *to affect*, connotes a pervious state, to be susceptible to influence (as in Flatley's definition, earlier in this note). A similar pervious sense adheres in the most influential classical account of emotion, Aristotle's *Rhetoric*, where the preferred term is *pathos* (πάθος), sometimes translated as "suffering." For a useful guide to the evolution of these terms, see Rorty, "Explaining Emotions." Teresa Brennan surveys the meaning of negative affects in Egyptian, Hebrew, and early Christian writings in *The Transmission of Affect*, 97–115. On "ugly feelings," see Ngai, *Ugly Feelings*. Little of this scholarship theorizes how processes of racialization inform structures of feeling; on this point, see Hong, *Minor Feelings*, esp. 56–57. Gregory J. Seigworth and Carolyn Pedwell map out the terminology of related but nonidentical genealogies for affect (*affectio/affectus/*immanence) in "A Shimmer of Inventories," though they also thoughtfully refuse to resolve the differences: "One of the lingering side-effects of spending serious time wandering in and through 'the affective' is its capacity to render the act of theorization itself (whatever its basis) haptic, multi-sensory, synesthetic" (10).

16 Berlant, *Female Complaint*, 160.

17 Fantasy, writes Lauren Berlant, is a "way to move through the uneven field of our ambivalent attachments to our sustaining objects, which possess us and thereby dispossess us of our capacity to idealize ourselves or them as consistent or benign simplicities"; it is "about the plotting of intensities that hold up a world that the unconscious deems worth living in" (*Desire/Love*, 69, 72). Similarly, Joan Wallach Scott advocates consideration of "fantasy as a formal mechanism for the articulation of scenarios that are at once historically specific in their representation and details and transcendent of historical specificity" (*Fantasy of Feminist History*, 49).

18 Fantasy, Darieck Scott helpfully reminds us, names "both the process and its product" (*Keeping It Real*, 10).

19 Winnicott, *Home Is Where We Start From*, 107. While Winnicott stresses the relational nature of subjectivity and the crucial role that fantasy plays for individual development, the psychic relationality of fantasy—the ways we relate to one another's fantasies, or our own fantasies of what those might be—is more strongly articulated in Berlant, *On the Inconvenience of Other People*, and in other of Berlant's work, cited throughout.

20 On the distinction between manifest and latent content in dream interpretation, see Freud, *Interpretation of Dreams*, esp. 311–85.

21 Laplanche and Pontalis, *Language of Psychoanalysis*, s.v. "Phantasy." Kant's discussion appears in his writings on transcendental deduction; see *Critique of Pure Reason*, esp. 219–66.

22 Laplanche and Pontalis, *Language of Psychoanalysis*, s.v. "Phantasy."

23 Segal, *Dream, Phantasy, and Art*, 16.

24 Debates about the significant historical and moral argument about Freud's "seduction theory"—the argument outlined in his paper "The Aetiology of Hysteria" (1896) that hysterical symptoms were a result of sexual abuse (that is, violence inflicted on the child from an external source), a position he later abandoned in favor of the idea of imaginary seductions that take place in unconscious fantasy (that are, as it were, inflicted by an internal source)— exceed the scope of the present argument. Freud discussed this change of position in a letter to Wilhelm Fliess dated September 21, 1897 (in *Complete Letters of Sigmund Freud to Wilhelm Fliess*, 264–67), a shift that is widely taken to be a key point for the development of psychoanalysis. When a new English translation of this letter came to light in the 1980s, it was the subject of a public reckoning due to Jeffrey Moussaieff Masson's dramatic account in *The Assault on Truth*. Among the many responses was Janet Malcolm's *New Yorker* profile of Masson, "Trouble in the Archives," expanded into *In the Freud Archives*.

25 "Repetition," writes Berlant, "is what enables you to recognize, even unconsciously, your desire as a quality of yours" (*Desire/Love*, 20). Freud's best-known theorization appears in "Remembering, Repeating, and Working-Through." But repetition is a major motif in much post-Freudian thought as well.

26 Belcourt, *History of My Brief Body*, 81.

27 "The first wishing seems to have been a hallucinatory cathecting of the memory of satisfaction" (Freud, *Interpretation of Dreams*, 637).

28 Freud, *Introductory Lectures on Psycho-Analysis*, 419. Strachey's translation captures the pathos of Freud's German but not the compassion: "Es ist kein Zweifel, daß das Verweilen bei den Wunscherfüllungen der Phantasie eine Befriedigung mit sich bringt, obwohl das Wissen, es handle sich nicht um Realität, dabei nicht getrübt ist," more literally rendered into English: "There is no doubt that dwelling on the wish-fulfillments of the fantasy brings with it a satisfaction, although the knowledge that it is not about reality is not thereby clouded" (Freud, *Vorlesungen zur Einführung in die Psychoanalyse*, 416).

29 Freud tended to use the word in compound nouns, as in primal scene (*Urszene*) or scene of seduction (*Verführungsszene*). The former term is theorized in "From the History of an Infantile Neurosis," the so-called Wolf-Man case. For the latter term, see *Complete Letters of Sigmund Freud to Wilhelm Fliess*.

30 Laplanche and Pontalis, *Language of Psychoanalysis*, s.v. "Phantasy." See also Laplanche and Pontalis, "Fantasy and the Origins of Sexuality."

31 Kaplan, "Thorn Birds," 149, 150.

32 Abraham and Torok, "Poetics of Psychoanalysis."

33 Rose, *States of Fantasy*, 5.

34 Scott, *Fantasy of Feminist History*, 51.

35 There are props too—Melanie Klein calls them phantasmatic objects or "part-objects." See, for example, "Oedipus Complex in the Light of Early Anxieties," 408–9. The quiddity of the Kleinian object was important to Eve Kosofsky Sedgwick's attempts to pivot queer theory away from representation and toward affect. See "Melanie Klein and the Difference Affect Makes," esp. 629. See also Green, *Fabric of Affect in Psychoanalytic Discourse*, 184–85.

36 On the "loosening" of attachments, see Berlant, *On the Inconvenience of Other People*, 27–29.

37 Berlant, *Desire/Love*, 70.

38 Berlant, *Desire/Love*, 69–70.

39 A coherent self, or a broken one, the acknowledgment of whose condition the ego cannot abide. Fantasy thus occupies a place in Heinz Kohut's theorization of narcissism, a condition whose extreme forms develop in relation to deprivations, and whose subjects often use fantasy as a compensatory space for staging various kinds of scenes that deny deprivation, including grandiosity, self-satisfaction, and other enlivenments. See *Search for the Self*, esp. 427–60. More generally, see Berlant: "recognition is the misrecognition you can bear" (*Cruel Optimism*, 26).

40 Laplanche and Pontalis, *Language of Psychoanalysis*, s.v. "Phantasy."

41 Freud, *Five Lectures on Psycho-Analysis*, 36.

42 Given these working definitions of fantasy, there won't be much to say in what follows about Jacques Lacan's writings, which generally privilege desire in psychic life and dismiss fantasy as a defense against desire. For the curious: Lacan, in his fourth seminar (1956–57), understood fantasy as defensive posture, screening the threat of castration (*Object Relation*). By the eighth seminar (1960–61), he spoke of the "fundamental fantasy" against which all of a subject's myriad expressions were defenses, and he argued that the work of the analyst was to traverse the fundamental fantasy, to expose to the analysand what this subject was organized to avoid, modifying the subject's mode of defense and also its mode of jouissance (*Transference*). By the fourteenth seminar (1966–67), titled "The Logic of Fantasy," Lacan, riffing off Benedict de Spinoza's claim in the *Ethics* that "desire is the essence of man [cupiditas est ipsa hominis essential]," argues that "desire is the essence of reality [*le désir, c'est l'essence de la réalité*]" and that fantasy becomes one of the ways we veer away from reality (*Le séminaire livre XIV*, 6).

Lacanian fantasy is a tall order. Saying so does not mean Lacan's theories are without value—I elaborate the opposite view in *Avidly Reads Theory*, 99–124—but it's worth noting for the present discussion that Lacan's place in literary theory is considerably greater than his place in contemporary clinical analytic practice, at least in the United States. For forceful attempts to reconcile Lacan with black studies, see Marriott, *Lacan Noir*, and Edelman, *Bad Education*, esp. 1–34.

43 The most magisterial history of this concept remains Robinson, *Black Marxism*. For a succinct summary, see Melamed, "Racial Capitalism." The entwined histories of race and modernity, including global capitalism, are powerfully articulated in Mbembe, *Critique of Black Reason*. In addition to those of many of the works cited in what follows, I'm indebted to the analyses in Puar, *Right to Maim*.

44 It may be worth stressing here that fantasy is not the only juncture where history meets the unconscious. For one, Jean Laplanche theorizes that unconscious expressions by adults (e.g., a shift in tone or mood, body language, alterations in the firmness or pressure of a touch) are registered by infants in rudimentary ways as meaningful, and that this meaningfulness can become introjected as the child develops, despite the inevitable gap between the meaning the child unconsciously ascribes and the meaning the adult may unconsciously have expressed. Laplanche calls these expressions "enigmatic signifiers" and describes the process of their communication as "translated" from adult to infant (*New Foundations for Psychoanalysis*, 45, 130–31). Such a process can account for a subject's impossible-to-fully-uproot internalization of historical and social phenomena like homophobia or racism. One can also locate junctures where history meets in the unconscious in more sociological terms, for example, in the personal-historical conjunction of Kathleen Stewart's "ordinary affects," defined as "public feelings that begin and end in broad circulation, but they are also the stuff that seemingly intimate lives are made of" (*Ordinary Affects*, 2).

45 Spillers et al., "'Whatcha Gonna Do?,'" 300. In a related though more focused critique, Jennifer C. Nash argues that in the United States the field of women's studies is "organized around the symbol of the black woman, even as the field retains little interest in the materiality of black women's bodies, the complexities of black women's experiences, or the heterogeneity of black women's intellectual and creative production" (*Black Feminism Reimagined*, 3–4).

46 Spillers et al., "'Whatcha Gonna Do?,'" 302.

47 The secondary literature on black women as medical subjects is extensive, and the following list represents points of departure only. On anatomy, see Fausto-Sterling, "Gender, Race, and Nation." On gynecology, see Owens, *Medical Bondage*. On genetics, see Skloot, *Immortal Life of Henrietta Lacks*. On nineteenth-century environmental sciences, see Schuller, *Biopolitics of Feeling*.

48 On the perennial "lack of fit between discourse and example," see Spivak, *Outside in the Teaching Machine*, 28.

49 Sharpe, *Ordinary Notes*, 97.

50 Abbot, "What Do Cases Do?"; Berlant, "On the Case."

51 Terada, *Metaracial*.

52 What's an archive? Good question: I use the term here to mean (1) a physical or metaphoric location of artifacts or objects, frequently noncirculating or not commonly circulating, on the basis of which one can make historical claims; and (2) the same, but as a site where consciously or not meaning gets made. In that second sense, Ann Laura Stoler has done perhaps the most to get scholars to think about the "distribution of sentiments" and the emotional textures of archival constitution (*Along the Archival Grain*, 58). Arlette Farge's *Allure of Archives*, while published quite a bit earlier than Stoler's work (1989) was translated into English later (2015). See also Arondekar, *For the Record*, which draws on the influential account laid out in Derrida, *Archive Fever*; and for elaborations of Derrida's argument that lead back in the direction of my working definition number 1, see Steedman, *Dust*; Fleming, *Cultural Graphology*. On archival longing, see Singh, *No Archive Will Restore You*. For useful challenges to the presumptively evidentiary quality of my working definition number one, see Vogel, *Scene of Harlem Cabaret* (esp. 104–7); Edwards, "Taste of the Archive." While all of these accounts are thinking about human emotion in relation to the constitution of archives and what is subsequently found in them, only Derrida lays emphasis on the unconscious per se.

53 Preservation plans for Simone's childhood home at 30 East Livingston Street, in Tryon, North Carolina, are discussed in a later section, "Fantasies."

54 *What Happened, Miss Simone?* (dir. Liz Garbus, Netflix, 2015).

55 "All #BlackLivesMatter. This Is Not a Moment, but a Movement," accessed January 8, 2024, https://web.archive.org/web/20150109182206/http://blacklivesmatter.com/about.

56 Garza, "Herstory of the #BlackLivesMatter Movement."

57 Khan-Cullors and Bandele, *When They Call You a Terrorist*, 200.

58 For a moving meditation on this predicament, see Quashie, *Black Aliveness*.

59 For a development of this claim in relation to black studies, see Stein, "Present Waver."

60 Spivak, "Psychoanalysis in Left Field and Fieldworking."

61 Wynter, "Unsettling the Coloniality of Being/Power/Truth/Freedom," 282.

62 Wynter, "Unsettling the Coloniality of Being/Power/Truth/Freedom," 317.

63 Wynter, "Unsettling the Coloniality of Being/Power/Truth/Freedom," 331; Wynter, "No Humans Involved," 66–67.

64 Weheliye, *Habeas Viscus*, 2. Zakiyyah Iman Jackson conceptualizes the problem similarly: "Antiblackness has also been diasporically challenged and refused, making it central to what comprises the very notion of the African diaspora and of blackness. It is precisely *through* rather than *against* historically demarcated regional, national, linguistic, and state preoccupations that this discourse cyclically reorganizes itself" (*Becoming Human*, 19). In a related argument, C. Riley Snorton has theorized that fungible flesh can become the basis for fugitive actions and possibilities (*Black on Both Sides*, 55–97).

65 I'm a longtime reader of early Derrida, which has oriented my thinking about phenomena toward self-difference; I value the apprehension of the self in

phenomenological terms, and the kinds of psychoanalysis I'm drawn to and that I draw on tend in this direction. Those are my cards, and now they're on the table.

Such an orientation is compatible with but arguably contrasts one through line in much recent and influential work in black studies, which has been around the question of ontology. Black studies, as Fred Moten cogently argues, sets as its task "the critique of Western civilization" ("Black Op," 1743). Blackness often designates the limit of what is possible in this domain, and so, by this line of thinking, it would be the attempt to ascertain the nature of that limit, its character and contour, its properties and contents, that sends black studies toward ontology. Rightly or wrongly, I register this interest in ontology as well in the coordinates of black studies that argue the point from the other direction, identifying not (or not just) blackness as the limit of Western civilization, but antiblackness as its structuring condition. Thus, as Frank B. Wilderson III argues, "Afro-pessimists are theorists of Black positionality who share Fanon's insistence that, though Blacks are indeed sentient beings, the structure of the entire world's semantic field . . . is sutured by anti-Black solidarity" (*Red, White, and Black*, 58); or again, in Calvin L. Warren's assertion that "the form of antiblackness might alter, but antiblackness itself will remain a constant—despite the power of our imaginations and political yearnings" (*Ontological Terror*, 3).

I recognize antiblackness as historical and social, embedded in institutions and reproduced unconsciously, and in these ways as pervasive and often apparently intractable. Christina Sharpe's generative metaphor "the weather is the total climate; and that climate is antiblack" helpfully envisions antiblackness as a condition in which we all exist (*In the Wake*, 104). But I think her claim's power and efficacy has to do with the fact that it is a metaphor, not a causal or necessarily a metaphysical claim. And though many interdisciplinary scholars now do use "ontology" to encompass relational or subjective aspects of the world including knowledge and perception (more traditionally treated by epistemology and phenomenology, respectively), my sense is that there are other ways of apprehending relation that may have still broader applicability. The turn to fantasy in these pages is a way of smudging the edges of ontological questions.

In general, and at least by comparison with classically ontological questions of priority, identity, or modality, *relation* in psychoanalytic discourse tends to describe contact or interpenetration—it uses words like *consume, include, enclose, incorporate, introject,* or *occupy.* These kinds of relations take forms like breastfeeding, fucking, mouthing, metabolizing, learning language or behavior or custom or style as absorbed into your mind, your ear, your eye. (I suppose you could think about these relations as ontologies, but it seems to me that road leads to something like Chomsky-esque universals.) Whatever else fantasy relations are, then, they will tend to function more like a phenomenal incorporation than a relation between two metaphysically distinct entities. Accordingly, part of the heuristic value of fantasy for this study is that it is pervasive without being total, inevitably just one part of a process by which someone hitches a ride on their way to being something that they aren't yet. We are always in proximity to what we are not yet but might to some extent become, and I presume that this phenomenal reality is what makes possible the invaluable task in which many black studies scholars are engaged, to recuperate some of what antiblackness relegates to the unthought.

Those skeptical of routing concerns from black studies through notions of fantasy, or of psychoanalysis more generally, might consider another route toward a similar conclusion as outlined by Achille Mbembe in the context of a critique of Martin Heidegger's account of ontology: "In ancient African traditions, for example, the point of departure for the questioning of human existence is not the question of being but that of relation, of mutual implication, that is to say of the discovery and the recognition of a different flesh from mine" (*Necropolitics*, 28).

66 Wynter's most fascinating discussion of objectivity happens in the context of what she calls the sociogenic principle: "The natural scientific description of the human experience of *sound* as a 'wave phenomenon' provides an extrahuman viewpoint description which does not, in any way, negate the reality of the human's *subjective* experiencing of the phenomenon as *sound*, is also able to provide the possibility of an objective description of these two opposed yet parallel qualitative mental states or modes of subjective experience. . . . Unlike the 'common reality' of a wave phenomenon, however, the sociogenic principle is not a natural scientific object of knowledge" ("Towards the Sociogenic Principle," 58–59).

67 Ellison, *Invisible Man*, 581.

68 Nina Simone, "Sunday in Savannah," '*Nuff Said!* (RCA, 1968).

69 Žižek, *Sublime Object of Ideology*, 108.

70 Stewart, *Ordinary Affects*, 112.

71 Berlant, "'68 or Something," 145.

72 Balint, *Basic Fault*, 25.

73 Jameson, "Reification and Utopia in Mass Culture," 142.

74 Chambers-Letson, *After the Party*, 8.

75 Singh, *The Breaks*, 85.

76 Hartman, *Wayward Lives, Beautiful Experiments*, 46.

77 Vološinov, *Marxism and the Philosophy of Language*, 39.

78 For a lucid account of how psychoanalysts gain evidence of mental process, by way of observations of behavior, context, and detail, see Isaacs, "Nature and Function of Phantasy." Or, as Hortense J. Spillers elaborates, "Inasmuch as classical psychoanalytic practice works to transform symptomaticity into a narrative, I take it that discourse constitutes its primary value. The raced subject in an American context must, therefore, work his way through a *layered* imperative and impediment, which deeply implicates History in any autobiographical itinerary" ("'All the Things You Could Be by Now If Sigmund Freud's Wife Was Your Mother,'" 732). In a generative historiographical move, Tara A. Bynum has recently argued for attention to expressions of personal pleasure,

including in writing, as a means of understanding the interiority of another person (*Reading Pleasures*, esp. 1–4).

79 Bollas, *Shadow of the Object*, 9. Transference, an often unconscious but frequently intense emotional investment by the patient or analysand in the analyst, was first theorized by Freud in *Fragment of an Analysis of a Case of Hysteria*, the so-called Dora case, though the phenomenon itself was detected earlier in Freud and Breuer's *Studies on Hysteria*. Freud's accounting for transference in analytic technique was revisited many times over the course of his career, particularly in a series of metapsychological essays, "Dynamics of Transference," "Remembering, Repeating, and Working-Through," and "Observations on Transference-Love."

Subsequent to Freud, transference is widely understood to be central to analytic technique, but the nature, attributes, and ethical best practices associated with psychoanalytic transference are subject to ongoing consideration. The idea that transference could serve as a "working alliance" between analyst and analysand was popularized by Greeson, "Working Alliance and the Transference Neurosis." A history of the concept in analytic practice, particularly the late twentieth-century debates within Freudian circles between Leo Stone and Charles Brenner, is neatly summarized by Malcolm in *Psychoanalysis*, esp. 35–47. My own thinking has been deepened by the theoretical account in Davies, "Erotic Overstimulation and the Co-construction of Sexual Meanings in Transference-Countertransference Experience." On the clinical side, a particularly interesting exploration of the use of the therapist's countertransference can be found in the case studies that constitute Orbach's *Impossibility of Sex*.

80 As the book historian–turned–psychoanalyst Ben Kafka writes, "For reasons personal and professional, I am committed to the idea that people are ruled by unconscious processes, which is simply not true of even the most 'agentic' things" (*Demon of Writing*, 14. His citation is to Johnson, *Persons and Things*.

81 Sedgwick, *Epistemology of the Closet*, 22; Pratt, *Stranger's Book*, 7, 81.

82 Althusser and Balibar, *Reading Capital*, 13.

83 Althusser and Balibar, *Reading Capital*, 29 (emphasis retained).

84 Althusser and Balibar, *Reading Capital*, 29 (emphasis retained); on "lacunae" see 19, 28.

85 Best and Marcus, "Surface Reading," 1. See also the account of Althusser detailed in Rooney, "Live Free or Describe."

86 Althusser and Balibar, *Reading Capital*, 16.

87 Simone, *I Put a Spell on You*, 87.

88 This emphasis on shifting contexts for Simone's performance and source material is distinct from, but should not be read as antithetical to, studies that work to embed her performances in thick histories of Afro-diasporic and Afro-American musical expression. See, for example, Herbert, "Rhythm and Blues, 1968–1972"; Bratcher, *Words and Songs of Bessie Smith, Billie Holiday, and Nina Simone*; Barnett, "'Learning How to Listen'"; in the context of music education, see McCall, Davis, Regus, and Dekle, "'To Be Young, Gifted and Black.'"

89 Tsing, *Mushroom at the End of the World*, viii.

90 Berlant, "Genre Flailing."

91 I remain intrigued and persuaded by Elizabeth A. Povinelli's account of subjective identifications that proceed without legible identities:

> "That's me, I thought, when I saw two women kissing in Santa Fe, New
> Mexico. "This is me," I thought when I went hunting with a group of
> women and men from Belyuen [Northern Territory, Australia]. But
> what is "this" and "that"?—an identity, a mode of life, a form of associa-
> tion? Surely I was hailed in both. But as surely, I was not hailed into
> an equivalent social form or mode of being. When I said, looking at
> Codey and Tasha kissing, "That's me," I found waiting at the end of the
> demonstrative an intelligible identity organized by a language game,
> widely available to others with whom I interacted. I am gay; this is
> homosexuality. When I said, "This is me," as I slogged through a dense
> mangrove with friends from Belyuen cooperatively and competitively
> looking for mud crabs, what identity dangled at the end of this? . . . But
> no matter how these nativity scenes overdetermined the identifications
> that felt like recognition when I first showed up at Belyuen, they do not
> provide me with an available name for this mode of social being. Nor
> do I think that they should—that the ethical, political, or social task is
> to find an identity that can retroactively constitute the truthful name of
> this mode of life that so rivets me." ("Disturbing Sexuality," 567–68)

92 On writing one's way into something, Svetlana Boym offers the term *graphomania* in her study of the copying, list making, and obsessive writing practices
of ordinary citizens in post-Soviet Russia (*Common Places*, 168–214), and
Kathleen Stewart develops the urgency of the concept, glossing *graphomania*
as "the incessant practice of recording the details of the everyday in order to
gain access to it" ("Still Life," 412).

BIOGRAPHY

1 The official album count is thirty-one, though it depends a bit on how you
count, since rights for Simone's earliest recordings were not hers and conse-
quently some of these thirty-one albums were released without her control
or in some cases even her knowledge. In addition, during Simone's lifetime,
nearly two dozen unauthorized or bootleg albums were released. The number
of posthumous authorized albums that include previously unreleased material,
plus remixes and compilations of previously released material, or some combination, is more than thirty. For those keeping track, all this means that as of
the time of this writing, there are north of seventy-five Nina Simone albums
in circulation across vinyl, cassette, CD, VHS, DVD, and audio and audiovisual
streaming platforms.

2 Simone, *I Put a Spell on You*.

3 Feldstein, "'I Don't Trust You Anymore,'" esp. 1355–56.

4 Richard Elliott contends that "*I Put a Spell on You* remains a vital contribution to her work, just as Billie Holliday's *Lady Sings the Blues* or Charles Mingus's *Beneath the Underdog* do to theirs" (*Nina Simone*, 6). By contrast, David Brun-Lambert calls *I Put a Spell on You* "a contrived, sterilized autobiography" (*Nina Simone*, 329).

5 Brun-Lambert's biography was originally published in French as *Nina Simone: Une vie* (2005); a Dutch translation was published in 2006, followed by an English translation in 2009.

6 Phillips, *Missing Out*.

7 James, *Black Jacobins*, 291.

8 Cohodas, *Princess Noire*, 198.

9 Light, *What Happened, Miss Simone?*, 144.

10 I learned to think about the social meaning and ethical stakes of listening to others though Stauffer's *Ethical Loneliness*.

11 Bass, *Difference and Disavowal*, 37.

12 Spillers, "Interstices," 87.

13 "No Opportunity Necessary, No Experience Needed" was recorded in 1969 in the sessions that also recorded the material released as *Black Gold* (RCA, 1970) but was not included on that album. It was first released on the CD compilation *Do Nothin' Till You Hear from Me* (Double Play, 1990) and has been included on subsequent releases of *Black Gold* as bonus material. A live recording, also from 1969, appeared on *Live at Berkeley* (Stroud, 1973).

14 Simone, *I Put a Spell on You*, 28.

15 Simone, *I Put a Spell on You*, 29.

16 Simone, *I Put a Spell on You*, 76.

17 Simone, *I Put a Spell on You*, 82.

18 Simone, *I Put a Spell on You*, 32.

19 Simone, *I Put a Spell on You*, 86.

20 Simone, *I Put a Spell on You*, 124.

21 Lakoff and Johnson, *Metaphors We Live By*.

22 Maria Torok has stressed, "If we claim that there is underlying unconscious fantasy behind every human act, we strip fantasy of its specificity and operational value," and furthermore that "*to understand the meaning of an unconscious fact or gesture does not entail the discovery of an unconscious fantasy.*" In her account, fantasies are more specifically characterized by three criteria (intrusion, imagination, and misfit), and these are present across different states of consciousness, including unconscious acts, prereflexive fantasies, and conversational fantasies. Notably, for Torok, these criteria align masturbatory fantasies with "varieties of imaginative activity such as stories, play, drawing, inner characters, fictions" and not with fantasies proper ("Fantasy," all quotations from 31 [emphasis retained]). The fact that, in her account, fantasy is an affective experience, and that for the affect to be represented the ego gets involved in fantasy expression, makes her definition overall narrower than any that I'm working with.

23 Simone, *I Put a Spell on You*, 124.

24 Simone, *I Put a Spell on You*, 89, 90.

25 Brooks, "Nina Simone's Triple Play," 180. On the banning, see *I Put a Spell on You*, 90.

26 For a formal reading of the song, see Brooks, "Nina Simone's Triple Play," 182–87; Iton, *In Search of the Black Fantastic*, 72; Kernodle, "'I Wish I Knew How It Would Feel to Be Free,'" 302–3; Elliott, *Nina Simone*, 49–51; Bruce, *How to Go Mad without Losing Your Mind*, 201–4; Fleming, *Black Patience*, 104–19. See also Lynskey, *33 Revolutions per Minute*, 70–84; Ward, *Just My Soul Responding*, 301; Judd, "Sapphire as Praxis," 191–93.

27 Maxwell identifies the major chord as A-flat and the relative minor as F ("When Nina Simone Sang What Everyone Was Thinking"). Kernodle calls this change "a significant modulation to the relative minor" but identifies the song beginning in C major and shifting to A minor ("'I Wish I Knew How It Would Feel to Be Free,'" 303). My ear is insufficiently trained to sort out this discrepancy.

28 Harney and Moten, *Undercommons*, 48.

29 Berlant, *Female Complaint*, 211.

30 Tongson, *Why Karen Carpenter Matters*, 5; citing Smucker, "Boring and Horrifying Whiteness."

31 All quotations in this paragraph are from Nina Simone, "My Father/Dialog," which was first released on the compilation *The Very Best of Nina Simone, 1967–1972: Sugar in My Bowl* (RCA BMG, 1998). It was added as bonus material to digital releases of *Here Comes the Sun* in 2005. It also appears on the compilation *Tell It Like It Is—Rarities and Unreleased Recordings: 1967–1973* (Sony BMG, 2008). Simone did eventually record "My Father" for *Baltimore* (CTI, 1978).

32 Gillespie, "Nina Simone, 'My Father/Dialog,'" n. 4 (ellipses in original). The quotation is to *Jet Magazine*, "Nina Simone Ends Voluntary Exile from U.S.," 54.

33 Nina Simone, "Don't Smoke in Bed," *Little Girl Blue* (Bethlehem, 1959). This album was recorded in late 1957 and released in February 1959.

34 Simone, *I Put a Spell on You*, 119.

35 Nathan, *Soulful Divas*, 45.

36 Nathan's term is suggestive but also muddies the already less than clear line between a mental state like dissociation (often understood to be a defensive response to past trauma) and a mental process like fantasy, which can be "distorted" by a defense (Laplanche and Pontalis, *Language of Psychoanalysis*, s.v. "Phantasy") but isn't necessarily a defense. For a useful overview of the concept of dissociation, see Tarnopolsky, "Concept of Dissociation in Early Psychoanalytic Writers." A pathologically extreme indulgence in fantasy, often as a defensive process, was identified in the early 1980s by the clinical researchers Sheryl C. Wilson and Theodore X. Barber in "The Fantasy-Prone Personality."

37 In the space where violent fantasy is enacted, one person's pleasure becomes another person's terror. Histories of race in the United States can be written from this premise. See, for example, Hartman, *Scenes of Subjection*; Tompkins, *Racial Indigestion*.

38 Freud, "'A Child Is Being Beaten,'" 98.

39 See, for example, Winnicott, "Transitional Objects and Transitional Phenomena."

40 Klein, "Love, Guilt and Reparation."

41 Leclaire, *A Child Is Being Killed*, 2.

42 Spillers, "'The Permanent Obliquity of an In(pha)lliby Straight,'" 146.

43 Simone, *I Put a Spell on You*, 49.

44 Simone, *I Put a Spell on You*, 49.

45 Simone, *I Put a Spell on You*, 49.

46 Hampton, *Nina Simone*, 158.

47 For some of what it may have meant to Lisa, see Braggs, "The Two Simones at Montreux."

48 Freud, "Special Type of Choice of Object Made by Men."

49 Bollas, *Shadow of the Object*, 110–12.

50 Hughes, "Nina Simone," 38.

51 Qtd. In Hampton, *Nina Simone*, 174.

52 Durham, "A Loving Reclamation of the Unutterable," 42.

53 On Simone's many avatars, see Elliott, "Reincarnation of an Egyptian Queen," esp. 26–27.

54 Freud discussed multipositionality as a feature of fantasies of identification in "'A Child Is Being Beaten.'" Many of Freud's readers have noticed the ways this essay echoes elements of the case study "From the History of an Infantile Neurosis" (e.g., 183); see also the discussion in that case of "transposition" (192).

55 Laplance and Pontalis, "Fantasy and the Origins of Sexuality"; Berlant, *Desire/Love*, 74.

56 Simone recorded the song ten years later on *Fodder on My Wings* (Carrere, 1982).

57 Simone, *I Put a Spell on You*, 126. She recorded the song with the modified lyrics for *Fodder on My Wings*.

58 Gaines, *Black Performance on the Outskirts of the Left*, 22.

59 Lordi, *Meaning of Soul*, 54 (emphasis retained). Lordi's reference is to the title of Alexis De Veaux's biography of Audre Lorde, *Warrior Poet* (2006).

60 Berlant, *On the Inconvenience of Other People*, 17. Rizvana Bradley reads a related but differently inflected emotion here: "Simone's dysphoric performance sketches out a singular impasse: the racially gendered predicament of being held before a world which demands an unbearable bearing and castigates the negative emotionality which is inevitably borne in and through that bearing" (*Anteaesthetics*, 21).

61 All quotations from Janis Ian, "Stars," *Stars* (Columbia, 1974); see also *Nina Simone: Live at Montreux 1976* (dir. Jean Bovon, Eagle Rock Entertainment, 2006) and, for remastered audio of the same performance, "Stars," *Nina Simone: The Montreux Years* (BMG, 2021).

62 Simone, *I Put a Spell on You*, 111.

63 Simone, *I Put a Spell on You*, 111.

64 Or, as Michelle Ann Stephens more exactly puts it, "Skin is a heuristic representing the intersectional meeting point of a black body subject to

symbolic and imaginary capture in racializing discourse and imagery (race as social construction) and a bodily subject whose sensory and relational (re-)presentation of self (race as inscription on the flesh) occurs in the experiential space of performance" (*Skin Acts*, 4).

65 Fanon, *Black Skin, White Masks*, 11. (Unless otherwise noted, all translations are from the 1967 edition). Fanon uses *sociogeny*, a developmental principle based in social influence, to distinguish from Freud's *phylogeny*, a developmental principle based in interorganismal relationships; both terms are distinct from *ontogeny*, a developmental principle based in organismal identity. The most consequential reading of Fanonian sociogeny is Wynter, "Towards the Sociogenic Principle." On the complex social factors influencing Freud's commitments to phylogeny, see Gillman, *Freud, Race, and Gender*, 70–71; for some recent, expansive attempts to locate Freud's circumstances in relation to a global colonial-capitalist framework, see Eng, "Colonial Object Relations"; Dillon, "Ante-Oedipus."

66 Fanon, *Black Skin, White Masks*, 109. *Nègre* is a nearly untranslatable word, as its multiple significations can include everything from a racial slur to a philosophical sense of "blackness." Markman's 1967 translation accordingly uses a number of different English words, interpreting Fanon's local meanings in terms of contemporary idioms from southern US speech. The result is a sharper set of semantic distinctions than exist in the French original.

67 Althusser, *Lenin and Philosophy and Other Essays*, 174; "Idéologie et appareils idéologiques d'État," 31. For attempts to understand Fanon and Althusser together, see Macherey, "Figures of Interpellation in Althusser and Fanon"; Martel, *Misinterpellated Subject*.

68 Riley, *Impersonal Passion*, 13.

69 Markman translated the fifth chapter of *Black Skin, White Masks*, "L'expérience vécue du Noir," most literally "the lived experience of the Black," as "The Fact of Blackness," in what is generally agreed to be a poor translation. The 2008 revised translation by Richard Philcox emphasizes the gender of the final noun, rendering the chapter title "The Lived Experience of the Black Man." It is likely that Fanon is channeling *experience vécue* from Jean-Paul Sartre, who (borrowing the phrase from Simone de Beauvoir, whom Fanon had not read by 1952 but later knew) tended to use it to translate Edmund Husserl's *Erlebnis*, a term that means experience but philosophically signifies a particular kind of consciousness around one's experience. In English, *fact* draws from a comparatively empirical, rather than phenomenological, vocabulary, though its sociological thrust is arguably Fanonian in its way. For a succinct summary of the intellectual derivation of this phrase as it came to Fanon, see Macey, *Frantz Fanon*, 164; a generative riff on this tension between the juridical and the sociological in Fanon can be found in Moten, "Case of Blackness."

70 Sharpe, *In the Wake*, 41.

71 Anzieu, *Skin-Ego*.

72 Cf. Spillers: "Overdetermined nominative properties . . . demonstrate a sort of telegraphic coding; they are markers so loaded with mythical prepossession

that there is no easy way for the agents buried beneath them to come clean" ("Mama's Baby, Papa's Maybe," 65).

73 Davis, *Women, Race, and Class*, 5.

74 Spillers, "Mama's Baby, Papa's Maybe," 68.

75 Sharpe, *In the Wake*, 105.

76 Simone, *I Put a Spell on You*, 110.

77 Simone, *I Put a Spell on You*, 87.

78 Simone, *I Put a Spell on You*, 118. This is the only time in *I Put a Spell on You* that Simone uses any paronym of the word *fuck*.

79 Qtd. in Hagan, "I Wish I Knew How It Felt to Be Free," 8.

80 Nina Simone, "Four Women," *Wild Is the Wind* (Philips, 1966). For other interpretations of "Four Women," see Gaines, *Black Performance on the Outskirts of the Left*, 36–42; Brooks, "Afro-Sonic Feminist Praxis," 209–15.

81 Toni Cade Bambara's anthology *The Black Woman* was published in 1970. *This Bridge Called My Back: Writings by Radical Women of Color*, edited by Cherríe Moraga and Gloria Anzaldúa, with a foreword by Bambara, was published in 1981. *All the Women Are White, All the Blacks Are Men, But Some of Us Are Brave*, edited by Akasha Gloria Hull, Patricia Bell-Scott, and Barbara Smith, appeared in 1982. The Combahee River Collective was founded in 1974 and published its "Statement" in 1977. Even that other contemporary anthem of black womanhood, Aretha Franklin's "Respect," was not released until early 1967, about six months after "Four Women."

82 For the response to "Four Women," see, for example Calwell, "Nina Simone's Lyrics Stir Storm of Protest."

83 Brooks, "Afro-Sonic Feminist Praxis," 210–11. Patricia Hill Collins champions the expression of anger in these lyrics in *Black Feminist Thought*, 112–13. I. Augustus Durham argues that Simone's personae in the song perform a reclamation of what cannot be expressed, in "A Loving Reclamation of the Unutterable."

84 *Nina Simone: Live in '65 and '68* (Reelin' in the Years, 2008).

85 Nina Simone, "Images," *Let It All Out* (Philips, 1966). Cuney's poem, titled "No Images," was first published in *Opportunity* magazine in 1926. It was then widely anthologized, including in Countee Cullen's *Caroling Dusk: An Anthology of Verse by Black Poets of the Twenties* (1927) and in James Weldon Johnson's 1931 reissue of *The Book of American Negro Poetry* (originally 1922). It did not appear in a collection of Cuney's own poetry until *Storefront Church* (1973), nearly fifty years after its composition. In 1967, a *Los Angeles Times* reporter noted, "For 'Images,' [Simone] set to music some lines she first heard in an LP of Negro poetry. She has yet to find the poet, one W. Cuney, and would like him to know that royalties await him" (Feather, "Nina"). Simone might easily have encountered the poem elsewhere, however, as she was close to Langston Hughes, with whom Cuney was lifelong friends, and during her years in New York, Simone also frequented Louis Michaux's African National Memorial Bookstore in Harlem. On that store's legacy, see *Afro-American*, "50-Year-Old Bookstore to Close in Harlem"; Fraser, "Lewis Michaux, 92, Dies."

86 Marcus R. Pyle argues for greater continuity between Simone's performance of these songs, and specifically that in "Images": "Simone counters Cuney's poetic erasure and instead presents a sonically multidimensional Black woman" ("Nina Simone as Poet and Orchestrator," 132).

87 *Nina Simone: Live in '65 and '68.*

88 Nina Simone, "Four Women," *Live at Berkeley* (Stroud, 1972). According to its liner notes, this album was recorded live at the University of California, Berkeley, in October 1969; Simone also played the Berkeley Jazz Festival in April 1969, and by some accounts some of the album's tracks were recorded in April. The confusion may stem in part from the fact that the album was released years after it was recorded, as one of three semiauthorized compilations on by-then-ex-husband Andy Stroud's record label. Bootlegs of the album also exist under the alternative titles *Live at Berkeley/Gifted and Black* and *Berkeley Concert*; the same recording of "Four Women" appears on *A Portrait of Nina* (Disques Festival, 1975).

It may or may not be relevant that at age 107 in 1969, Aunt Sarah would have been born in 1862, the year before the Emancipation Proclamation.

89 See Pyle's fantastic reading of these lyrics, "Nina Simone as Poet and Orchestrator," esp. 146–47.

90 Spillers, "Mama's Baby, Papa's Maybe," 65.

91 Spillers, "Interstices," 76.

92 Simone, *I Put a Spell on You*, 26.

93 Simone, *I Put a Spell on You*, 26.

94 Simone, *I Put a Spell on You*, 26–27.

95 Elliott, *Nina Simone*, 16; *La Légende* (dir. Frank Lords, 1992).

96 *What Happened, Miss Simone?* (dir. Liz Garbus, Netflix, 2015); *The Amazing Nina Simone* (dir. Jeff L. Lieberman, Re-Emerging Films, 2015). The former says Simone received her honorary degree from Curtis two days before she died; the latter says one month after.

97 The song title listed on the album uses the word *child*, and in most cases during the recording Simone can be heard clearly to enunciate the final *d*. However, in some moments in this and other versions of the song, Simone arguably substitutes the colloquial *chile*, an idiom of (especially southern) black speech, whose referent is not necessarily a juvenile person at all. For a useful discussion of this phrase and its uptake, see Jackson, *White Negroes*, 74–75.

98 For a helpful overview, see Jackson, "History of Freud's Concepts of Regression." Michael Balint distinguishes between benign and malignant regressions in *The Basic Fault*.

99 Muñoz, *Cruising Utopia*, 100.

100 Nina Simone, "O-o-h Child," *Here Comes the Sun* (RCA, 1971).

101 Mitchell, "Theory as Object."

102 And this distance can confound the ways or means we who encounter difficulty have for approaching it. In the case of art that provokes difficult

emotion, as Jennifer Doyle rightly argues, the distance that difficulty creates is not something to immediately close or contract, for it may be the very point of difficult art to work on emotion "because this is where ideology does its most devastating work" (*Hold It Against Me*, xi). The same point could, I think be extended beyond art to many difficult ideas or experiences.

103 On the undisciplined excess produced by shadows, see Musser, *Between Shadows and Noise*.

104 Winston, "Whole Technology of Dyeing"; Gonzalez, "Morphologies"; Roth, "Looking at Shirley, the Ultimate Norm." On the ways black street photographers work with this limitation, see Thompson, *Shine*.

105 Ladner, *Tomorrow's Tomorrow*.

106 Christopher Bollas remarks that "we have tended to regard regressive reactions to the analytic space as resistances to the working alliance or the analytic process," but if that were the case, it's unlikely that patients would so often resist "the very 'invitation' of the analytic space and process towards regression" (*Shadow of the Object*, 25).

107 Moten, "Black Op," 1745.

108 Morrison, *Song of Solomon*, 173.

109 Simone, *I Put a Spell on You*, 89.

110 Hartman, *Scenes of Subjection*, 64.

111 Hampton, *Nina Simone*, 38. Simone repeats the claim in *La Légende* and in a 1999 episode of the BBC's HARDtalk interview show (HARDtalk, "Nina Simone" BBC, 25 mins., March 25, 1999). Nikki Giovanni's poem "Howl (for Nina Simone)" includes the lines:

> Sure the feds will try to trap you
> Sure the feds will run you out of the country
> Yes J. Edgar Hoover will try to ruin your career
> With the same lies he told on King.
> (*Acolytes*, 6)

112 Brooks, "Afro-Sonic Feminist Praxis," 206.

113 Moten, *In the Break*, 14.

COVERING

1 Simone covered Cole Porter's "You'd Be So Nice to Come Home To" on *Nina at Newport* (1960); "The Laziest Gal in Town" on *Broadway-Blues-Ballads* (1964); and his "Ev'rytime We Say Goodbye," first issued on the 2005 CD release of *Forbidden Fruit* (1961). Hoagy Carmichael's "Memphis in June" was on the original issue of *Forbidden Fruit*, and his "I Get Along without You Very Well (Except Sometimes)" appears on *Nina Simone and Piano* (1969). Dorothy Fields and Jimmy McHugh's "Exactly Like You" is covered on *Nina Simone at Town Hall* (1959), and their "Porgy" appears on *Nina at Newport*.

2 Circumstances of Simone's recording change considerably after the end of her RCA contract in 1974. However, the pattern I'm identifying largely holds true from *Baltimore* (1978) to *A Single Woman* (1993). The latter album includes "Marry Me," a song Simone wrote that explicitly rebuts Leon Carr and Earl Shuman's "Marriage Is for Old Folks," which she had recorded on *I Put a Spell on You* (1965); the 2008 "extended album" bonus material indicates Simone wrote and recorded several other songs that did not make the album's original release.

3 She's listed with a writing credit for "Nobody's Fault but Mine" on *Nina Simone and Piano*, but another version of the song had been recorded by Blind Willie Johnson in 1927 and released as a single by Columbia Records. It later was incorporated into the album *Blind Willie Johnson—His Story* (Folkways, 1957).

4 On Cuney, see "Biography," n. 85. Dunbar's "Compensation" was first published in *The Smart Set: A Magazine of Cleverness* (1901). It also appeared in *Lippincott's Monthly Magazine* (1904) and was collected into *Lyrics of Sunshine and Shadow* (1905). It has since been widely anthologized.

5 In a recently released 1966 concert recording, Simone prefaces "Blues for Mama" by noting she wrote the music, and Lincoln wrote the lyrics ("Blues for Mama," *You've Got to Learn* [Verve/UMe, 2023]).

6 For a moving reading of this performance, see Chambers-Letson, *After the Party*, 76–78.

7 Mitchell's originality in pop song structure, in particular her departure from the Tin Pan Alley "verse-verse-chorus" format, is discussed in Yaffe, *Reckless Daughter*, 58 and passim; while on Nyro's recently released 1966 audition tapes, we hear producer Milt Okun ask, "Do you do any songs other than those that you've written?" to which Nyro replies, "Of course I know, you know, there are other songs" ("Luckie/Studio Talk," *Go Find the Moon: The Audition Tape* [Omnivore, 2021]). Meanwhile, between 1974 and 1978, Ronstadt released five top-five charting albums, all of which have been certified platinum by the Recording Industry of America. These include very few original songs (one or two per album, mostly written by J. D. Souther), only two songs that Ronstadt herself cowrote ("Try Me Again" and "Lo Siento Mi Vida," both on *Hasten Down the Wind* [1976]), alongside covers of artists from Chuck Berry to Hank Williams to the Everly Brothers to Jimmy Cliff.

8 For example: "Nina Simone did not write all of her lyrics, although she wrote some of her songs and was probably involved in the selection of others. Our intention is not to gloss over this basic fact, but to point out that this fact alone is not sufficient to discredit the power of a collection of intentionally selected pieces" (Mena and Saucier, "'Don't Let Me Be Misunderstood,'" 262).

9 Goldman, "Return of the Queen of Shebang"; Jewell, "Cries of Joy"; Morrison, *Love*, 164.

10 For a fantastic reading of Simone's holding, in contrast to Billie Holiday's, when recording "Strange Fruit," see Crawley, *Blackpentecostal Breath*, 63–64.

11 Martha Feldman calls this phenomenon in Simone's oeuvre "harmonic restraint" ("Love, Race and Resistance," 85).

12 Though it exceeds the present discussion, it's worth noting that music theory itself, at the time of this writing, is undergoing its own disciplinary considerations about the overrepresentation of whiteness among its practitioners and its canon. See Ewell, "Music Theory and the White Racial Frame." For a related pedagogical argument, see Hines, "Incorporating Intersectional Musicality within the Classroom."

13 Adele, "Someone Like You," *21* (XL Columbia, 2011).

14 "Often described in liner notes as a 'Norwegian folk song,' 'Black Is the Color . . .' had been part of the American folk repertoire for a considerable period before Simone offered her interpretation of it. It appears in Jean Ritchie's 1965 anthology *Folk Songs of the Southern Appalachians*, where it is listed as having been collected by Cecil Sharp in 1916 in North Carolina, Simone's home state" (Elliott, *Nina Simone*, 38). See also Ritchie, *Folk Songs of the Southern Appalachians*, 88. "Black Is the Color of My True Love's Hair" is recorded as number 3103 in the Roud Folk Song Index, which identifies its origin as Scottish. Ingrid Monson has called the "transformations of non-African-American popular songs (standards), quotation of tunes (or solos), and exaggerated, humorous references to well-known musical features of jazz and other African-American musical genres" a form of "musical irony" ("Doubleness and Jazz Improvisation," 285).

15 Contrast Simone's tendency to stick to the script here with Emile Latimer's lyrical improvisations in their concert duets in late 1969, for example, when he sings "Black is her body / So firm, so bold / Black is her beauty / Her soul of gold." Versions of this duet can be heard in a concert video recorded at the University of Massachusetts Amherst on October 4, 1969 (Nina Simone, "Nina Simone: Black Is the Color Of My True Love's Hair," YouTube, February 15, 2013, https://www.youtube.com/watch?v=bfQF-H3knLw) and on Simone's *Black Gold* (RCA, 1970) recorded live at Philharmonic Hall on October 19, 1969. It would seem that Latimer's lyrics lend the album its title.

16 Wilson, "Nina Simone and Trio, at Hunter, Blend Jazz, Pop and Stage Music."

17 Stadler, "Cover Art."

18 Simone recorded "Sign o' the Times" in the sessions that produced *A Single Woman* (Elektra, 1993), though it was first released on the expanded version of that album in 2008. The song was written by Prince and was the lead single on his *Sign o' the Times* (1987).

19 "Killing Me Softly with His Song" was written by Charles Fox and Norman Gimbel, based on lyrics by Lori Lieberman and first recorded on her eponymous 1972 album. It was quickly covered by Roberta Flack for her album *Killing Me Softly* (1972) and by Anne Murray on *Danny's Song* (1973).

20 Edgers, "She Sang 'Killing Me Softly.'"

21 Emily J. Lordi emphasizes the context of soul music as a space for covers: "The meaning of *to cover* thus gains depth in the soul context. It signifies not just a remake but also a process of *covering over* or supplanting an original record-

ing, and of creating cover *behind which* to stage subversive, if not unspeakable, conversations about racial influence, recognition, and profit, as well as intraracial struggles for power and love" (*Meaning of Soul*, 49).

22 Flack was barely four years younger than Simone but began her recording career in 1968, more than ten years later. Simone first recorded "Suzanne" and "To Love Somebody" on *To Love Somebody* (1969); Flack on *Killing Me Softly* (1973) and *Quiet Fire* (1971), respectively. Simone's "If He Changed My Name" appears on *Nina Simone at the Village Gate* (1962), while Flack's "I Told Jesus" appears on her debut album, *First Take* (1969). "Do What You Gotta Do" was first recorded by Johnny Rivers in 1967 but is better known as a hit for Al Wilson that year. Simone recorded it on *'Nuff Said!* (1968), and Flack on *Chapter Two* (1970). For a more complete list of recording overlaps between Simone, Flack, and Judy Collins, see Elliott, *Nina Simone*, 92. James Baldwin uses the epigraph "I told Jesus it would be all right / if He changed my name" for the second chapter of *No Name in the Street* (82) but attributes it to "traditional." Magdelena J. Zaborowska connects Baldwin's use of the epigraph to the version "popularized under the same title by Roberta Flack," though she elsewhere credits Baldwin's references in the same text to the spiritual "Take Me to the Water" to the version "sung by the queer diva Nina Simone, who was Baldwin's friend" (*James Baldwin's Turkish Decade*, 319n52, 45).

23 Flack recorded "Just Like a Woman" on *Chapter Two* (1970), Simone on *Here Comes the Sun* (1971).

24 Simone, *I Put a Spell on You*, 116.

25 "Please Don't Let Me Be Misunderstood" was one of five songs written by Bennie Benjamin and Sol Marcus, arranged by Horace Ott, and recorded on Simone's *Broadway-Blues-Ballads* (1964); she was the first person to record it, though The Animals' version was recorded the same year. "I Don't Want Him" refers to Irving Berlin's "You Can Have Him" from the 1949 musical *Miss Liberty*; it was recorded by Doris Day (1949), Dinah Shore (1949), and Ella Fitzgerald (1958) before Simone released it on *Nina Simone at Town Hall*. "I Put a Spell on You" was written and recorded by Jalacy "Screamin' Jay" Hawkins in 1956; Simone's album of the same name was released in 1965, and her version of the single was rereleased in 1969, one year after Alan Price's recording. "The Other Woman" was one of the last songs penned by the prolific Jessie Mae Robinson; it was a hit for Sarah Vaughn in 1957 before Simone recorded it on *Nina Simone at Town Hall* and rerecorded it in concert many times.

26 Simone, *I Put a Spell on You*, 116.

27 Awkward, *Soul Covers*, xvi (emphasis retained).

28 Michael Coyle distinguishes the Presley-era, pre–rock and roll phenomenon as "hijacking" in "Hijacked Hits and Antic Authenticity."

29 Jackson, *White Negroes*.

30 Lott, *Love and Theft*.

31 Baraka, "Changing Same," 205 (ellipses retained).

32 Stover, *Sonic Color Line*.

33 Frith, *Performing Rites*, 69–70.

34 Awkward, *Soul Covers*, 9.

35 Brooks, *Jeff Buckley's Grace*, 125.

36 Brooks, *Jeff Buckley's Grace*, 127.

37 Barthes, *Preparation of the Novel*, 134; subsequent quotations are also from this page.

38 Simone, *I Put a Spell on You*, 23.

39 Nina Simone, "Nina Simone: To Love Somebody (Live in Antibes, 1969)," YouTube, September 11, 2022, https://www.youtube.com/watch?v=LymNICNvaH8.

40 "Pirate Jenny," *The Threepenny Opera, 1954 New York Cast* (Verve, 2000). Though Blitzstein's translation was the first to be performed on Broadway, another had been published in 1949 for Grove Press, with the book translated by Desmond Vesey and the lyrics by Eric Bentley. Prepared more for reading than singing, however, Bentley's lyrics generally work to preserve the end-line rhyme scheme rather than the meter necessary to keep time to the music. The liberties of Blitzenstein's translation are discussed in detail in Kraaz, "With 'Pirate Jenny' from Schiffbauerdamm to Carnegie Hall," esp. 371–74.

41 Nina Simone, "Pirate Jenny," *Nina Simone in Concert* (Philips, 1964); Brecht, *Die Dreigroschenoper*, 31. Bentley gives the line somewhat more literally as "When you see my tatty clothing and this tatty old hotel" (Brecht, *Threepenny Opera*, 24).

42 Brooks, "Nina Simone's Triple Play," 181.

43 Berman, "Sounds Familiar?," 178–79.

44 Though Berman argues her performance is not Brechtian, he concedes, "Simone's approach highlights the dialectic's nuance" ("Sounds Familiar?," 177). By contrast, Kraaz argues that it is only in Simone's version that "the song's inherent political potential is eventually realized" ("With 'Pirate Jenny' from Schiffbauerdamm to Carnegie Hall," 367).

45 *Nina Simone: Live in '65 and '68* (Reelin' in the Years, 2008).

46 For example, Brooks: "Simone's invocation of their work, I argue, is a project less invested in remaining faithful to the literal tenets of Brechtian ideology and more focused on producing interpretative deformations of Brechtian text that paradoxically generate an alienation effect; her work dares audiences to see and hear 'America' differently and on a different frequency" ("Nina Simone's Triple Play," 182). See also Heard's interpretation of Simone as a kind of avant-garde performance artist in "'Don't Let Me Be Misunderstood,'" esp. 1069–71.

47 Feldstein, "'I Don't Trust You Anymore,'" 1363.

48 Gaines, *Black Performance on the Outskirts of the Left*, 33.

49 Taylor, "Nina Simone," 148. She gives a different account in *I Put a Spell on You*: "Singing disturbed me in a way I had never experienced with classical music" (83).

50 Smitherman, *Talkin and Testifyin*, 3. This alternative spelling of the song title is Smitherman's.

51 Hagan, "I Wish I Knew How It Felt to Be Free," 8–9.

52 Hagan, "I Wish I Knew How It Felt to Be Free," 9.

53 "Quoting ourselves," remarks Leo Bersani, "far from being an enslavement to our past, creates what may be the only free relation we can have to our past: the freedom of continually repeating its intrinsic inconclusiveness" (*Receptive Bodies*, 126).

54 Freud, *Three Case Histories*, 204.

55 Berlant, *Cruel Optimism*, 286n12.

56 Hampton, *Nina Simone*, 39, 43, 47, 56–57.

57 Ford, *Liberated Threads*, 3. See also Tsuruta, "I Ain't About to Be Non-violent, Honey."

58 Feldstein, "'I Don't Trust You Anymore,'" 1374.

59 Simone, *I Put a Spell on You*, 98; for a more detailed interpretation, see Ford, *Liberated Threads*, 28–30.

60 Pierpont, "Raised Voice."

61 Bion, "Psycho-Analytic Study of Thinking."

62 Langston Hughes Papers, James Weldon Johnson Collection, Yale Collection of American Literature, Beinecke Rare Book and Manuscript Library, Box 147, Folder 2724.

63 Bion relates thought, much as Hanna Segal relates symbolism, to the capacity to recognize and experience absence. See Segal, *Dream, Phantasy, and Art*, esp. 57–58.

64 On the difference between deliberate, intentional, and purposeful action, see Austin, "Three Ways of Spilling Ink."

65 As usual, I agree with Richard Elliott: "*Nina Simone and Piano* offers an ideal candidate for considering Simone as an album artist, distilling as it does the components that made her such a compelling performer and concentrating them into the 'pure' or secret world of a solo artist engaged in the delicate art of interpretation" ("Reincarnation of an Egyptian Queen," 31).

66 Tom (The Master Blaster) Reed, liner notes to *Nina Simone and Piano* (RCA, 1969).

67 Simone, *I Put a Spell on You*, 50–51.

68 Chambers-Letson, *After the Party*, 47.

69 *Los Angeles Sentinel*, "Record Review: Nina Simone, Nina Simone and Piano."

70 Elliott again: "In terms of style, genre and musical habitation, we might think of all the songs on *Piano* as portals to other artists and other musical communities, and to the continuities and discontinuities foregrounded by musical comparison" ("Reincarnation of an Egyptian Queen," 36).

71 "Another Spring" was written by Angelo Badalamenti, the composer later associated with David Lynch's works, under the pseudonym Andy Badale. It doesn't matter to the rest of the story, but I just had to tell you.

72 *Folksy Nina* includes "Hush, Little Baby" and attributes it to Pete Seeger. However, the song was not written by Seeger, though it was recorded in 1950 by the folk quartet The Weavers, of which Seeger was a member, and he continued to perform it after leaving the group. It is likely Simone found inspiration in one of these versions, and her attribution gives the sense that she was listening to contemporary music years before she was covering it. "Hush, Little Baby" is

listed as number 470 in the Roud Folk Song Index, which identifies it as of US origin, with nineteenth-century examples from Virginia and North Carolina.

73 "I Shall Be Released" was written by Dylan but first recorded by The Band in 1968. For one version of that song's history, see Stein, "Pop Politics."

74 On Simone's performance of "Who Knows Where the Time Goes?," see Bruce, *How to Go Mad without Losing Your Mind*, 214–15.

75 Lordi locates *Emergency Ward* among albums that "united the mellow sensibility of singers like Smokey Robinson and Nat King Cole with innovations in psychedelic rock and innovative production techniques associated with Charles Stepney and Norman Whitfield to create longer, more elaborately orchestrated works—a turn that was initiated by [Isaac] Hayes's 1969 *Hot Buttered Soul*" (*Meaning of Soul*, 33).

76 "Funkier Than a Mosquita's Tweeter" was a B-side for Ike and Tina Turner's 1971 single "Proud Mary," off one of their albums of the previous year, *Working Together*. The song was original to the group, written by Tina Turner's sister and creative partner, Alline Bullock. However, Simone's subsequent cover was so definitive, so much better known, that her spelling of "Mosquito's" is usually taken to be the song's title, despite its alteration from the original.

77 Nor did Simone assume a public persona as a means of realizing identifications across race or gendered lines, as, for example, Joni Mitchell did between 1976 and 1982 in the guise of a black man she named Art Nouveau. See Grier, "Only Black Man at the Party."

78 See, for example, Freud, "Negation."

79 The best—I mean, *the best*—version was recorded live in audio and video at the Teatro Sistina in Rome, November 3, 1969. Though never officially released, a video recording of parts of the concert are available at Nina Simone, "Live at Teatro Sistina in Rome, 1969," YouTube video, June 24, 2021, https:// www.youtube.com/playlist?list=PLg4blegEv8Zcr-FyTrivQaN0gQxe7T1hq. Allegedly there is a bootleg record of the audio for the whole concert, but I have never been able to verify this. The single track, "Suzanne," shows up on side-B of a different bootleg, misleadingly titled *Nina Simone in Concert: Live in Las Vegas 1965* (Oxford, 1976). Simone only later played in Las Vegas, during a September 29–October 26 residency at Caesar's Palace in 1967. The same track also appears on a Japanese bootleg, *Nina Simone in Paris* (Joker, 1978), later reissued in Italy as *Suzanne* (Moon, 1990). Liner notes for both albums erroneously claim the recordings were done in Paris in 1968.

80 Wilson, "Museums in Tune with Nina Simone."

81 Nina Simone, "Nina Simone: Just Like a Woman," YouTube, February 3, 2013, https://www.youtube.com/watch?v=UB_Y82u_T84. All subsequent quotations are from this performance.

82 Indigo Girls, "Tangled Up in Blue," *1200 Curfews* (Epic, 1995).

83 Berlant, "National Brands/National Body."

84 Tinsley, "Black Atlantic, Queer Atlantic," 199.

85 David Brun-Lambert sets the tone: "It is hard to suppose that Andy Stroud was in the dark about his wife's intimacy with Marie-Christine Dunham[-

Pratt], but no one can say how he reacted to the news" (*Nina Simone*, 173). See also Cohodas, *Princess Noire*, 119; Hagan, "I Wish I Knew How It Felt to Be Free," 11; Light, *What Happened, Miss Simone?*, 72. Hagan also quotes Stroud suggesting that Simone had a sexual and later financial relationship with Faith Jackson, aka Kevin Matthias, whom she knew in Philadelphia in the early 1950s ("I Wish I Knew How It Felt to Be Free," 10). Simone's description of Matthias in *I Put a Spell on You* retrospectively places emphasis in a significantly different erotic register: "I never envy other people's careers or money, I envy their freedom, and I think I was more envious of Kevin than of any woman I ever knew" (47–48). *The Amazing Nina Simone* (dir. Jeff L. Lieberman, Re-Emerging Films, 2015) includes an interview with Marie-Christine Dunham-Pratt, whom the film identifies as Simone's lover in the period after her marriage to Stroud ended, circa 1970; Dunham-Pratt's interview describes their meeting but demurs on further details. In the same film, Simone's brother and bandmate Samuel Waymon reports that Simone dated a woman in 1960, after her separation from first husband, Don Ross, but "it was not a big deal in her world. She didn't feel guilty over it." This claim is different than the account offered by Imani Perry who writes, regarding Simone, Hansberry, and James Baldwin, that "all three were, according to early twenty-first-century terminology, queer, though only Jimmy's sexuality was publicly known." She later adds: "I do not know whether Nina and Lorraine discussed sexuality. Nina was tortured by her own. She felt a deep shame over her desire for women, and Andy's rage about it made things even worse" (*Looking for Lorraine*, 118, 131). It remains the case, regardless, that even if Simone was "queer," she did not live a queer life in the ways that Hansberry did. On the complexities of Hansberry's emergent identity as a black lesbian in the 1950s, see Higashida, "To Be(come) Young, Gay, and Black"; Colbert, *Radical Vision*, 54; Pollak, "Lorraine Hansberry's Queer Archive."

86 Trude Heller's is mentioned briefly in the inventory of gay bars and businesses in Mitchell, "Transformation of Gay Life from the Closet to Liberation," 452; and in Ryan, *Women's House of Detention*, 282. At the corner of Sixth Avenue and West Ninth Street in Greenwich Village, Trude Heller's was directly across the street from the Women's House of Detention (now the Jefferson Market Garden) that stood on the site from 1932 until 1974. If someone ever tells you we can't tear down prisons and plant flowers on the spot, show them this endnote.

87 Davis and Sarlin, "No One Is Sovereign in Love."

88 Qtd. in Hagan, "I Wish I Knew How It Felt to Be Free," 12.

89 Scott, *Fantasy of Feminist History*, 5; Freud, "Some Psychological Consequences of the Anatomical Distinction between the Sexes."

90 Butler, "Melancholy Gender," 168.

91 Glück, *Margery Kempe*, 57.

92 Berlant, "Starved," 435.

93 For one lucid case study, see Musser, "From Our Body to Yourselves."

94 Simone's final cover of "The Times They Are a-Changing" was released on the expanded version of *A Single Woman* in 2008. In 1991, Simone recorded a duet with Miriam Makeba, "Thulasizwe/I Shall Be Released" on the latter's album *Eyes on Tomorrow* (Gallo, 1991).

95 Garland, *Sound of Soul*, 188. In a 1973 interview, James Baldwin returned the compliment to Simone: "When I say poet, it's an arbitrary word. It's a word I use because I don't like the word artist. Nina Simone is a poet. Max Roach is a poet. There is a whole list of people. I'm not talking about literature at all. I'm talking about the recreation of experience, you know, the way that it comes back. Billie Holiday was a poet. She gave you back your experience. She refined it, and you recognized it for the first time because she was in and out of it and she made it possible for you to bear it. And if you could bear it, then you could begin to change it. That's what a poet does. I'm not talking about books. I'm talking about a certain kind of passion, a certain kind of energy which people produce and they secrete in certain people like Billie Holiday, Nina Simone, and Max Roach because they need it and these people give it back to you and they get you from one place to another" ("Black Scholar Interviews James Baldwin," 40–41).

96 There can sometimes be a rush among contemporary critics to want to decenter the kind of abstract universal that Simone evokes here, but there may be good reasons to historicize it instead. As Darby English has noted in a surprising and subtle history, modernist strategies of representational abstraction were finding expression at this moment in the New York art world, as resources for experiments to think about aesthetics in non-segregationist terms. See English, *1971*.

97 Fanon, *Black Skin, White Masks*, 229.

98 Nyong'o, *Afro-Fabulations*, 4.

99 Toni Morrison describes such a double movement in her own creative works as "race-specificity without race prerogative" ("Home," 5). See also Fleming, "Anticipating Blackness," 135.

100 Gleason, "Imaginative Nina Simone Album."

101 West, "Closer Look at the Styles of Nina and Aretha."

102 Holden, "Younger Generation's Homage to a Soulful Diva."

103 Holden, "Younger Generation's Homage to a Soulful Diva."

1972

1 Simone told Arthur Taylor in a 1970 interview, "The Beatles were good inasmuch as they drew attention to our [i.e., black people's] music in the white world. They made white people listen to our music with a different attitude than they had before. It could be that they give their respect only to the Beatles and that they are as racist as they've ever been, but I think we are listened to more and given more respect than before the Beatles. I do not know if this is true, and if it's not true we're in worse shape than we were. It would mean that whites are only listening to whites, as before, and that

youngsters who listen to the Beatles' music don't even know what good music is. Only history will prove whether the Beatles were a good thing" (Taylor, "Nina Simone," 153–54).

Simone's claim that the Beatles took from black music is more than just her opinion. In August 1980, John Lennon told David Sheff, "[Paul McCartney] and I were staying somewhere and he walked in and hummed the first few bars, with the words, and he says, 'Where do I go from here?' I had been listening to (blues singer) Nina Simone. I think it was 'I Put A Spell On You.' There was a line in it that went, *I love you, I love you, I love you.* That's what made me think of the middle-eight for 'Michelle.' So my contribution to Paul's songs was always to add a little bluesy edge to them. Otherwise, 'Michelle' is a straight ballad, right? He provides a lightness, an optimism, while I would always go for the sadness, the discords, the bluesy notes" (Sheff, "Interview with John Lennon and Yoko Ono"). Likewise, in his 1980 autobiography, George Harrison writes that he was directly influenced and later took inspiration from Simone's cover of his own original song "Isn't It a Pity' (*I Me Mine*, 300).

2 Berlant, *Female Complaint*, 88.

3 Mauro Boscarol, "Nina Simone at Sesame Street, 18 February 1972," YouTube, August 17, 2012, https://www.youtube.com/watch?v=I-f3PYJT5mU.

4 Rayman and Tracy, "Evidence Disappears in Case of Two NYPD Officers Killed in East Village." The history of Attica and its aftermath is magisterially told in Thompson, *Blood in the Water*.

5 *New York Times*, "Travel Notes"; Range, "The Pinnacle of Kitsch."

6 Ebert, "The Harder They Come."

7 Davis, *Angela Davis*, 363.

8 Two years earlier, Chisholm published an autobiography with the same title, *Unbought and Unbossed.*

9 What Hortense Spillers has called "raising, in the depths of his being, a question that his culture could not answer" ("'All the Things You Could Be by Now If Sigmund Freud's Wife Was Your Mother,'" 725).

10 The song "22nd Century" was recorded in 1971 for the RCA sessions that produced *Here Comes the Sun.* It was first released on the CD compilation *The Very Best of Nina Simone: Sugar in My Bowl, 1967–1972* (RCA BMG, 1998) and subsequently added as bonus material to streaming versions of *Here Comes the Sun.* It is also included on *Tell It Like It Is—Rarities and Unreleased Recordings: 1967–1973* (Sony BMG, 2008).

OBEAH

1 Simone, *I Put a Spell on You*, 137.

2 Nina Simone, "Liberian Calypso," *Fodder on My Wings* (Carrere, 1982).

3 Nina Simone, "Backlash Blues," *Nina Simone: Live at Montreux 1976* (dir. Jean Bovon, Eagle Rock Entertainment, 2006).

4 West, "Return of Nina Simone."

5 HARDtalk, "Nina Simone" BBC, 25 mins., March 25, 1999.

6 Simone, *I Put a Spell on You*, 138.

7 West, "Return of Nina Simone." On the two senses of cultural identity, see Hall, "Cultural Identity and Diaspora."

8 Hartman, *Lose Your Mother*, 98.

9 For the richest account of the Liberia in which Simone lived, see Thomas, "Nina Simone in Liberia."

10 Berlant, *Anatomy of National Fantasy*, 5.

11 McKittrick, *Demonic Grounds*.

12 In a 1988 interview, Simone claimed that the song was written "the night [Hansberry] passed away" in 1965. Nina Simone, "Nina Simone interviewed on The Wire," YouTube, February 26, 2013, https://www.youtube.com/watch?v=ZbYX83_yZNI.

13 *Summer of Soul*, dir. Questlove (Searchlight, 2021).

14 The other Grammy nomination Simone received during her lifetime was three years prior for "Go to Hell," off *Silk and Soul* (1967). In both cases she was nominated in vocalist categories. See "Artists: Nina Simone," Grammy Awards, accessed January 8, 2024, https://www.grammy.com/artists/nina-simone/16055.

15 Redmond, *Anthem*, 191–92. In her autobiography, Simone locates these events in Chicago in mid-January 1966 (*I Put a Spell on You*, 108), but she is possibly conflating two episodes into one.

16 Redmond, *Anthem*, 192, citation to Rollins and Matthews, "Candidates Warned"; Simone, *I Put a Spell on You*, 108.

17 Simone, *I Put a Spell on You*, 108–9.

18 Simone, *I Put a Spell on You*, 95. For more on the genesis of the SNCC, see Ransby, *Ella Baker and the Black Freedom Movement*, 239–98.

19 "Environment" was a concept D. W. Winnicott used across a large body of work to describe the conditions in which developmental processes take place. One influential account appears as *The Child, the Family and the Outside World*.

20 Kernodle, "'I Wish I Knew How It Would Feel to Be Free,'" 296–97. The Albany movement was a SNCC-sponsored desegregation campaign that took place in Albany, Georgia, during October and November 1961 in partnership with local communities and students at Albany State College (now Albany State University).

21 Redmond, *Anthem*, 192. For more on Simone's performances at fundraising events in the mid-1960s, see Monson, *Freedom Sounds*, esp. 218–20.

22 Reid-Pharr, *Once You Go Black*.

23 Anderson, *Imagined Communities*, 149.

24 Heard, "'Don't Let Me Be Misunderstood,'" 1066.

25 Sikov, *Laughing Hysterically*, 17.

26 See, for starters, Dayan, *Haiti, History, and the Gods*.

27 On the long history of racial meanings associated with obeah, see Khan, *Deepest Dye*.

28 Ranko Tintor Fiko, "Nina Simone—I Put a Spell on You—Live in England—14.09.1968," YouTube, June 6, 2012, https://www.youtube.com

/watch?v=W7mBQhfkqHs. The performance seems improvised, but it wasn't a one-off. Simone uses the same revised lyrics in a performance at the Montreal Jazz Festival in 1992; see Nina Simone, "Nina Simone: I Put a Spell on You," YouTube, February 6, 2013, https://www.youtube.com/watch?v=Hn3FfH9jq3c.

29 James, *Holding Aloft the Banner of Ethiopia*.

30 Scaramuzzo, "Passings"; Ehrlich, "'Exuma' at 50."

31 For wider histories of this scene, see Banes, *Greenwich Village 1963*; Colby and Fitzpatrick, *Bitter End*; Petrus and Cohen, *Folk City*; Duncan, *Rebel Café*.

32 *New York Times*, "Black Performers Set for 2-Week Fete."

33 Lucas, "Disc Data"; *New York Amsterdam News*, "Easter Show at Radio City"; Palmer, "Music: Irresistible 'Junkanoo Drums.'"

34 Lucas, "Disc Data."

35 *Philadelphia Tribune*, "Series Look at the Roots of Black Music."

36 Palmer, "Music: Irresistible 'Junkanoo Drums.'"

37 Justin Vivian Bond, "22nd Century," *Denrophile* (Whimsymusic, 2011); Rahne Alexander, "22nd Century," performance at The Voxel, Baltimore, 2023.

38 The song "22nd Century" was first released on the compilation *The Very Best of Nina Simone, 1967–1972: Sugar in My Bowl* (RCA BMG, 1998). It was added as bonus material to digital releases of *Here Comes the Sun* in 2005. It also appears on the compilation *Tell It Like It Is—Rarities and Unreleased Recordings: 1967–1973* (Sony BMG, 2008).

39 Richard Elliott thereby argues that Simone's "22nd Century" is utopian as much as it's apocalyptic ("Reincarnation of an Egyptian Queen," 41).

40 Nina Simone, "Westwind," *Black Gold* (RCA, 1970). Philharmonic Hall is a venue that still exists despite several name changes. It opened in 1962 as part of the complex of buildings that made up the Lincoln Center redevelopment project on Manhattan's Upper West Side. In 1973, Philharmonic Hall was rechristened Avery Fisher Hall after the philanthropist who made a major gift. In 2014, the Lincoln Center for the Performing Arts corporation paid the Fisher family $15 million for the rights to rescind the name, which was then auctioned off to the highest bidder. After a $100 million gift, the space was renamed David Geffen Hall in 2015. See Salmon, "Naming Wrongs."

41 Daphne A. Brooks: "The compositional structure of 'Four Women' manifests what musicologist Guy Ramsey has helpfully identified for me in conversation as an embellished minor blues form: twelve bars with a four-bar tag on each chorus. Ramsey calls 'Four Women' a moderate hard bop from the bebop family of styles, one that holds the remnants of Latin beats that were very popular among hard bop musicians of the 1950s. I hear a hint of calypso in the framework of the composition as well (but that could just be me!)" ("Afro-Sonic Feminist Praxis," 210–11). Daphne, it's not just you.

42 Vogel, *Stolen Time*.

43 Jameson, *Marxism and Form*, esp. 306–416.

44 In addition to Redmond, *Anthem*, and Monson, *Freedom Sounds*, see Gilroy, *Black Atlantic*, esp. 72–110; Floyd, Zeck, and Ramsey, *Transformation of Black Music*. See also Powell, *Sounds from the Other Side*, esp. 19–64.

45 Mercer, *Welcome to the Jungle*, 53–66.

46 Hall, *Familiar Stranger*, 138.

47 Edwards, *Practice of Diaspora*, 4–5.

48 Pinto, *Difficult Diasporas*.

49 Simone, understood as representative of a militant, distinctly African American identity, was reciprocally used by Africans and members of the African diaspora in their own creative self-fashioning. For example, Celeste Day Moore details Simone's reception among Algerians in 1969 in *Soundscapes of Liberation*, 181–82. See also Youcef, "Nina Simone in Algiers."

50 Yes, this is a critique of the New Historicism.

51 Harney and Moten, *Undercommons*, 96.

52 Carby, *Imperial Intimacies*, 84; Hartman, "Venus in Two Acts," 10.

53 Nina Simone, "Damballa," *It Is Finished* (RCA, 1974).

54 Hurston, *Tell My Horse*, 168.

55 Haitians often represent Damballa with the figure or association of a snake. The image of the three-toed frog may be an inflection of this serpent figure, though it may also speak to an aspect of vodun ritual. The difficulty of my being able to say with any certainty has to do with the fact that, while vodun practices are widely regarded as an authoritative source for Haitian history (in addition to Dayan, *Haiti, History, and the Gods*, see Dubois, "Thinking Haiti's Nineteenth Century"), they exist in ritual and oral transmission far more than in the kinds of documentation considered authoritative in the European academy and its spheres of influence. However, one possibility emerges with Mayra Montero's novel *In the Palm of Darkness* (1995), which unfolds its explorations of Haitian history and folklore around a search for the *grenouille du sang* (blood frog) and apparently tells its story effectively enough to have become a reference point for subsequent Haitian artists and critics.

56 Hurston, *Tell My Horse*, 219.

57 Brel was born Belgian but spent his adulthood and professional career in France. Meanwhile, through the course of her career, Simone recorded songs in multiple languages in addition to French, including Hebrew ("Eretz Zavat Chalav U'dvash" in unreleased studio sessions from 1961–62 and released as "Eretz Zavat Chalav" on *Folksy Nina* [Colpix, 1964]); Italian ("Cosi Ti Amo" released in Italy by RCA on an album of the same title in 1970, recorded in the studio sessions for *To Love Somebody*); Yoruba ("Zungo" on *Nina at the Village Gate* [1962] and again on the expanded edition of *It Is Finished*, recorded in 1974 but released in 2013); and Zulu (in her collaboration with Miriam Makeba, "Thulasizwe/I Shall Be Released," on the latter's album *Eyes on Tomorrow* [1991]). According to Ruth Feldstein, "Europeans echoed [Langston] Hughes when they tended to regard Simone as quintessentially African American—emblematic of racial and national specificity—at the same time that they positioned her as a cosmopolitan figure whose affiliations were not tethered to any one nation" ("'I Don't Trust You Anymore,'" 1358).

58 Simone, *I Put a Spell on You*, 166.

59 Simone, *I Put a Spell on You*, 166–67.

60 Simone, *I Put a Spell on You*, facing page 119.

61 Nina Simone, "I Was Just a Stupid Dog to Them," *Fodder on My Wings* (Carrere, 1982).

62 Nina Simone, "No Woman, No Cry," *Nina Simone: The Montreux Years* (BMG, 2021).

63 Cohodas, *Princess Noire*, 371.

64 "At Berkeley, Hartman wanted to reckon with the ways in which violence had been used to enforce social order. She also wanted to write with a resonance that was uncommon in scholarly literature. 'I wanted to be a Wailer,' she said—a member of Bob Marley's band. 'What does it mean to describe Trench Town, in Jamaica, but be describing the world? What does it mean to have that kind of power articulating a condition, with poetry and beauty?'" (Okeowo, "Secret Histories").

65 Farred, *What's My Name?*, 215–74.

66 HARDtalk, "Nina Simone."

67 Pareles, "A Diva's Day, Rich with Love, Prayer and Politics."

68 Barnett, "Nina Simone," 149.

69 See, for instance, Fairbairn, "The Repression and the Return of Bad Objects"; Bowlby, "Nature of the Child's Tie to His Mother"; Ainsworth, Blehar, Waters, and Wall, *Patterns of Attachment*.

70 Bob Marley and the Wailers' "Sinner Man" was a B-side for two different singles with two different record labels, "Lonesome Track" (Coxone, 1966) and "Let Him Go" (Island, 1966). The song never found its way onto an album in Marley's lifetime but was eventually released on the compilation/reissue album *The Wailing Wailers at Studio One* (Heartbeats, 1994). The complexities of recording music in Jamaica in the 1960s and 1970s and the differences from standard US practices at the time are documented by White in *Catch a Fire*; in particular, most Jamaican music publication was of singles, and most longer albums were semiannual compendia of singles by various artists (250). See also Steffens and Pierson, *Bob Marley and the Wailers*.

71 Veal, *Dub*.

72 Cassidy and Le Page, *Dictionary of Jamaican English*, 322, s.v. "no."

73 Although not packaged as such, *It Is Finished* is essentially a live album, with all but three tracks recorded on July 28, 1973, at Philharmonic Hall. Simone appeared onstage that night accompanied by just two other performers, her longtime guitarist Al Schackman, credited on the album as Avram Schackman, and the Nigerian American percussionist Babatunde Olatunji, who had known Simone since 1961 and had composed music for *A Raisin in the Sun*, but who goes uncredited on *It Is Finished* (though the concert included a cover of his "Zungo," which can be heard on the album's 2013 expanded edition). Nadi Qamar, the percussionist who did get credit on the 1974 album, played on the three studio tracks also included there. See Olatunji, *Beat of My Drum*, 197; Cohodas, *Princess Noire*, 277.

74 Garland, *Sound of Soul*, 188.

75 Nina Simone, "Obeah Woman," *It Is Finished* (RCA, 1974). All subsequent quotations are from this version of the song.

76 Richard Elliott reads "Obeah Woman" as a performance of reconciliation, but he observes how the song stops very suddenly: "As if realizing the façade could easily crumble, she suddenly commands her musicians to finish" (*Nina Simone*, 85).

77 Winnicott, *Home Is Where We Start From*, 50.

AUDIENCE

1 Freud, "On Narcissism," 42.

2 For Heinz Kohut, the narcissist does not look in the mirror so much as assumes the other is a mirror. See *Analysis of the Self*.

3 Lacan, *Formations of the Unconscious*, 330. The full passage: "Ce dont il s'agit pour l'homme selon la définition même de l'amour, *c'est de donner ce qu'on n'a pas*, c'est de donner ce qu'il n'a pas, le phallus, à un être qui ne l'est pas" (*Le séminaire, livre V*, 351).

4 "It seems at this stage of development the unification of external and internal, loved and hated, real and imaginary objects is carried out in such a way that each step in the unification leads again to a renewed splitting of the imagos. But, as the adaptation to the external world increases, this splitting is carried out on planes which gradually become increasingly nearer and nearer to reality. This goes on until love for the real and the internalized objects and trust in them are well established. Then ambivalence, which is partly a safeguard against one's own hate and against the hated and terrifying objects, will in normal development again diminish in varying degrees" (Klein, "Contribution to the Psychogenesis of Manic-Depressive States," 288).

5 Sherman, "Nina Simone Casts Her Moody Spells"; Wilson, "Two Faces of Nina Simone"; Walsh and Hutton, "Antibes Jazz Festival Report"; *New Journal and Guide*, "Let Nina Simone Tell You about Soul Music"; West, "Closer Look at the Styles of Nina and Aretha."

6 Qtd. in Hagan, "I Wish I Knew How It Felt to Be Free," 8. See also Shepard, *Motel Chronicles*, 79–80.

7 Brun-Lambert, *Nina Simone*, 84. See also Aznavour, *Le temps des avants*, 258.

8 Robinson, "Nina Simone Thrills, Oscar Brown Chills."

9 Yablonsky, "Nina Simone at the Village Gate," 65.

10 Angelou, "Nina Simone," 77.

11 Hampton, *Nina Simone*, 34, 54.

12 Nick Cave, foreword to Ellis, *Nina Simone's Gum*, 2.

13 Taylor, "Nina Simone," 152.

14 Simone, *I Put a Spell on You*, 94; see also 93.

15 Harris, *My Soul Looks Back*, 90.

16 Elliott, "So Transported."

17 Projection is a storied concept in European thought and predates Freud's alignment of it with his theories of the unconscious. The idea that a projection is the result of unconsciously splitting off parts of the self that one wishes to repudiate is typically distinguished as *projective identification*, a term first used by Melanie Klein in her 1946 essay "Notes on Some Schizoid Mecha-

nisms." Many subsequent Kleinians do not, however, distinguish between projection and projective identification. For the clinical context, see Ogden, *Projective Identification and Psychotherapeutic Technique.*

18 Qtd. in Hagan, "I Wish I Knew How It Felt to Be Free," 13.

19 Hampton, *Nina Simone*, 39. *Often* is of course a relative term.

20 Warner, "Publics and Counterpublics"; Brennan, *Transmission of Affect*, 51.

21 Kosner, "To Nina Simone Respect Means More Than Flattery."

22 *Nina Simone: Live at Montreux 1976* (dir. Jean Bovon, Eagle Rock Entertainment, 2006).

23 Barnett, "Nina Simone," 147.

24 Wilson, "Two Faces of Nina Simone." See also Holden, "Cabaret": "Rooted in extreme emotional ambivalence, her performances have the aura of sacramental rites, in which a priestess and her flock work to establish a mystical communion. Because of Miss Simone's fabled temperament, however, communion is not a foregone conclusion. Each performance becomes a group psychodrama that could as easily topple into disaster as soar into triumph."

25 Nina Simone, "To Be Young, Gifted and Black," *Live at Berkeley* (Stroud, 1972).

26 Hampton, *Nina Simone*, 39, 56–57.

27 Nina Simone, "To Be Young, Gifted and Black," *Black Gold* (RCA, 1970). Another recorded moment happens before a 1990 concert performance of "Four Women": "These next two tunes are dedicated to the blacks of America. The blacks of Switzerland. The blacks of the Middle East. The blacks of Africa. And we're all very happy that Nelson Mandela is free. Right?" (*Nina Simone: The Montreux Years* [BMG, 2021]).

28 *Village Voice*, March 5, 1970, 35.

29 Smith, "The Other (More Serious) Side of Nina."

30 Berlant, "Momentary Anesthesia of the Heart."

31 Garland, *Sound of Soul*, 169–70.

32 Berlant: "We wouldn't need defenses if relations really failed: defenses are against something or someone that's still there, whether 'there' is just in one's head or appreciable by others or verifiable via research" (*On the Inconvenience of Other People*, 26).

33 Angelou, "Nina Simone," 132.

34 For on- and off-Broadway production details, see Horn, *Age of "Hair."*

35 According to one British report from 1968, "She and her husband, Andy Stroud, were involved with the staging of Hair! in America. They knew the people putting the show on and saw it four times, twice off-Broadway in its infancy" (Walsh, "Fantasy World of Nina Simone"). "Ain't Got No/I Got Life" was recorded twice at RCA studios in May 1968: version one, which starts with a repeated piano hook, was released on *'Nuff Said!* (1968), cross-faded with live applause from the Westbury Music Fair where much of the rest of that album's material was recorded; version two starts with a guitar and horn section riff and was first released on *Tell It Like It Is—Rarities and Unreleased Recordings: 1967–1973* (Sony BMG, 2008). The 1968 single is version one without the applause.

36 Walsh, "Fantasy World of Nina Simone."

37 This list and the next one proceed in roughly the order that Simone mentions each item for the first time across subsequent recordings. These include the version on 'Nuff Said!; a performance live in London (summer 1968); live at the Olympia in Paris (summer 1968); from the album *The Great Show: Live in Paris* (Disques Festival, 1975), also released under the title *Live in Europe*, recorded at the Montreux Jazz Festival in summer 1968, and officially released on *Nina Simone: The Montreux Years* (BMG, 2021); live at the Antibes Jazz Festival (summer 1969); live at the Harlem Cultural Fair (August 1969); live in Amherst, Massachusetts (June 1969); on *Black Gold* (1970), recorded at New York's Philharmonic Hall (October 1969); in the documentary *Nina Simone—A Historical Perspective* (dir. Peter Rodis, 1970); on *Live at Berkeley* (1972), recorded in 1968; and on *A Very Rare Evening* (PM Records, 1979), recorded in Hamburg in 1969. Non-album, nondocumentary performances accessed via https://www.youtube.com/user/NinaSimoneMusic.

38 Brooks, "'Ain't Got No/I Got Life.'"

39 Keeling, *Queer Times, Black Futures*, 152.

40 Lordi, *Meaning of Soul*, 53.

41 Musser, *Sensational Flesh*, 183.

42 Chambers-Letson, *After the Party*, 79.

43 McKittrick, *Dear Science and Other Stories*, 163.

44 Brooks, *Liner Notes for the Revolution*, 20.

45 Freud imagined, more than fifteen books into his own prolific career, that writing came from longing, that it "was in its origin the voice of an absent person" (*Civilization and Its Discontents*, 41).

46 Simone, *I Put a Spell on You*, 68.

47 Simone, *I Put a Spell on You*, 69.

48 Nina Simone, "Nina Simone interview with Mavis Nicholson," YouTube, February 5, 2013, https://www.youtube.com/watch?v=V7gXcSYN5ZE. For the *Times* review, see Holden, "Rare Gig for Nina Simone, Diva of Pop." In a late interview, Simone repeated, "I recall reading the comparisons of myself to Holiday and thinking a comparison to Maria Callas was more apt, but in American society a black woman's talents are never truly seen for what they are" (Barnett, "Nina Simone," 147).

49 Morrison, *Beloved*, 225.

50 Smith, "The Other (More Serious) Side of Nina."

51 Taylor, "Nina Simone," 156.

52 Feather, "Nina."

53 Lloyd, "Nina Simone"; Holden, "Rare Gig for Nina Simone, Diva of Pop"; Blau, "Three Singers Reflect on Music and Careers"; Bardin, "Simone Says."

54 Feldstein, "'I Don't Trust You Anymore,'" 1349; Brooks, "Nina Simone's Triple Play," 179; Garland, *Sound of Soul*, 170; Elliott, *Nina Simone*, 21; Kernodle, "'I Wish I Knew How It Would Feel to Be Free,'" 300; Nathan, *Soulful Divas*, 46; Feldman, "Love, Race and Resistance," 85; Redmond, *Anthem*, 182.

55 Liaison to Honorable Alexander P. Butterfield, July 6, 1970, documents obtained via FOIA request 1560551-000. On the bureau's terms of art, see Maxwell, *F. B. Eyes.*

56 Elliott, *Nina Simone*, 41.

57 For example, Simone's quotation of Franz Shubert's "Der Doppelgänger" in her 1965 recording of "Strange Fruit" is discussed briefly in Ross, *Listen to This*, 343; and in Tillet, "Strange Sampling," 122–23. On the Bach fugue in an early live performance of "Love Me or Leave Me," see Macdonald, "Nina Simone Plays a Stunning Bach-Style Fugue." For Simone's incorporation of counterpoint and classical themes into her 1976 Montreux concert, see Scribner, "1968, Take Two," esp. 70, 73. On the practice of quoting more generally, see Monson, "Doubleness and Jazz Improvisation."

58 Elliott, *Nina Simone*, 41.

59 Garland, *Sound of Soul*, 183 (emphasis retained).

60 Taylor, "Nina Simone," 150.

61 Nina Simone, "Nina Simone interviewed on The Wire," YouTube, February 26, 2013, https://www.youtube.com/watch?v=ZbYX83_yZNI.

62 Nina Simone, "Go Limp," *Nina Simone in Concert* (Philips, 1964).

63 Nyong'o, "Unforgiveable Transgression of Being Caster Semenya," 98.

64 Rowell, "'Words Don't Go There,'" 962.

65 Simone, "Nina Simone Interviewed on The Wire."

66 Glissant, "For Opacity," 190, 193.

67 Blas, "Opacities." See also León, "Forms of Opacity"; Tremblay, *Breathing Aesthetics*, 135–36; Post, *Deadpan*, 103–38; Saketopoulou, *Sexuality beyond Consent.*

68 Snorton, *Black on Both Sides*, 10.

69 Berlant, "The Traumic."

70 Kramer, *Against Depression*, 73.

71 Vaillant, *Adaptation to Life*, 120–21.

72 Miller, *Drama of the Gifted Child*; Burnett-Zeigler, *Nobody Knows the Trouble I've Seen.*

73 "It doesn't bother me that people call me angry. If you're a black person and you're not angry, you're damned mad. Damned mad" (Barnett, "Nina Simone," 154). See also Bettina Judd: "To continue, I have to make this point perfectly clear: Black women are no angrier than any other group of people. I'm pissed that I even have to tell you this" ("Sapphire as Praxis," 180).

74 For the landmark account of the ways that mental health diagnosis can be used as a means of social control, see Szasz, *Myth of Mental Illness.* Contemporary accounts of what is now called *neurodiversity* can be said to originate in the popularization of Szasz's critique. In addition to the psychobiological insight that a mental function can be compromised or disciplined but cannot, properly speaking, be "ill," contemporary social scientific literature, especially qualitative ethnography, robustly documents the contribution of social factors in shaping individual behavior, motivation, and mood. There is, in short, a

lot of evidence that the story of mental function is more like "we're all in this together" than terms like *individual* admit.

75 Simone's use of antidepressants is mentioned in Cohodas, *Princess Noire*, 341, 353; "depression": Light, *What Happened, Miss Simone*, 107, 123; "schizophrenia": Cohodas, *Princess Noire*, 337; "multiple personality disorder": Cohodas, *Princess Noire*, 330; "chemical imbalance": Hampton, *Nina Simone*, 11; "bipolar disorder": Brun-Lambert, *Nina Simone*, 275–76.

76 For a significant counterpoint, see Bruce, *How to Go Mad without Losing Your Mind*, esp. 50–51, 74–75, 201–4.

77 For example, Hampton, *Nina Simone*, 11; Brun-Lambert, *Nina Simone*, 275–76; Cohodas, *Princess Noire*, 245, 330, 337.

78 On the question of how people narrate their experiences of changes in mental health, and how that narration impacts mental health, see Adler, "Living Into the Story." See also Oedegaard et al., "'It Means So Much for Me to Have a Choice.'"

79 *Consent* is Glissant's term; my use of it here is informed by Moten, *Black and Blur*, xv.

80 Hampton, *Nina Simone*, 140.

81 Winnicott, "Ego Distortion in Terms of True and False Self," 140–57.

82 van der Kolk, *Body Keeps the Score*, 213; Berlant, *Cruel Optimism*, 10.

83 Berlant, *Cruel Optimism*, 1.

84 Hagan, "I Wish I Knew How It Felt to Be Free," 16.

85 Berlant, "The Traumic."

86 Dembart, "Nina Simone."

FANTASIES

1 Baldwin, "Discovery of What It Means to Be an American," 22.

2 Simone, *I Put a Spell on You*, 118.

3 See Love, *Feeling Backward*. Thanks to Caroline Doyle for helping me phrase this.

4 Mazzeo, *Secret of Chanel No. 5*; Helleu, *Jacques Helleu and Chanel*; Adrian, *Nina Simone*, 203–4. The airdate of the commercial is unclear, in part because sources contradict, though this may be due to the fact that it circulated in more than one country though not necessarily simultaneously—my best educated guess is that it was filmed in 1985 and first aired in 1986 and may have stayed on air into 1987. Chanel's rebranding campaign had been going since the mid-1970s, with Catherine Deneuve as Bouquet's predecessor.

5 Charly had reissued the song in multiple formats since 1982, though without the commercial success that began in late 1987. See Adrian, *Nina Simone*, 204.

6 The rights holder, Bethlehem Records, was sold and absorbed at least five times before becoming part of Salsoul Records in 1974, which became defunct ten years later in 1984, immediately before "My Baby Just Cares for Me" was used by Chanel. Salsoul was revived in 1992, and the rights for the jazz back catalog, including the Bethlehem Records recordings, were eventually acquired by Verse music group, which was in turn acquired by BMG in 2015.

7 *Billboard*, "Nina Simone Recovers Masters."

8 Aardman Animations was responsible more or less contemporaneously for the animation sequences on the US Saturday-morning variety show/sitcom *Pee-Wee's Playhouse* (1986–91) and the internationally popular animated shorts starring the man-dog duo Wallace and Gromit, including "The Wrong Trousers" (1993) and "A Close Shave" (1995). The video for "My Baby Just Cares for Me" was one of several Claymation music videos released by Aardman in 1987, all for singles or rereleased singles that year, including Robert Parker's "Bare-footin'" (1966) and what's possibly the most decorated animated music video of all time, Peter Gabriel's "Sledgehammer" (1987). Peter Lords, the director of "My Baby Just Cares for Me," went on to direct a number of feature-length films with Aardman, including *Chicken Run* (2000).

9 HARDtalk, "Nina Simone" BBC, 25 mins., March 25, 1999.

10 In a helpful formulation, Daphne Brooks attributes to Simone "uniquely articulated forms of sonic black womanhood" ("Nina Simone's Triple Play," 179). On the racialized sound of African American performers, see Griffin, "When Malindy Sings," esp. 108–9. On gendered assumptions about the "acousmatic nature" of vocal sound, see Eidsheim, *Race of Sound*, 6–7. On Simone's "fugitive voice," see Feldman, "Love, Race and Resistance." See also Moten, *Black and Blur*, esp. 130.

11 Redmond, *Anthem*, 208.

12 The conspicuous and stereotype-fueled blackness of the club setting and trio playing in the animated video for Jay-Z's "The Story of O. J." (dir. Mark Romanek, 2017), which samples Simone's "Four Women," would appear to be a direct talkback to the racial elisions of Aardman's "My Baby Just Cares for Me."

13 Cf. Bow, *Racist Love*.

14 Cohodas, *Princess Noire*, 334.

15 Brown, *Cult of the Saints*, 78.

16 *Irish Times*, "Hundreds at Nina Simone Funeral in France"; Pierpont, "Raised Voice"; Ellis, *Nina Simone's Gum*, 79.

17 BBC News, "Funeral Held for Singer Simone."

18 Davis, "Nina Simone's Music Was So Much More Than the Soundtrack to a Movement."

19 Hahn, "What Do Reliquaries Do for Relics?"

20 Ellis, *Nina Simone's Gum*, 178.

21 Ellis, *Nina Simone's Gum*, 136.

22 Menconi, *Step Up and Go*, 241–42.

23 Menconi, *Step Up and Go*, 231–32.

24 "Nina Simone Childhood Home," National Trust for Historic Preservation, accessed January 8, 2024, https://savingplaces.org/places/ninasimone.

25 Chow, "Nina Simone's Childhood Home Gets 'National Treasure' Designation"; Bradley, "Home Coming."

26 Qtd. in Maxwell, "Nina Simone."

27 Qtd. in Maxwell, "Nina Simone."

28 E.g., Simone, *I Put a Spell on You*, 137; West, "Return of Nina Simone"; HARDtalk, "Nina Simone" BBC, 25 mins., March 25, 1999. See also section 4, "Obeah."

29 For the classic outline of the latter, see McNulty, "Revitalizing Industrial Cities through Cultural Tourism." On the ways small museums lend social capital to regional areas—areas that may otherwise fail to measure up to the standards of a globalizing world more inclined to recognize urban areas as seats of the kind of culture whose cachet isn't simply local—see Burton and Griffin, "More Than a Museum?"

30 Tryon Downtown Development Association, "Historic Tryon Walking Tour," accessed January 8, 2024, https://web.archive.org/web/20110213034611 /http://downtowntryon.org/index.php/download_file/45/84/.

31 Giovanni, *Acolytes*, 5.

32 On messianic time, see Benjamin, "Theses on the Philosophy of History."

33 Giovanni, *Acolytes*, 6.

34 Giovanni, *Acolytes*, 7.

35 Ginsberg, *Howl and Other Poems*, 9.

36 Collins and Skover, *The People v. Ferlinghetti*.

37 Giovanni, *Acolytes*, 6. Michael Schwerner, James Chaney, and Andrew Goodman were three CORE activists who were murdered in Philadelphia, Mississippi, on June 21, 1964.

38 Hand, *me and Nina*.

39 DuBurke, "Nina Simone."

40 Hampton, *Nina Simone*, 109.

41 Simone, *I Put a Spell on You*, 99–100.

42 Alago, "The Day I Shared a Bubble Bath with Nina Simone." The story is told with varying details in multiple places, including in an interview in *Bad Feeling Magazine* (2020) and by Warren Ellis in *Nina Simone's Gum*, 41. The most detailed account appears in Alago's autobiography:

> I arrived with two dozen white roses and a bottle of champagne because I knew she would love both of them. I hadn't seen her in a while and we were both thrilled to see each other.
>
> There was a lot of activity in her room. A few people were making sure her clothes were pressed; another woman was cornrowing her hair, braiding it close to her scalp so she could wear a turban for that evening's performance. But once she saw me, she kicked everyone out of the room and threw open her arms. We hugged, we kissed, and then she said to me, "Oh, my dear, we should take a bubble bath!"
>
> "*What?*" I asked, a little shocked. But then I thought to myself, *Well, it is Nina Simone—we're going to take a bubble bath.*
>
> I went into the bathroom and checked the medicine cabinet, but of course—no bubbles. I called the concierge and asked them to call the chemist and see if they have any bubble bath products and, if so, would they purchase it, put it on the bill, and bring it up to Nina Simone's room.
>
> After the porter brought the bottle to us, I poured it into the tub and waited for the bubbles to rise up. Nina came in, and without a thought

took off all her clothes and climbed into the bathtub. I wasn't too hot about taking off all my clothes, so I kept my boxers on and got in with her.

I had brought the champagne with me and poured out two glasses. We started drinking and laughing and telling each other completely silly stories. We felt totally free, without a care in the world.

Eventually, the bubbles disappeared, and we climbed out of the tub. Her assistants and hair stylists returned to dress her and finish her hair.

I gave her a big kiss and left. I returned to the hotel at 6 P.M. to take her to the show at The Royal Festival Hall. She rose to the occasion that night. Her performance was unspeakably remarkable. (*I Am Michael Alago*, 157–58)

43 Phillips, *On Flirtation*, xvii, xxii.
44 According to Sanchez: "Reena has the multiple personalities. That's how we see Mama B (who is Bessie Smith), Toni (who is Billie Holiday), and Malika (who takes the baton from Nina Simone)" (qtd. in Forsgren, *Sistuhs in the Struggle*, 193). On *The Welcome Table*, see Leeming, *James Baldwin*, 377; Zaborowska, *James Baldwin's Turkish Decade*, 251, 327n6; and Zaborowska, *Me and My House*, 193. Other possible inspirations for the character Edith Hemings include Gülriz Sururi, Eartha Kitt, Betrice Reading, Josephine Baker, Maya Angelou, Verta Mae Grosvenor, Paule Marshall, and Eleanor Traylor.
45 Scafidi, "Speaking from the Heart."
46 Foucault, *Discipline and Punish*, 31.
47 Beyoncé, "Sandcastles," *Lemonade* (Parkwood/Columbia, 2016). "The Look of Love" was written by Burt Bacharach and Hal David and first recorded in 1966 by Springfield for the soundtrack to the James Bond film *Casino Royale* (1967). Springfield rerecorded the track the same year, and elsewhere in 1967 it was covered in recordings by Claudine Longet on *The Look of Love*, Lainie Kazan on *Love Is Lainie*, and Morgana King on *Gemini Rising*—all in addition to Simone's cover that year, and many, many subsequent covers by other artists.
48 Klein, "Love, Guilt and Reparation."
49 For some of the range of debate, and excellent resources that fuel it, see Candace Benbow, "Lemonade Syllabus," May 7, 2016, https://issuu.com /candicebenbow/docs/lemonade_syllabus_2016.
50 Berlant, "Humorlessness (Three Monologues and a Hairpiece)," 339. See also Bastién, "The Silence Is the Loudest Part."
51 Krieger, *Ekphrasis*.
52 Marshall, *Praisesong for the Widow*, 19.
53 *Four Women* (dir. Julie Dash, UCLA Film Archives, 1975).
54 On "the afterlife of slavery," see Hartman, *Lose Your Mother*, 6, 133.
55 "Four Women," *For Colored Girls: Music from and Inspired by the Original Motion Picture Soundtrack* (Atlantic, 2010).
56 Latrice Royale, "Four Women—HD," YouTube, June 9, 2020, https://www .youtube.com/watch?v=SN67–1C-8bk. The video captions describe Royale's performance as a lip sync to a Nina Simone song, but the audio is of a cover

by Kelly Price, Marsha Ambrosius, Jill Scott, and Ledisi from the television special "Live BET Black Girls Rock" (2010).

57 *To Be Free* (dir. Adepero Oduye, Harbor Films, 2017).

58 See Elliott, *Nina Simone*, 136.

59 Elliott discusses the tendency to create cover albums "with no Simone originals and an absence of any of the explicitly political material that the artist was known for" (*Nina Simone*, 135).

60 Mark Richardson, for example, found something nice to say when he concluded of *Remixed and Reimagined*, "it could have been worse" ("Remixed and Reimagined").

61 Amerigo Gazaway, "Soul Mates: Nina Simone & Lauryn Hill—The Miseducation of Eunice Waymon," accessed January 8, 2024, https://soulmatesproject .bandcamp.com/album/nina-simone-lauryn-hill-the-miseducation-of-eunice -waymon.

62 See Heard, "'Don't Let Me Be Misunderstood.'"

63 Rose, *Black Noise*, 79.

64 Tillet, "Strange Sampling," 120; see also Ponomareff, "ForeWomen."

65 Schoemer, "Smoldering, and Still Singing about It."

66 For the most thoughtful articulation of the connections between Hill and Simone, see Tillet, "Strange Sampling."

67 Barnett, "Nina Simone," 152.

68 Barnett, "Nina Simone," 152–53.

69 Powell, "You Al Capone, I'm Nina Simone."

70 E.g., "Miss Simone is a mood-setter rather than a singer of songs" (Sherman, "Nina Simone Casts Her Moody Spells"); "she is building a mood and drawing her audience into that mood" (Wilson, "Two Faces of Nina Simone").

71 At the time of this writing, imdb.com lists Simone's songs in 254 film and television appearances, 240 of which are from 1993 or later.

72 "That Went Well," episode 3.12 of *Bojack Horseman*, (dir. Amy Winfrey, 2016, Netflix).

73 Heidegger, *Being and Time*, 172–73.

74 Bollas, *Shadow of the Object*, 103.

75 Flatley, "How a Revolutionary Counter-mood Is Made"; Flatley, "Reading for Mood."

76 OK, Brian Massumi sort of does. See "Autonomy of Affect."

77 Greeson, "On Moods and Introjects."

78 Berlant, "Genre Flailing."

79 "My Heart Will Go On" was originally recorded for the film's soundtrack but was released as the lead single to Dion's album *Let's Talk about Love* (1997) mere weeks later. Since I will probably never write an endnote about Céline Dion again, this is my chance to acknowledge how much my appreciation for her was transformed by Carl Wilson's *Let's Talk about Love*.

80 Berlant, *Cruel Optimism*, 64; Keeling, "Looking for M—," 579.

81 Kushner, *Flamethrowers*, 46.

82 Kushner, *Flamethrowers*, 27.

83 Cohodas, *Princess Noire*, 354–55.

84 Brooks, "Soul Survivor."

85 *The Point of No Return* (dir. John Badham, Warner Bros., 1993).

86 *Before Sunset* (dir. Richard Linklater, Warner Independent, 2004).

87 *Witch Hunt* (dir. Paul Schrader, HBO Pictures, 1994).

88 On wearing someone's body like a prosthesis, see Berlant, "National Brands/ National Body," 111. To better understand the problem set into a historical trajectory, see Berlant, *Female Complaint*. I remain a big fan of Berlant's early essay on the same topic, "The Female Woman."

89 Schuller, *Trouble with White Women*.

90 *Black Panther: Wakanda Forever* (dir. Ryan Coogler, Marvel Studios, 2022).

91 Feldstein, "'I Don't Trust You Anymore,'" 1372; Moore, *Soundscapes of Liberation*, 181–82.

92 Al-Joundi, *The Day Nina Simone Stopped Singing*, 9.

93 For critiques of contemporary political uses of Simone, see Elliott, *Nina Simone*, 135; Scribner, "1968, Take Two," 69–70.

94 Simone was not wearing an Afro in the summer of 1969, nor by mid-1970. This most iconic look of hers represents her in about seven or eight months of her life, albeit very well documented months. As noted in "Obeah," the existing recordings and documents that capture Simone's life and career cluster heavily into the two or three years on either side of 1970.

95 Scott, *Conscripts of Modernity*, 5.

96 Berlant, *Cruel Optimism*, 227.

97 Nina Simone, "Nina Simone: Mississippi Goddam," YouTube, February 6, 2013, https://www.youtube.com/watch?v=1eaxFES2YXA.

98 "Selma, Alabama," episode 2.4 of *We're Here* (dir. Peter Logreco, 2021, HBO).

99 Feel Tank Chicago, "The Present Is What We Are Doing Together."

100 Hartman, *Lose Your Mother*, 108; Huerta, *Magical Habits*, 27.

101 Santoro, "Nina Simone."

102 Baldwin, "Faulkner and Desegregation," 572.

103 Baldwin, "Faulkner and Desegregation," 568.

104 *Nina Simone—A Historical Perspective* (dir. Peter Rodis, 1970); this documentary first aired on WOR, New York City public television, on August 24, 1970. Scenes may have been filmed as early as 1969. All quotations in this paragraph are from this film.

105 Walcott, *Long Emancipation*, 108. For an alternate reading that concentrates on the "negative underside of that interdiction," see Bradley, *Anteaesthetics*, 27.

106 Fleming, "Anticipating Blackness," 136–40.

107 Freeburg, *Black Aesthetics and the Interior Life*, 139–43.

108 Sharpe, *Ordinary Notes*, 145.

109 Moten, *In the Break*, 12; Kelley, *Freedom Dreams*.

110 Elliott, "Reincarnation of an Egyptian Queen," 41–45.

111 Most readily available at Combahee River Collective, "The Combahee River Collective Statement," accessed January 8, 2024, http://historyisaweapon.com /defcon1/combrivercoll.html.

112 Shakur, *Assata*, 155

113 Lorde, "Uses of the Erotic," 59.

114 Morrison, *Love*, 164.

115 Ferreira da Silva, "Toward a Black Feminist Poethics," 84; Weheliye, *Habeas Viscus*, 40.

116 Hartman, *Wayward Lives, Beautiful Experiments*, 366.

117 Davis, *Freedom Is a Constant Struggle*.

118 Mbembe, *Necropolitics*, 29.

119 *Vogue*, "Filmmaker and Activist Tourmaline on How to Freedom Dream."

SOMETHING (REPRISE)

1 Nina Simone (@NinaSimoneMusic), "My music is the essence of my being . . ."—#ninasimone," Twitter, March 16, 2023, 2:55 p.m., https://twitter.com/NinaSimoneMusic/status/1636440982513172485.

2 *Tongues Untied* (dir. Marlon Riggs, Frameline, 1989). The text is from Essex Hemphill's poem "Homocide" (*Ceremonies*, 144–45).

3 Lauren Berlant, as always, captures some of it: "Take Marlon Riggs's *Tongues Untied* (1989), where the specific beauty and self-pleasure of protestors in parades is a form of sexual *and* political happiness, a part of the erotics of public personhood that queer politics imagines as central to the world of un-humiliated sexuality (at least for gay men) it means to bring forth in America" (*Queen of America Goes to Washington City*, 189–90).

Abbot, Andrew. "What Do Cases Do?" In *Time Matters: On Theory and Methods*, 129–60. Chicago: University of Chicago Press, 2001.

Abraham, Nicolas, and Maria Torok. "A Poetics of Psychoanalysis: 'The Lost Object—Me.'" 1978. Translated by Nicholas Rand. *SubStance* 13, no. 2 (1984): 3–18.

Acker, Kerry. *Nina Simone*. Philadelphia: Chelsea House, 2004.

Adler, Jonathan M. "Living Into the Story: Agency and Coherence in a Longitudinal Study of Narrative Identity Development and Mental Health over the Course of Psychotherapy." *Journal of Personality and Social Psychology* 102, no. 2 (2012): 367–89.

Adrian, Frédéric. *Nina Simone*. Paris: Le mot et le reste, 2021.

Adriansen, Sophie. *Nina Simone, mélodie de la lutte: Jeune, douée & noire: L'origine d'une légende*. Paris: Charleston, 2022.

Afro-American. "50-Year-Old Bookstore to Close in Harlem." December 14, 1974.

Ainsworth, Mary D. Salter, Mary C. Blehar, Everett Waters, and Sally N. Wall. *Patterns of Attachment: A Psychological Study of the Strange Situation*. Hillsdale, NJ: Lawrence Erlbaum, 1978.

Alago, Michael. "The Day I Shared a Bubble Bath with Nina Simone." *Guardian*, November 19, 2017. https://www.theguardian.com/lifeandstyle/2017/nov/19/the-day-i-shared-a-bubble-bath-with-nina-simone.

Alago, Michael, with Laura Davis-Chanin. *I Am Michael Alago: Breathing Music. Signing Metallica. Beating Death*. Guilford, CT: Backbeat Books, 2020.

Al-Joundi, Darina, with Mohamed Kacimi. *The Day Nina Simone Stopped Singing*. 2008. Translated by Marjolijn de Jager. New York: Feminist Press, 2011.

Althusser, Louis. "Idéologie et appareils idéologiques d'État." *La Pensée* 151 (June 1970): 3–38.

Althusser, Louis. *Lenin and Philosophy and Other Essays*. Translated by Ben Brewster. New York: Monthly Review Press, 1971.

Althusser, Louis, and Étienne Balibar. *Reading Capital*. 1968. Translated by Ben Brewster. London: Verso, 2009.

Anderson, Benedict. *Imagined Communities: Reflections on the Origin and Spread of Nationalism*. Rev. ed. London: Verso, 1991.

Angelou, Maya. "Nina Simone: High Priestess of Soul." *Redbook*, November 1970, 77, 132–34.

Anzieu, Didier. *The Skin-Ego*. Rev. ed. 1995. Translated by Naomi Segal. London: Karnac Books, 2016.

Arondekar, Anjali. *For the Record: On Sexuality and the Colonial Archive in India*. Durham, NC: Duke University Press, 2009.

Austin, J. L. "Three Ways of Spilling Ink." *Philosophical Review* 75, no. 4 (1966): 427–40.

Awkward, Michael. *Soul Covers: Rhythm and Blues Remakes and the Struggle for Artistic Identity (Aretha Franklin, Al Green, Phoebe Snow)*. Durham, NC: Duke University Press, 2007.

Aznavour, Charles. *Le temps des avants*. Paris: Flammarion, 2003.

Baldwin, James. "The Black Scholar Interviews James Baldwin." *Black Scholar* 5, no. 4 (1973–74): 33–42.

Baldwin, James. "The Discovery of What It Means to Be an American." *New York Times Book Review*, January 25, 1959.

Baldwin, James. "Faulkner and Desegregation." *Partisan Review* 23 (1956): 568–73.

Baldwin, James. *No Name in the Street*. 1972. New York: Vintage, 2000.

Balint, Michael. *The Basic Fault: Therapeutic Aspects of Regression*. London: Tavistock, 1968.

Banes, Sally. *Greenwich Village 1963: Avant-Garde Performance and the Effervescent Body*. Durham, NC: Duke University Press, 1993.

Baraka, Amiri. "The Changing Same." 1966. In *Black Music*, by LeRoi Jones, 180–211. New York: William Morrow, 1968.

Bardin, Brantley. "Simone Says." *Details Magazine*, January 1997, 66–67.

Barnett, LaShonda Katrice. "'Learning How to Listen': Analyzing Style and Meaning in the Music of Abbey Lincoln, Nina Simone, and Cassandra Wilson." PhD diss., College of William and Mary, 2012.

Barnett, LaShonda Katrice. "Nina Simone." In *I Got Thunder: Black Women Songwriters on Their Craft*, 141–54. New York: Thunder's Mouth Press, 2007.

Barthes, Roland. *The Preparation of the Novel: Lecture Courses and Seminars at the Collège de France (1978–1979 and 1979–1980)*. Edited by Nathalie Léger. 2003. Translated by Kate Briggs. New York: Columbia University Press, 2011.

Bass, Alan. *Difference and Disavowal: The Trauma of Eros*. Stanford, CA: Stanford University Press, 2000.

Bastién, Angelica Jade. "The Silence Is the Loudest Part of *Renaissance: A Film*." *Vulture*, December 4, 2023. https://www.vulture.com/article/renaissance-a-film-by-beyonce-review.html.

BBC News. "Funeral Held for Singer Simone." April 25, 2003. http://news.bbc.co.uk/2/hi/entertainment/2975871.stm.

Belcourt, Billy-Ray. *A History of My Brief Body*. Columbus, OH: Two Dollar Radio, 2020.

Benjamin, Walter. "Theses on the Philosophy of History." In *Illuminations*. 1955. Translated by Harry Zohn, edited with an introduction by Hannah Arendt, 253–64. New York: Schocken, 1968.

Berlant, Lauren. *The Anatomy of National Fantasy: Hawthorne, Utopia, and Everyday Life*. Chicago: University of Chicago Press, 1991.

Berlant, Lauren. *Cruel Optimism*. Durham, NC: Duke University Press, 2011.

Berlant, Lauren. *Desire/Love*. Brooklyn: Punctum Books, 2012.

Berlant, Lauren. *The Female Complaint: The Unfinished Business of Sentimentality in American Culture*. Durham, NC: Duke University Press, 2008.

Berlant, Lauren. "The Female Woman: Fanny Fern and the Form of Sentiment." *American Literary History* 3, no. 1 (1991): 429–54.

Berlant, Lauren. "Genre Flailing." *Capacious: Journal for Emerging Affect Inquiry* 1, no. 2 (2018): 156–62.

Berlant, Lauren. "Humorlessness (Three Monologues and a Hairpiece)." *Critical Inquiry* 43, no. 2 (2017): 305–40.

Berlant, Lauren. "A Momentary Anesthesia of the Heart." *International Journal of Politics, Culture, and Society* 28 (2015): 273–81.

Berlant, Lauren. "National Brands/National Body: *Imitation of Life*." In *Comparative American Identities: Race, Sex, and Nationality in the Modern Text*, edited by Hortense J. Spillers, 110–30. New York: Routledge, 1991.

Berlant, Lauren. "On the Case." *Critical Inquiry* 33, no. 4 (2007): 663–72.

Berlant, Lauren. *On the Inconvenience of Other People*. Durham, NC: Duke University Press, 2022.

Berlant, Lauren. "Poisonality." In *The Affect Theory Reader II: Worldings, Tensions, Futures*, edited by Gregory J. Seigworth and Carolyn Pedwell, 451–63. Durham, NC: Duke University Press, 2023.

Berlant, Lauren. *The Queen of America Goes to Washington City: Essays on Sex and Citizenship*. Durham, NC: Duke University Press, 1997.

Berlant, Lauren. "'68 or Something." *Critical Inquiry* 21, no. 1 (1994): 124–55.

Berlant, Lauren. "Starved." *South Atlantic Quarterly* 106, no. 3 (2007): 433–44.

Berlant, Lauren. "The Traumic: On *Bojack Horseman*'s 'Good Damage.'" *Post45: Contemporaries*, November 22, 2020. http://post45.org/2020/11/the-traumic-on-bojack-horsemans-good-damage/.

Berman, Russell A. "Sounds Familiar? Nina Simone's Performances of Brecht/Weill Songs." In *Sound Matters: Essays on the Acoustics of Modern German Culture*, edited by Nora M. Alter and Lutz Koepnick, 171–82. New York: Berghahn Books, 2004.

Bersani, Leo. *Receptive Bodies*. Chicago: University of Chicago Press, 2018.

Best, Stephen, and Sharon Marcus. "Surface Reading: An Introduction." *Representations* 108 (2009): 1–21.

Billboard. "Nina Simone Recovers Masters." March 18, 1995, 90.

Bion, W. R. "The Psycho-Analytic Study of Thinking." *International Journal of Psycho-Analysis* 43 (1962): 306–10.

Blas, Zach. "Opacities: An Introduction." *Camera Obscura* 31, no. 2 (2016): 149–53.

Blau, Eleanor. "Three Singers Reflect on Music and Careers." *New York Times*, March 8, 1985.

Bollas, Christopher. *The Shadow of the Object: Psychoanalysis of the Unthought Known*. 1987. New York: Columbia University Press, 2017.

Bow, Leslie. *Racist Love: Asian Abstraction and the Pleasures of Fantasy.* Durham, NC: Duke University Press, 2022.

Bowlby, John. "The Nature of the Child's Tie to His Mother." *International Journal of Psycho-Analysis* 39 (1958): 350–73.

Boym, Svetlana. *Common Places: Mythologies of Everyday Life in Russia.* Cambridge, MA: Harvard University Press, 1994.

Bradley, Adam. "A Home Coming." *T Magazine*, March 27, 2022, 100.

Bradley, Rizvana. *Anteaesthetics: Black Aesthesis and the Critique of Form.* Stanford, CA: Stanford University Press, 2023.

Braggs, Rashida K. "The Two Simones at Montreux." *Jazz Research Journal* 15, nos. 1–2 (2022): 126–31.

Bratcher, Melanie E. *Words and Songs of Bessie Smith, Billie Holiday, and Nina Simone: Sound Motion, Blues Spirit, and African Memory.* New York: Routledge, 2007.

Brecht, Bertolt. *Die Dreigroschenoper.* 1928. Berlin: Suhrkamp Verlag, 1955.

Brecht, Bertolt. *The Threepenny Opera.* 1928. Translated by Desmond Vesey and Eric Bentley. New York: Grove Press, 1949.

Brennan, Teresa. *The Transmission of Affect.* Ithaca, NY: Cornell University Press, 2004.

Brooks, Daphne A. "Afro-Sonic Feminist Praxis: Nina Simone and Adrienne Kennedy in High Fidelity." In *Black Performance Theory*, edited by Thomas F. DeFrantz and Anita Gonzalez, 204–22. Durham, NC: Duke University Press, 2014.

Brooks, Daphne A. "'Ain't Got No/I Got Life': #OscarsSoWhite & the Problem of Women Musicians on Film." *Los Angeles Review of Books*, February 28, 2016. https://lareviewofbooks.org/article/aint-got-no-i-got-life-oscarssowhite-the-problem-of-women-musicians-film/.

Brooks, Daphne A. *Jeff Buckley's Grace.* New York: Continuum, 2005.

Brooks, Daphne A. *Liner Notes for the Revolution: The Intellectual Life of Black Feminist Sound.* Cambridge, MA: Belknap Press of Harvard University Press, 2021.

Brooks, Daphne A. "Nina Simone's Triple Play." *Callaloo* 34, no. 1 (2011): 176–97.

Brooks, Libby. "Soul Survivor." *Guardian*, August 6, 2001. https://www.theguardian.com/g2/story/0,3604,532415,00.html.

Brown, Elsa Barkley. "'What Has Happened Here': The Politics of Difference in Women's History and Feminist Politics." *Feminist Studies* 18, no. 2 (1992): 295–312.

Brown, Peter. *The Cult of the Saints: Its Rise and Function in Latin Christianity.* Chicago: University of Chicago Press, 1981.

Bruce, LaMarr Jurelle. *How to Go Mad without Losing Your Mind: Madness and Black Radical Creativity.* Durham, NC: Duke University Press, 2021.

Brun-Lambert, David. *Nina Simone: The Biography.* 2005. Translated by Paul Morris and Isabelle Villancher. London: Aurum Press, 2009.

Burnett-Zeigler, Inger. *Nobody Knows the Trouble I've Seen: The Emotional Lives of Black Women.* New York: Amistad, 2021.

Burton, Christine, and Janette Griffin. "More Than a Museum? Understanding How Small Museums Contribute to Social Capital in Regional Communities." *Asia Pacific Journal of Arts and Cultural Management* 5, no. 1 (2008): 314–32.

Butler, Judith. "Melancholy Gender—Refused Identification." *Psychoanalytic Dialogues* 5, no. 2 (1995): 165–80.

Bynum, Tara A. *Reading Pleasures: Everyday Black Living in Early America.* Urbana: University of Illinois Press, 2023.

Calwell, Earl. "Nina Simone's Lyrics Stir Storm of Protest." *New York Post*, September 2, 1966.

Carby, Hazel V. *Imperial Intimacies: A Tale of Two Islands.* London: Verso, 2019.

Carby, Hazel V. *Reconstructing Womanhood: The Emergence of the Afro-American Woman Novelist.* New York: Oxford University Press, 1987.

Cassidy, F. G., and R. B. Le Page, eds. *Dictionary of Jamaican English.* 2nd ed. Kingston, Jamaica: University of the West Indies Press, 2002.

Chambers-Letson, Joshua. *After the Party: A Manifesto for Queer of Color Life.* New York: New York University Press, 2018.

Chow, Andrew. "Nina Simone's Childhood Home Gets 'National Treasure' Designation." *New York Times*, June 18, 2018.

Coates, Ta-Nehisi. "Nina Simone's Face." *Atlantic*, March 15, 2016. http://www.theatlantic.com/entertainment/archive/2016/03/nina-simone-face/472107/.

Cohodas, Nadine. *Princess Noire: The Tumultuous Reign of Nina Simone.* New York: Pantheon, 2010.

Colbert, Soyica Diggs. *Radical Vision: A Biography of Lorraine Hansberry.* New Haven, CT: Yale University Press, 2021.

Colby, Paul, and Martin Fitzpatrick. *The Bitter End: Hanging Out at America's Nightclub.* New York: Cooper Square Press, 2000.

Collins, Patricia Hill. *Black Feminist Thought: Knowledge, Consciousness, and the Politics of Empowerment.* 2nd ed. New York: Routledge, 2000.

Collins, Ronald K. L., and David M. Skover. *The People v. Ferlinghetti: The Fight to Publish Allen Ginsberg's Howl.* Lanham, MD: Rowman and Littlefield, 2019.

Coyle, Michael. "Hijacked Hits and Antic Authenticity: Cover Songs, Race, and Postwar Marketing." In *Rock over the Edge Transformations in Popular Music Culture*, edited by Roger Beebe, Denise Fulbrook, and Ben Saunders, 133–60. Durham, NC: Duke University Press, 2002.

Crawley, Ashon T. *Blackpentecostal Breath: The Aesthetics of Possibility.* New York: Fordham University Press, 2017.

Davies, Jody. "Erotic Overstimulation and the Co-construction of Sexual Meanings in Transference-Countertransference Experience." *Psychoanalytic Quarterly* 70, no. 4 (2001): 757–88.

Davis, Angela Y. *Angela Davis: An Autobiography.* New York: International Publishers, 1974.

Davis, Angela Y. *Freedom Is a Constant Struggle: Ferguson, Palestine, and the Foundations of a Movement.* Chicago: Haymarket Books, 2016.

Davis, Angela Y. "Nina Simone's Music Was So Much More Than the Soundtrack to a Movement." *Mail & Guardian*, September 5, 2016. https://mg.co.za/article/2016-09-05-00-angela-davis-nina-simones-music-was-so-much-more-than-the-soundtrack-to-a-movement.

Davis, Angela Y. *Women, Race, and Class.* New York: Vintage, 1981.

Davis, Heather, and Paige Sarlin. "No One Is Sovereign in Love: A Conversation between Lauren Berlant and Michael Hardt." *No More Potlucks* 18 (2011). http://nomorepotlucks.org/site/no-one-is-sovereign-in-love-a-conversation-between-lauren-berlant-and-michael-hardt/.

Dayan, Colin Joan. *Haiti, History, and the Gods.* Berkeley: University of California Press, 1995.

Dembart, Lee. "Nina Simone: Soul on Ice." *New York Post*, March 15, 1969.

Derrida, Jacques. *Archive Fever: A Freudian Impression.* 1995. Translated by Eric Prenowitz. Chicago: University of Chicago Press, 1996.

Dillon, Elizabeth Maddock. "Ante-Oedipus: Gender and Racial Capitalism in Plantation Modernity." *History of the Present* 12, no. 1 (2022): 4–33.

Doyle, Jennifer. *Hold It Against Me: Difficulty and Emotion in Contemporary Art.* Durham, NC: Duke University Press, 2013.

Dubois, Laurent. "Thinking Haiti's Nineteenth Century." *Small Axe* 18, no. 2 (2014): 72–79.

DuBurke, Randy. "Nina Simone: CIVIL JAZZ!" In *Playing for Keeps: Improvisation in the Aftermath*, edited by Daniel Fischlin and Eric Porter, 121–28. Durham, NC: Duke University Press, 2020.

Duncan, Stephen R. *The Rebel Café: Sex, Race, and Politics in Cold War America's Nightclub Underground.* Baltimore: Johns Hopkins University Press, 2018.

Durham, I. Augustus. "A Loving Reclamation of the Unutterable: Patricia Hill Collins, Hortense J. Spillers, and Nina Simone as Excellent Performers of Nomenclature." *Palimpsest* 2, no. 1 (2013): 28–46.

Ebert, Roger. "The Harder They Come." *Chicago Sun-Times*, February 9, 1973.

Edelman, Lee. *Bad Education: Why Queer Theory Teaches Us Nothing.* Durham, NC: Duke University Press, 2023.

Edgers, Geoff. "She Sang 'Killing Me Softly' before Roberta Flack. Now She Just Wants You to Hear Her Side of the Story." *Washington Post*, January 24, 2020.

Edwards, Brent Hayes. *The Practice of Diaspora: Literature, Translation, and the Rise of Black Internationalism.* Cambridge, MA: Harvard University Press, 2003.

Edwards, Brent Hayes. "The Taste of the Archive." *Callaloo* 35, no. 4 (2012): 944–72.

Ehrlich, Brenna. "'Exuma' at 50: How a Bahamian Artist Channeled Island Culture into a Strange Sonic Ritual." Rollingstone.com, November 5, 2020. https://www.rollingstone.com/music/music-features/exuma-obeah-man-album-tony-mackey-1083973/.

Eidsheim, Nina Sun. *The Race of Sound: Listening, Timbre, and Vocality in African American Music.* Durham, NC: Duke University Press, 2019.

Elliott, Richard. *Nina Simone.* Sheffield, UK: Equinox, 2013.

Elliott, Richard. "The Reincarnation of an Egyptian Queen: Dystopian Lateness and Speculation in Nina Simone's Afrofuturism." *Jazz Research Journal* 15, nos. 1–2 (2022): 25–50.

Elliott, Richard. "So Transported: Nina Simone, 'My Sweet Lord' and the (Un)folding of Affect." In *Sound, Music, Affect: Theorizing Sonic Experience*, edited by Marie Thompson and Ian Biddle, 75–90. London: Bloomsbury, 2013.

Ellis, Warren. *Nina Simone's Gum*. London: Faber and Faber, 2021.

Ellison, Ralph. *Invisible Man*. 1952. New York: Vintage, 1995.

Eng, David L. "Colonial Object Relations." *Social Text* 34, no. 1 (2016): 1–19.

English, Darby. *1971: A Year in the Life of Color*. Chicago: University of Chicago Press, 2016.

Ewell, Phillip A. "Music Theory and the White Racial Frame." *MTO: A Journal for the Society for Music Theory* 26, no. 2 (2020). https://doi.org/10.30535/mto.26.2.4.

Fairbairn, W. R. D. "The Repression and the Return of Bad Objects (With Special Reference to 'War Neuroses')." 1943. In *Psychoanalytic Study of the Personality*, 59–81. 1952. New York: Routledge, 1994.

Fanon, Frantz. *Black Skin, White Masks*. 1952. Translated by Charles Lam Markman. New York: Grove Press, 1967.

Fanon, Frantz. *Black Skin, White Masks*. 1952. Translated by Richard Philcox. New York: Grove Press, 2008.

Fanon, Frantz. *Peau noire, masques blancs*. 1952. Paris: Éditions de Seuil, 2015.

Farge, Arlette. *The Allure of Archives*. 1989. Translated by Thomas Scott-Railton. New Haven, CT: Yale University Press, 2015.

Farred, Grant. *What's My Name? Black Vernacular Intellectuals*. Minneapolis: University of Minnesota Press, 2003.

Fausto-Sterling, Anne. "Gender, Race, and Nation: The Comparative Anatomy of 'Hottentot' Women in Europe, 1815–1817." In *Deviant Bodies: Critical Perspectives on Difference in Science and Popular Culture*, edited by Jennifer Terry and Jacqueline Urla, 19–48. Bloomington: Indiana University Press, 1995.

Feather, Leonard. "Nina: Pianist by Plan, Chanteuse by Chance." *Los Angeles Times*, March 5, 1967.

Feel Tank Chicago. "The Present Is What We Are Doing Together." In *Re/Imagining Depression: Creative Approaches to "Feeling Bad,"* edited by Julie Hollenbach and Robin Alex McDonald, 195–214. Cham, Switzerland: Palgrave Macmillan, 2021.

Feldman, Martha. "Love, Race and Resistance: The Fugitive Voice of Nina Simone." In *The Female Voice in the Twentieth Century: Material, Symbolic and Aesthetic Dimensions*, edited by Serena Facci and Michela Garda, 83–101. London: Routledge, 2021.

Feldstein, Ruth. "'I Don't Trust You Anymore': Nina Simone, Culture, and Black Activism in the 1960s." *Journal of American History* 91, no. 4 (2005): 1349–79.

Ferreira da Silva, Denise. "Toward a Black Feminist Poethics." *Black Scholar* 44, no. 2 (2014): 81–97.

Field, Corinne T., and LaKisha Michelle Simmons, eds. *The Global History of Black Girlhood*. Champaign: University of Illinois Press, 2022.

Flatley, Jonathan. *Affective Mapping: Melancholia and the Politics of Modernism*. Cambridge, MA: Harvard University Press, 2008.

Flatley, Jonathan. "How a Revolutionary Counter-mood Is Made." *New Literary History* 43, no. 3 (2012): 503–25.

Flatley, Jonathan. "Reading for Mood." *Representations* 140 (2017): 137–58.

Fleming, Juliet. *Cultural Graphology: Writing after Derrida*. Chicago: University of Chicago Press, 2016.

Fleming, Julius B., Jr. "Anticipating Blackness: Nina Simone, Lorraine Hansberry, and the Time of Black Ontology." *South Atlantic Quarterly* 121, no. 1 (2022): 131–52.

Fleming, Julius B., Jr. *Black Patience: Performance, Civil Rights, and the Unfinished Project of Emancipation*. New York: New York University Press, 2022.

Floyd, Samuel A., Jr., with Melanie L. Zeck and Guthrie P. Ramsey Jr. *The Transformation of Black Music: The Rhythms, the Songs, and the Ships of the African Diaspora*. New York: Oxford University Press, 2017.

Ford, Tanisha C. *Liberated Threads: Black Women, Style, and the Global Politics of Soul*. Chapel Hill: University of North Carolina Press, 2015.

Forsgren, La Donna. *Sistuhs in the Struggle: An Oral History of Black Arts Movement Theater and Performance*. Evanston, IL: Northwestern University Press, 2020.

Foucault, Michel. *Discipline and Punish: The Birth of the Prison*. 1975. Translated by Alan Sheridan. New York: Vintage, 1995.

Fraser, C. Gerald. "Lewis Michaux, 92, Dies; Ran Bookstore in Harlem." *New York Times*, August 27, 1976.

Freeburg, Christopher. *Black Aesthetics and the Interior Life*. Charlottesville: University of Virginia Press, 2017.

Freud, Sigmund. "'A Child Is Being Beaten.'" 1919. In *Sexuality and the Psychology of Love*, edited by Philip Rieff, 97–122. New York: Touchstone, 1997.

Freud, Sigmund. *Civilization and Its Discontents*. 1930. Translated and edited by James Strachey. New York: W. W. Norton, 1989.

Freud, Sigmund. *The Complete Letters of Sigmund Freud to Wilhelm Fliess, 1887–1904*. Edited and translated by Jeffrey Moussaieff Masson. Cambridge, MA: Belknap Press, 1986.

Freud, Sigmund. "Dynamics of Transference." 1912. In *The Standard Edition of the Complete Psychological Works of Sigmund Freud*. Translated from the German under the general editorship of James Strachey, in collaboration with Anna Freud, assisted by Alix Strachey and Alan Tyson, 12:97–108. London: Hogarth, 1950.

Freud, Sigmund. *Five Lectures on Psycho-Analysis*. 1909. Translated and edited by James Strachey. New York: W. W. Norton, 1961.

Freud, Sigmund. *Fragment of an Analysis of a Case of Hysteria*. 1905. In *Dora: An Analysis of a Case of Hysteria*, edited by Philip Rieff, 1–112. New York: Touchstone, 1963.

Freud, Sigmund. "From the History of an Infantile Neurosis." 1918. In *Three Case Histories*, edited by Philip Rieff, 161–280. New York: Touchstone, 1996.

Freud, Sigmund. *The Interpretation of Dreams*. 1900. Translated by James Strachey. New York: Avon, 1965.

Freud, Sigmund. *Introductory Lectures on Psycho-Analysis*. 1917. Translated and edited by James Strachey. New York: W. W. Norton: 1989.

Freud, Sigmund. "Negation." 1925. In *General Psychological Theory: Papers on Metapsychology*, edited by Philip Rieff, 217–21. New York: Touchstone, 1991.

Freud, Sigmund. "Observations on Transference-Love: Further Recommendations on the Technique of Psycho-Analysis." 1915. In *The Standard Edition of the Com-

plete Psychological Works of Sigmund Freud. Translated from the German under
the general editorship of James Strachey, in collaboration with Anna Freud,
assisted by Alix Strachey and Alan Tyson, 12:159–73. London: Hogarth, 1950.

Freud, Sigmund. "On Narcissism: An Introduction." 1914. In *General Psychological Theory: Papers on Metapsychology*, edited by Philip Rieff, 41–69. New York:
Touchstone, 1991.

Freud, Sigmund. "Remembering, Repeating, and Working-Through." 1914. In
The Standard Edition of the Complete Psychological Works of Sigmund Freud.
Translated from the German under the general editorship of James Strachey,
in collaboration with Anna Freud, assisted by Alix Strachey and Alan Tyson,
12:145–57. London: Hogarth, 1950.

Freud, Sigmund. "Some Psychological Consequences of the Anatomical Distinction between the Sexes." 1925. In *Sexuality and the Psychology of Love*, edited by
Philip Rieff, 173–83. New York: Touchstone, 1997.

Freud, Sigmund. "A Special Type of Choice of Object Made by Men." 1910. In
Sexuality and the Psychology of Love, edited by Philip Rieff, 39–48. New York:
Touchstone, 1997.

Freud, Sigmund. *Three Case Histories.* Edited by Philip Rieff. New York: Touchstone, 1996.

Freud, Sigmund. *Vorlesungen zur Einführung in die Psychoanalyse.* 1917. Berlin:
Gustav Kiepenheuer Verlag, 1955.

Freud, Sigmund, and Josef Breuer. *Studies on Hysteria.* 1895. Translated by James
Strachey, in collaboration with Anna Freud. New York: Basic Books, 2000.

Frith, Simon. *Performing Rites: On the Value of Popular Music.* Cambridge, MA:
Harvard University Press, 1996.

Gaines, Malik. *Black Performance on the Outskirts of the Left: A History of the
Impossible.* New York: New York University Press, 2017.

Garland, Phyl. *The Sound of Soul.* Chicago: Henry Regnery, 1969.

Garza, Alicia. "A Herstory of the #BlackLivesMatter Movement." *Feminist Wire*,
October 7, 2014. https://thefeministwire.com/2014/10/blacklivesmatter-2/.

Gillespie, Michael Boyce. "Nina Simone, 'My Father/Dialog.'" *ASAP Journal*,
April 2, 2020. http://asapjournal.com/nina-simone-my-father-dialog/.

Gillman, Sander L. *Freud, Race, and Gender.* Princeton, NJ: Princeton University
Press, 1995.

Gilroy, Paul. *The Black Atlantic: Modernity and Double-Consciousness.* Cambridge, MA: Harvard University Press, 1993.

Ginsberg, Allen. *Howl and Other Poems.* San Francisco: City Lights Pocket Book-
shop, 1956.

Giovanni, Nikki. *Acolytes.* New York: HarperCollins, 2007.

Gleason, Ralph J. "An Imaginative Nina Simone Album." *New York Post*, June 20, 1969.

Glissant, Édouard. "For Opacity." 1990. In *Poetics of Relation*, translated by Betsy
Wing, 189–94. Ann Arbor: University of Michigan Press, 1997.

Glück, Robert. *Margery Kempe.* 1994. New York: NYRB, 2020.

Goldman, Albert. "Return of the Queen of Shebang." *Life*, October 2, 1970.

González, Jennifer A. "Morphologies: Race as Visual Technology." In *Only Skin Deep: Change Visions of the American Self*, edited by Coco Fusco and Brian Wallis, 379–93. New York: Harry N. Abrams, 2003.

Green, André. *The Fabric of Affect in Psychoanalytic Discourse*. 1973. Translated by Alan Sheridan. New York: Routledge, 1999.

Greeson, Ralph R. "On Moods and Introjects." *Bulletin of the Menninger Clinic* 18 (1954): 1–11.

Greeson, Ralph R. "The Working Alliance and the Transference Neurosis." *Psychoanalytic Quarterly* 34, no. 1 (1965): 155–81.

Grier, Miles Parks. "The Only Black Man at the Party: Joni Mitchell Enters the Rock Canon." *Genders* 56 (2012). https://www.colorado.edu/gendersarchive1998 -2013/2012/11/01/only-black-man-party-joni-mitchell-enters-rock-canon.

Griffin, Farah Jasmine. "When Malindy Sings: A Meditation on Black Women's Vocality." In *Uptown Conversations: The New Jazz Studies*, edited by Robert G. O'Meally, Brent Hayes Edwards, and Farah Jasmine Griffin, 102–25. New York: Columbia University Press, 2004.

Hagan, Joe. "I Wish I Knew How It Felt to Be Free: The Secret Diary of Nina Simone." *The Believer* 73 (2010): 7–16.

Hahn, Cynthia. "What Do Reliquaries Do for Relics?" *Numen* 57, no. 3/4 (2010): 284–316.

Hall, Stuart. "Cultural Identity and Diaspora." *Framework* 36 (1989): 68–81.

Hall, Stuart. *Familiar Stranger: A Life between Two Islands*. Durham, NC: Duke University Press, 2017.

Hampton, Sylvia, with David Nathan. *Nina Simone: Break Down and Let It All Out*. London: Sanctuary, 2004.

Hand, Monica A. *me and Nina*. Farmington, ME: Alice James Books, 2012.

Harney, Stefano, and Fred Moten. *The Undercommons: Fugitive Planning and Black Study*. Brooklyn: Minor Compositions/Autonomedia, 2013.

Harris, Jessica B. *My Soul Looks Back: A Memoir*. New York: Scribner, 2017.

Harrison, George. *I Me Mine*. 1980. San Francisco: Chronicle Books, 2002.

Hartman, Saidiya. *Lose Your Mother: A Journey along the Atlantic Slave Route*. New York: Farrar, Straus and Giroux, 2007.

Hartman, Saidiya. *Scenes of Subjection: Terror, Slavery, and Self-Making in Nineteenth-Century America*. New York: Oxford University Press, 1997.

Hartman, Saidiya. "Venus in Two Acts." *Small Axe* 12, no. 2 (2008): 1–14.

Hartman, Saidiya. *Wayward Lives, Beautiful Experiments: Intimate Histories of Social Upheaval*. New York: W. W. Norton, 2019.

Heard, Danielle C. "'Don't Let Me Be Misunderstood': Nina Simone's Theater of Invisibility." *Callaloo* 35, no. 4 (2012): 1056–84.

Heidegger, Martin. *Being and Time*. 1927. Translated by John Macquarrie and Edward Robinson. New York: Harper and Row, 1962.

Helleu, Jacques. *Jacques Helleu and Chanel*. New York: Harry N. Abrams, 2006.

Hemphill, Essex. *Ceremonies: Prose and Poetry*. New York: Plume, 1992.

Herbert, Sharnine S. "Rhythm and Blues, 1968–1972: An African-Centered Rhetorical Analysis." PhD diss., Howard University, 2000.

Higashida, Cheryl. "To Be(come) Young, Gay, and Black: Lorraine Hansberry's Existentialist Routes to Anticolonialism." *American Quarterly* 60, no. 4 (2008): 899–924.

Hines, Jasmine. "Incorporating Intersectional Musicality within the Classroom: Black Feminism through Nina Simone and Janelle Monáe." *Journal of Popular Music Education* 4, no. 3 (2020): 311–28.

Hirsch, Mathilde, and Florence Noiville. *Nina Simone: Love Me or Leave Me.* Paris: Tallandier, 2019.

Holden, Stephen. "Cabaret: Nina Simone." *New York Times*, June 6, 1983.

Holden, Stephen. "A Rare Gig for Nina Simone, Diva of Pop." *New York Times*, June 3, 1983.

Holden, Stephen. "A Younger Generation's Homage to a Soulful Diva." *New York Times*, June 24, 2004.

Hong, Cathy Park. *Minor Feelings: An Asian American Reckoning.* New York: One World, 2020.

Horn, Barbara Lee. *The Age of "Hair": Evolution and the Impact of Broadway's First Rock Musical.* New York: Praeger, 1991.

Huerta, Monica. *Magical Habits.* Durham, NC: Duke University Press, 2021.

Hughes, Langston. "Nina Simone." *New York Post,* June 29, 1962.

Hurston, Zora Neale. *Tell My Horse: Voodoo and Life in Haiti and Jamaica.* 1938. New York: Harper Perennial, 2009.

Irish Times. "Hundreds at Nina Simone Funeral in France." April 25, 2003. https://www.irishtimes.com/news/hundreds-at-nina-simone-funeral-in-france-1.473882.

Isaacs, Susan. "The Nature and Function of Phantasy." *International Journal of Psycho-Analysis* 29 (1948): 73–97.

Iton, Richard. *In Search of the Black Fantastic: Politics and Popular Culture in the Post–Civil Rights Era.* New York: Oxford University Press, 2008.

Jackson, Lauren Michele. *White Negroes: When Cornrows Were in Vogue . . . and Other Thoughts on Cultural Appropriation.* Boston: Beacon, 2019.

Jackson, Stanley W. "The History of Freud's Concepts of Regression." *Journal of the American Psychoanalytic Association* 17, no. 3 (1969): 743–84.

Jackson, Zakiyyah Iman. *Becoming Human: Matter and Meaning in an Antiblack World.* New York: New York University Press, 2020.

James, C. L. R. *The Black Jacobins: Toussaint L'Ouverture and the San Domingo Revolution.* 2nd ed. New York: Vintage, 1963.

James, Winston. *Holding Aloft the Banner of Ethiopia: Caribbean Radicalism in Early Twentieth-Century America.* New York: Verso, 1999.

Jameson, Fredric. *Marxism and Form: Twentieth-Century Dialectical Theories of Literature.* Princeton, NJ: Princeton University Press, 1971.

Jameson, Fredric. "Reification and Utopia in Mass Culture." *Social Text* 1 (1979): 130–48.

Jet Magazine. "Nina Simone Ends Voluntary Exile from U.S." April 22, 1985, 54–55.

Jewell, Derek. "Cries of Joy." *Sunday Times*, March 30, 1969.

Johnson, Barbara. *Persons and Things*. Cambridge, MA: Harvard University Press, 2008.

Judd, Bettina. "Sapphire as Praxis: Toward a Methodology of Anger." *Feminist Studies* 45, no. 1 (2019): 178–208.

Kafka, Ben. *The Demon of Writing: Powers and Failures of Paperwork*. New York: Zone, 2012.

Kant, Immanuel. *Critique of Pure Reason*. 1781/1787. Translated and edited by Paul Guyer and Alan W. Wood. Cambridge: Cambridge University Press, 1998.

Kaplan, Cora. "The Thorn Birds: Fiction, Fantasy, Femininity." In *Formations of Fantasy*, edited by Victor Burgin, James Donald, and Cora Kaplan, 142–66. London: Methuen, 1986.

Keeling, Kara. "Looking for M—: Queer Temporality, Black Political Possibility, and Poetry from the Future." *GLQ: A Journal of Lesbian and Gay Studies* 15, no. 4 (2009): 565–82.

Keeling, Kara. *Queer Times, Black Futures*. New York: New York University Press, 2019.

Kelley, Robin D. G. *Freedom Dreams: The Black Radical Imagination*. Boston: Beacon Press, 2002.

Kernodle, Tammy L. "'I Wish I Knew How It Would Feel to Be Free': Nina Simone and the Redefining of the Freedom Song of the 1960s." *Journal of the Society for American Music* 2, no. 3 (2008): 295–317.

Khan, Aisha. *The Deepest Dye: Obeah, Hosay, and Race in the Atlantic World*. Cambridge, MA: Harvard University Press, 2021.

Khan-Cullors, Patrisse, and Asha Bandele. *When They Call You a Terrorist: A Black Lives Matter Memoir*. New York: St. Martin's, 2018.

Klein, Melanie. "A Contribution to the Psychogenesis of Manic-Depressive States." 1935. In *Love, Guilt and Reparation and Other Works 1921–1945*, 262–89. New York: Free Press, 1975.

Klein, Melanie. "Love, Guilt and Reparation." 1936. In *Love, Guilt and Reparation and Other Works 1921–1945*, 306–43. New York: Free Press, 1975.

Klein, Melanie. "Notes on Some Schizoid Mechanisms." 1946. In *Envy and Gratitude and Other Works 1946–1963*, 1–24. New York: Free Press, 1975.

Klein, Melanie. "The Oedipus Complex in the Light of Early Anxieties." 1945. In *Love, Guilt and Reparation and Other Works 1921–1945*, 370–419. New York: Free Press, 1975.

Kohut, Heinz. *The Analysis of the Self: A Systematic Approach to the Psychoanalytic Treatment of Narcissistic Personality Disorders*. New York: International Universities Press, 1971.

Kohut, Heinz. *The Search for the Self: Selected Writing of Heinz Kohut: 1950–1978*. 2 vols. Edited by Paul H. Ornstein. New York: International Press, 1978.

Kosner, Edward. "To Nina Simone Respect Means More Than Flattery." *Philadelphia Tribune*, April 11, 1961.

Kraaz, Eva Tanita. "With 'Pirate Jenny' from Schiffbauerdamm to Carnegie Hall: Nina Simone's Making of a Protest Song in 1964." *Monatshefte* 115, no. 3 (2023): 365–85.

Kramer, Peter D. *Against Depression*. New York: Viking, 2005.

Krieger, Murray. *Ekphrasis: The Illusion of the Natural Sign.* Baltimore: Johns Hopkins University Press, 1992.

Kushner, Rachel. *The Flamethrowers.* New York: Scribner, 2013.

Lacan, Jacques. *Formations of the Unconscious: The Seminar of Jacques Lacan, Book V.* Edited by Jacques-Alain Miller. Translated by Russell Grigg. London: Polity, 2017.

Lacan, Jacques. *Le séminaire, livre V: Les formations de l'inconscient.* Edited by Jacques-Alain Miller. Paris: Seuil, 1998.

Lacan, Jacques. *Le séminaire livre XIV: La logique du fantasme.* Edited by Jacques-Alain Miller. Paris: Seuil, 2023.

Lacan, Jacques. *The Object Relation: The Seminar of Jacques Lacan, Book IV.* Edited by Jacques-Alain Miller. Translated by Adrian Price. London: Polity, 2021.

Lacan, Jacques. *Transference: The Seminar of Jacques Lacan, Book VIII.* Edited by Jacques-Alain Miller. 1991. Translated by Bruce Fink. London: Polity, 2015.

Ladner, Joyce. *Tomorrow's Tomorrow: The Black Woman.* New York: Doubleday, 1971.

Lakoff, George, and Mark Johnson. *Metaphors We Live By.* Chicago: University of Chicago Press, 1980.

Laplanche, Jean. *New Foundations for Psychoanalysis.* 1987. Translated by David Macey. Oxford: Basil Blackwell, 1989.

Laplanche, Jean, and J.-B. Pontalis. "Fantasy and the Origins of Sexuality." *International Journal of Psychoanalysis* 49, no. 1 (1968): 1-18.

Laplanche, Jean, and J.-B. Pontalis. *The Language of Psychoanalysis.* 1967. Translated by Donald Nicholson-Smith. New York: W. W. Norton, 1973.

Leclaire, Serge. *A Child Is Being Killed: On Primary Narcissism and the Death Drive.* 1978. Translated by Marie-Claude Hays. Stanford, CA: Stanford University Press, 1998.

Leeming, David. *James Baldwin: A Biography.* New York: Arcade, 1994.

León, Christina A. "Forms of Opacity: Roaches, Blood, and Being Stuck in Xandra Ibarra's Corpus." *ASAP Journal* 2, no. 2 (2017): 369-94.

Leroy, Gilles. *Nina Simone, roman.* Paris: Mercure de France, 2010.

Light, Alan. *What Happened, Miss Simone? A Biography.* New York: Crown Archetype, 2016.

Lloyd, Jack. "Nina Simone: Back from Abroad with a Special Brand of Music." *Daily News,* May 27, 1980.

Lorde, Audre. "The Uses of the Erotic: The Erotic as Power." 1978. In *Sister Outsider: Essays and Speeches,* 53-59. Trumansburg, NY: Crossing Press, 1984.

Lordi, Emily J. *The Meaning of Soul: Black Music and Resilience since the 1960s.* Durham, NC: Duke University Press, 2020.

Los Angeles Sentinel. "Record Review: Nina Simone, Nina Simone and Piano!" February 27, 1969.

Lott, Eric. *Love and Theft: Blackface Minstrelsy and the American Working Class.* New York: Oxford University Press, 1993.

Loudermilk, A. "Nina Simone and the Civil Rights Movement: Protest at Her Piano, Audience at Her Feet." *Journal of International Women's Studies* 14, no. 3 (2013): 121-36.

Love, Heather. *Feeling Backward: Loss and the Politics of Queer History*. Cambridge, MA: Harvard University Press, 2007.

Lucas, Bob. "Disc Data." *Los Angeles Sentinel*, December 24, 1970.

Luepnitz, Deborah Anna. "Thinking in the Space between Winnicott and Lacan." *International Journal of Psychoanalysis* 90 (2009): 957–81.

Lynskey, Dorian. *33 Revolutions per Minute: A History of Protest Songs*. New York: HarperCollins, 2011.

Macdonald, Kyle. "Nina Simone Plays a Stunning Bach-Style Fugue in the Middle of One of Her Classic Songs." Classicfm.com, May 4, 2021. https://www .classicfm.com/discover-music/instruments/piano/nina-simone-improvises -bach-fugue-classic-song/.

Macey, David. *Frantz Fanon: A Biography*. New York: Picador, 2000.

Macherey, Pierre. "Figures of Interpellation in Althusser and Fanon." Translated by Zachary Luke Fraser. *Radical Philosophy* 173 (2012): 9–20.

Malcolm, Janet. *In the Freud Archives*. New York: Knopf, 1984.

Malcolm, Janet. *Psychoanalysis: The Impossible Profession*. New York: Vintage, 1981.

Malcolm, Janet. "Trouble in the Archives." *New Yorker*, November 28, 1983.

Marriott, David S. *Lacan Noir: Lacan and Afro-Pessimism*. Cham, Switzerland: Palgrave Macmillan, 2021.

Marshall, Paule. *Praisesong for the Widow*. New York: Plume, 1983.

Martel, James R. *The Misinterpellated Subject*. Durham, NC: Duke University Press, 2017.

Masson, Jeffrey Moussaieff. *The Assault on Truth: Freud's Suppression of the Seduction Theory*. New York: Farrar, Straus and Giroux, 1984.

Massumi, Brian. "The Autonomy of Affect." *Cultural Critique* 31 (Autumn 1995): 83–109.

Maxwell, Tom. "Nina Simone: Constructing a Legacy." *Longreads*, July 3, 2020. https://tommaxwell-32724.medium.com/nina-simone-constructing-a-legacy -564b9cd2dc7f.

Maxwell, Tom. "When Nina Simone Sang What Everyone Was Thinking." *Longreads*, April 20, 2017. https://longreads.com/2017/04/20/a-history-of -american-protest-music-when-nina-simone-sang-what-everyone-was-thinking/.

Maxwell, William J. *F. B. Eyes: How J. Edgar Hoover's Ghostreaders Framed African American Literature*. Princeton, NJ: Princeton University Press, 2015.

Mazzeo, Tilar J. *The Secret of Chanel No. 5: The Intimate History of the World's Most Famous Perfume*. New York: HarperCollins, 2010.

Mbembe, Achille. *Critique of Black Reason*. 2013. Translated by Laurent Dubois. Durham, NC: Duke University Press, 2017.

Mbembe, Achille. *Necropolitics*. 2016. Translated by Steven Corcoran. Durham, NC: Duke University Press, 2019.

McCall, Joyce M., Adrian Davis, Marjoris Regus, and James Dekle. "'To Be Young, Gifted and Black.'" *Teachers College Record* 125, no. 1 (2023): 56–83.

McKittrick, Katherine. *Dear Science and Other Stories*. Durham, NC: Duke University Press, 2021.

McKittrick, Katherine. *Demonic Grounds: Black Women and the Cartographies of Struggle*. Minneapolis: University of Minnesota Press, 2006.

McNulty, Robert H. "Revitalizing Industrial Cities through Cultural Tourism." *International Journal of Environmental Studies* 25, no. 4 (1985): 225–28.

McWilliams, Nancy. *Psychoanalytic Psychotherapy: A Practitioner's Guide*. New York: Guilford Press, 2004.

Melamed, Jodi. "Racial Capitalism." *Critical Ethnic Studies* 1, no. 1 (2015): 76–85.

Mena, Jasmine A., and P. Khalil Saucier. "'Don't Let Me Be Misunderstood': Nina Simone's Africana Womanism." *Journal of Black Studies* 45, no. 3 (2014): 247–65.

Menconi, David. *Step Up and Go: The Story of North Carolina Popular Music, from Blind Boy Fuller and Doc Watson to Nina Simone and Superchunk*. Chapel Hill: University of North Carolina Press, 2020.

Mercer, Kobena. *Welcome to the Jungle: New Positions in Black Cultural Studies*. New York: Routledge, 1994.

Miller, Alice. *The Drama of the Gifted Child: The Search for the True Self*. Rev. ed. New York: Basic Books, 1997.

Mitchell, Christopher Adam. "The Transformation of Gay Life from the Closet to Liberation, 1948–1980." PhD diss., Rutgers University, 2015.

Mitchell, Juliet. "Theory as Object." *October* 113 (2005): 27–38.

Monson, Ingrid. "Doubleness and Jazz Improvisation: Irony, Parody, and Ethnomusicology." *Critical Inquiry* 20, no. 2 (1994): 283–313.

Monson, Ingrid. *Freedom Sounds: Civil Rights Call Out to Jazz and Africa*. New York: Oxford University Press, 2007.

Moore, Celeste Day. *Soundscapes of Liberation: African American Music in Post-war France*. Durham, NC: Duke University Press, 2021.

Morrison, Toni. *Beloved*. 1987. New York: Vintage, 2004.

Morrison, Toni. "Home." In *The House That Race Built*, edited by Wahneema Lubiano, 3–12. New York: Pantheon, 1997.

Morrison, Toni. *Love*. New York: Vintage, 2003.

Morrison, Toni. *Song of Solomon*. 1975. New York: Vintage, 1998.

Moten, Fred. *Black and Blur*. Durham, NC: Duke University Press, 2017.

Moten, Fred. "Black Op." *PMLA* 123, no. 5 (2008): 1743–47.

Moten, Fred. "The Case of Blackness." *Criticism* 50, no. 2 (2008): 177–218.

Moten, Fred. *In the Break: The Aesthetics of the Black Radical Tradition*. Minneapolis: University of Minnesota Press, 2003.

Muñoz, José Esteban. *Cruising Utopia: The Then and There of Queer Futurity*. New York: New York University Press, 2009.

Musser, Amber Jamilla. *Between Shadows and Noise: Sensation, Situatedness, and the Undisciplined*. Durham, NC: Duke University Press, 2024.

Musser, Amber Jamilla. "From Our Body to Yourselves: The Boston Women's Health Book Collective and Changing Notions of Subjectivity, 1969–1973." *Women's Studies Quarterly* 35, nos. 1/2 (2007): 93–109.

Musser, Amber Jamilla. *Sensational Flesh: Race, Power, and Masochism*. New York: New York University Press, 2014.

Nash, Jennifer C. *Black Feminism Reimagined: After Intersectionality*. Durham, NC: Duke University Press, 2019.

Nathan, David. *The Soulful Divas*. New York: Billboard, 1999.

New Journal and Guide. "Let Nina Simone Tell You about Soul Music." July 12, 1969.

New York Amsterdam News. "Easter Show at Radio City." March 16, 1974.

New York Times. "Black Performers Set for 2-Week Fete." June 29, 1972.

New York Times. "Travel Notes: Beleaguered Shrines, King Tut to London, Lake Placid Games." January 9, 1972.

Ngai, Sianne. *Ugly Feelings*. Cambridge, MA: Harvard University Press, 2005.

Nyong'o, Tavia. *Afro-Fabulations: The Queer Drama of Black Life*. New York: New York University Press, 2019.

Nyong'o, Tavia. "The Unforgiveable Transgression of Being Caster Semenya." *Women and Performance* 20, no. 1 (2010): 95–100.

Oedegaard, Christine H., Larry Davidson, Brynjulf Stige, Marius Veseth, Anne Blindheim, Linda Garvik, Jan-Magne Sørensen, Øystein Søraa, and Ingunn Marie Stadskleiv Engebretsen. "'It Means So Much for Me to Have a Choice': A Qualitative Study Providing First-Person Perspectives on Medication-Free Treatment in Mental Health Care." *BMC Psychiatry* 20, no. 399 (2020). https://doi.org/10.1186/s12888-020-02770-2.

Ogden, Thomas H. *Projective Identification and Psychotherapeutic Technique*. Lanham, MD: Rowman and Littlefield, 1982.

Okeowo, Alexis. "Secret Histories." *New Yorker*, October 26, 2020.

Olatunji, Babatunde, with Robert Atkinson. *The Beat of My Drum: An Autobiography*. Philadelphia: Temple University Press, 2005.

Orbach, Susie. *The Impossibility of Sex: Stories of the Intimate Relationship between Therapist and Patient*. New York: Scribner, 2000.

Owens, Deirdre Cooper. *Medical Bondage: Race, Gender, and the Origins of American Gynecology*. Athens: University of Georgia Press, 2017.

Palmer, Robert. "Music: Irresistible 'Junkanoo Drums.'" *New York Times*, August 31, 1977.

Pareles, Jon. "A Diva's Day, Rich with Love, Prayer and Politics." *New York Times*, September 1, 1998.

Perry, Imani. *Looking for Lorraine: The Radiant and Radical Life of Lorraine Hansberry*. Boston: Beacon Press, 2018.

Petrus, Stephen, and Ronald D. Cohen. *Folk City: New York and the American Folk Music Revival*. New York: Oxford University Press, 2015.

Philadelphia Tribune. "Series Look at the Roots of Black Music." January 20, 1989.

Phillips, Adam. *Missing Out: In Praise of the Unlived Life*. New York: Picador, 2012.

Phillips, Adam. *On Flirtation: Psychoanalytic Essays on the Uncommitted Life*. Cambridge, MA: Harvard University Press, 1994.

Pierpont, Claudia Roth. "A Raised Voice: How Nina Simone Turned the Movement into Music." *New Yorker*, August 11 and 18, 2014.

Pinto, Samantha. *Difficult Diasporas: The Transnational Feminist Aesthetic of the Black Atlantic*. New York: New York University Press, 2013.

Pollak, Alec. "Lorraine Hansberry's Queer Archive." *Yale Review*, September 18, 2023. https://yalereview.org/article/alec-pollak-lorraine-hansberry-queer-archive.

Ponomareff, Alexander. "ForeWomen: Eunice Kathleen Waymon, Nina Simone, Talib Kweli, DJ Hi Tek, and the Politics of Self-Creation." *Journal of Popular Music Studies* 31, no. 1 (2019): 157–74.

Post, Tina. *Deadpan: The Aesthetics of Black Inexpression*. New York: New York University Press, 2022.

Povinelli, Elizabeth A. "Disturbing Sexuality." *South Atlantic Quarterly* 106, no. 3 (2007): 565–76.

Powell, Alison. "You Al Capone, I'm Nina Simone: The American Soul of Nina Simone." *Interview*, January 1997, n.p.

Powell, Elliott H. *Sounds from the Other Side: Afro–South Asian Collaborations in Black Popular Music*. Minneapolis: University of Minnesota Press, 2020.

Pratt, Lloyd. *The Stranger's Book: The Human in African American Literature*. Philadelphia: University of Pennsylvania Press, 2015.

Puar, Jasbir K. *The Right to Maim: Debility, Capacity, Disability*. Durham, NC: Duke University Press, 2017.

Pyle, Marcus R. "Nina Simone as Poet and Orchestrator: Black Female Subjectivity and the Exo(p)tic in 'Images' and 'Four Women.'" *Journal of Popular Music Studies* 33, no. 1 (2021): 130 –47.

Quashie, Kevin. *Black Aliveness, or A Poetics of Being*. Durham, NC: Duke University Press, 2021.

Range, Peter. "The Pinnacle of Kitsch. Southern-Style." *New York Times*, October 29, 1972.

Ransby, Barbara. *Ella Baker and the Black Freedom Movement: A Radical Democratic Vision*. Chapel Hill: University of North Carolina Press, 2003.

Rayman, Graham, and Thomas Tracy. "Evidence Disappears in Case of Two NYPD Officers Killed in East Village by 3 Members of the Black Liberation Army." *New York Daily News*, January 23, 2016. https://www.nydailynews.com/new-york/nypd-embarrassment-44-years-no-arrests-article-1.2507296.

Redmond, Shana L. *Anthem: Social Movements and the Sound of Solidarity in the African Diaspora*. New York: New York University Press, 2014.

Reid-Pharr, Robert F. *Once You Go Black: Choice, Desire, and the Black American Intellectual*. New York: New York University Press, 2007.

Richardson, Mark. "Remixed and Reimagined." *Pitchfork*, January 12, 2007. https://pitchfork.com/reviews/albums/9749-remixed-and-reimagined/.

Riley, Denise. *Impersonal Passion: Language as Affect*. Durham, NC: Duke University Press, 2005.

Ritchie, Jean. *Folk Songs of the Southern Appalachians*. 2nd ed. Lexington: University Press of Kentucky, 1997.

Robinson, Cedric J. *Black Marxism: The Making of the Black Radical Tradition*. 1983. Foreword by Robin D. G. Kelley. Chapel Hill: University of North Carolina Press, 2000.

Robinson, Raymond. "Nina Simone Thrills, Oscar Brown Chills." *New York Amsterdam News*, December 3, 1966.

Rollins, Bryant, and Les Matthews. "Candidates Warned: Must Deal with Both Black Nationalists and Integrationists or Get No Support." *New York Amsterdam News*, October 17, 1971.

Rooney, Ellen. "Live Free or Describe: The Reading Effect and the Persistence of Form." *differences: A Journal of Feminist Cultural Studies* 21, no. 3 (2010): 112–39.

Rorty, Amélie O. "Explaining Emotions." In *Explaining Emotions*, edited by Amélie O. Rorty, 103–26. Berkeley: University of California Press, 1980.

Rose, Jacqueline. *States of Fantasy*. Oxford: Clarendon Press, 1996.

Rose, Tricia. *Black Noise: Rap Music and Black Culture in Contemporary America*. Hanover, NH: Wesleyan University Press, 2004.

Ross, Alex. *Listen to This*. New York: Farrar, Straus and Giroux, 2010.

Roth, Lorna. "Looking at Shirley, the Ultimate Norm: Colour Balance, Image Technologies, and Cognitive Equity." *Canadian Journal of Communication* 34, no. 1 (2009): 111–36.

Rowell, Charles Henry. "'Words Don't Go There': An Interview with Fred Moten." *Callaloo* 27, no. 4 (2004): 954–66.

Ryan, Hugh. *The Women's House of Detention: A Queer History of a Forgotten Prison*. New York: Bold Type Books, 2022.

Saketopoulou, Avgi. *Sexuality beyond Consent: Risk, Race, Traumatophilia*. New York: New York University Press, 2023.

Salmon, Felix. "Naming Wrongs." *Slate*, March 6, 2015. https://slate.com/business /2015/03/david-geffen-gives-100-million-to-lincoln-center-why-the-sale-of -naming-rights-is-corrupting-cultural-philanthropy.html.

Santoro, Gene. "Nina Simone." *Daily News*, July 2, 2001.

Scafidi, Sarah. "Speaking from the Heart: Playwright Christina Ham on Nina Simone: Four Women." *DC Theatre Scene*, October 26, 2017. https://dctheatrescene .com/2017/10/26/speaking-heart-playwright-christina-ham-nina-simone-four -women/.

Scaramuzzo, Gene. "Passings: Tony 'Exuma' McKay." *The Beat* 16, no. 2 (1997): 73–74.

Schoemer, Karen. "Smoldering, and Still Singing about It." *New York Times*, July 1, 1992.

Schuller, Kyla. *The Biopolitics of Feeling: Race, Sex, and Science in the Nineteenth Century*. Durham, NC: Duke University Press, 2018.

Schuller, Kyla. *The Trouble with White Women: A Counter-history of Feminism*. New York: Bold Type Books, 2021.

Scott, Darieck. *Keeping It Real: Black Queer Fantasy and Superhero Comics*. New York: New York University Press, 2022.

Scott, David. *Conscripts of Modernity: The Tragedy of Colonial Enlightenment*. Durham, NC: Duke University Press, 2004.

Scott, Joan Wallach. *The Fantasy of Feminist History*. Durham, NC: Duke University Press, 2011.

Scribner, Charity. "1968, Take Two: The Militancy of Nina Simone." In *Gender, Emancipation, and Political Violence: Rethinking the Legacy of 1968* , edited by Sarah Colvin and Katharina Karcher, 63–75. New York: Routledge, 2019.

Sedgwick, Eve Kosofsky. *Epistemology of the Closet*. Berkeley: University of California Press, 1990.

Sedgwick, Eve Kosofsky. "Melanie Klein and the Difference Affect Makes." *South Atlantic Quarterly* 106, no. 3 (2007): 625–42.

Segal, Hanna. *Dream, Phantasy, and Art*. New York: Routledge, 1991.

Seigworth, Gregory J., and Carolyn Pedwell. "A Shimmer of Inventories." In *The Affect Theory Reader II: Worldings, Tensions, Futures*, edited by Gregory J. Seigworth and Carolyn Pedwell, 1–59. Durham, NC: Duke University Press, 2023.

Shakur, Assata. *Assata: An Autobiography*. Brooklyn: Lawrence Hill, 1987.

Sharpe, Christina. *In the Wake: On Blackness and Being*. Durham, NC: Duke University Press, 2016.

Sharpe, Christina. *Ordinary Notes*. New York: Farrar, Straus and Giroux, 2023.

Sheff, David. "Interview with John Lennon and Yoko Ono." *Playboy: Entertainment for Men*, January 1981, 75.

Shepard, Sam. *Motel Chronicles*. San Francisco: City Lights Books, 1983.

Sherman, Robert. "Nina Simone Casts Her Moody Spells." *New York Times*, November 23, 1966.

Sikov, Ed. *Laughing Hysterically: American Screen Comedy of the 1950s*. New York: Columbia University Press, 1994.

Simone, Nina, with Stephen Cleary. *I Put a Spell on You*. 1991. New York: Da Capo Press, 2003.

Singh, Julietta. *The Breaks*. Minneapolis: Coffee House Press, 2021.

Singh, Julietta. *No Archive Will Restore You*. Brooklyn: Punctum Books, 2018.

Skloot, Rebecca. *The Immortal Life of Henrietta Lacks*. New York: Broadway Books, 2010.

Smith, Michael. "The Other (More Serious) Side of Nina." *Melody Maker*, December 7, 1968.

Smitherman, Geneva. *Talkin and Testifyin: The Language of Black America*. Boston: Houghton Mifflin, 1977.

Smucker, Tom. "Boring and Horrifying Whiteness: The Rise and Fall of Reaganism as Prefigured by the Career Arcs of Carpenters, Lawrence Welk, and the Beach Boys, 1973–74." In *Pop When the World Falls Apart: Music in the Shadow of Doubt*, edited by Eric Weisbard, 47–61. Durham, NC: Duke University Press, 2012.

Snorton, C. Riley. *Black on Both Sides: A Racial History of Trans Identity*. Minneapolis: University of Minnesota Press, 2017.

Spillers, Hortense J. "'All the Things You Could Be by Now If Sigmund Freud's Wife Was Your Mother': Psychoanalysis and Race." *Critical Inquiry* 22, no. 4 (1996): 710–34.

Spillers, Hortense J. "Interstices: A Small Drama of Words." In *Pleasure and Danger: Exploring Female Sexuality*, edited by Carole A. Vance, 73–100. Boston: Routledge, 1984.

Spillers, Hortense J. "Mama's Baby, Papa's Maybe: An American Grammar Book." *Diacritics* 17, no. 2 (1987): 64–81.

Spillers, Hortense J. "'The Permanent Obliquity of an In(pha)lliby Straight': In the Time of Daughters and Fathers." In *Changing Our Own Words: Essays on Criticism,*

Theory, and Writing by Black Women, edited by Cheryl A. Wall, 127–46. New Brunswick, NJ: Rutgers University Press, 1987.

Spillers, Hortense J., with Saidiya Hartman, Farah Jasmine Griffin, Shelly Eversley, and Jennifer L. Morgan. "'Whatcha Gonna Do?': Revisiting 'Mama's Baby, Papa's Maybe: An American Grammar Book': A Conversation." *Women's Studies Quarterly* 35, no. 1/2 (2007): 299–309.

Spivak, Gayatri Chakravorty. *Outside in the Teaching Machine*. New York: Routledge, 1993.

Spivak, Gayatri Chakravorty. "Psychoanalysis in Left Field and Fieldworking: Examples to Fit the Title." In *Speculations after Freud: Psychoanalysis, Philosophy and Culture*, edited by Sonu Shamdasani and Michael Munchow, 41–75. New York: Routledge, 1994.

Stadler, Gustavus. "Cover Art." *Avidly*, June 25, 2013. http://avidly.lareviewofbooks .org/2013/06/25/cover-art/.

Stauffer, Jill. *Ethical Loneliness: The Injustice of Not Being Heard*. New York: Columbia University Press, 2015.

Steedman, Carolyn. *Dust: The Archive and Cultural History*. New Brunswick, NJ: Rutgers University Press, 2002.

Steffens, Roger, and Leroy Jodie Pierson. *Bob Marley and the Wailers: The Definitive Discography*. Nashville: Rounder Books, 2005.

Stein, Jordan Alexander. *Avidly Reads Theory*. New York: New York University Press, 2019.

Stein, Jordan Alexander. "Pop Politics." *Avidly*, June 30, 2014. https://avidly .lareviewofbooks.org/2014/06/30/pop-politics/.

Stein, Jordan Alexander. "The Present Waver." *Los Angeles Review of Books*, September 17, 2021. https://www.lareviewofbooks.org/article/the-present-waver-on -wake-the-hidden-history-of-women-led-slave-revolts/.

Stephens, Michelle Ann. *Skin Acts: Race, Psychoanalysis, and the Black Male Performer*. Durham, NC: Duke University Press, 2014.

Stewart, Kathleen. *Ordinary Affects*. Durham, NC: Duke University Press, 2007.

Stewart, Kathleen. "Still Life." In *Intimacy*, edited by Lauren Berlant, 405–20. Chicago: University of Chicago Press, 2000.

Stoler, Ann Laura. *Along the Archival Grain: Epistemic Anxieties and Colonial Common Sense*. Princeton, NJ: Princeton University Press, 2009.

Stover, Jennifer Lynn. *The Sonic Color Line: Race and the Politics of Listening*. New York: New York University Press, 2016.

Stroud, Andrew. *Nina Simone, "Black Is the Color . . ."* Bloomington, IN: Xlibris, 2005.

Szasz, Thomas. *The Myth of Mental Illness: Foundations of a Theory of Personal Conduct*. New York: Harper and Row, 1961.

Tarnopolsky, Alex. "The Concept of Dissociation in Early Psychoanalytic Writers." *Journal of Trauma and Dissociation* 4, no. 3 (2003): 7–25.

Taylor, Arthur. "Nina Simone." 1977. In *Notes and Tones: Musician-to-Musician Interviews*, 148–59. New York: Da Capo Press, 1993.

Terada, Rei. *Feeling in Theory: Emotion after the "Death of the Subject."* Cambridge, MA: Harvard University Press, 2001.

Terada, Rei. *Metaracial: Hegel, Antiblackness, and Political Identity*. Chicago: University of Chicago Press, 2023.

Thomas, Katherina Grace. "Nina Simone in Liberia." *Guernica*, June 19, 2017. https://www.guernicamag.com/nina-simone-in-liberia/.

Thompson, Heather Ann. *Blood in the Water: The Attica Prison Uprising of 1971 and Its Legacy*. New York: Vintage, 2016.

Thompson, Krista. *Shine: The Visual Economy of Light in African Diasporic Aesthetic Practice*. Durham, NC: Duke University Press, 2015.

Tillet, Salamishah. "Strange Sampling: Nina Simone and Her Hip-Hop Children." *American Quarterly* 66, no. 1 (2014): 119–37.

Tinsley, Omise'eke Natasha. "Black Atlantic, Queer Atlantic: Queer Imaginings of the Middle Passage." GLQ: *A Journal of Lesbian and Gay Studies* 14, nos. 2–3 (2008): 191–215.

Tompkins, Kyla Wazana. *Racial Indigestion: Eating Bodies in the 19th Century*. New York: New York University Press, 2012.

Tongson, Karen. *Why Karen Carpenter Matters*. Austin: University of Texas Press, 2019.

Torok, Maria. "Fantasy: An Attempt to Define Its Structure and Operation." 1959. In *The Shell and the Kernel: Renewals of Psychoanalysis*, by Nicolas Abraham and Maria Torok, edited and translated by Nicholas T. Rand, 1:27–36. Chicago: University of Chicago Press, 1994.

Tremblay, Jean-Thomas. *Breathing Aesthetics*. Durham, NC: Duke University Press, 2022.

Tsing, Anna Lowenhaupt. *The Mushroom at the End of the World: On the Possibility of Life in Capitalist Ruins*. Princeton, NJ: Princeton University Press, 2015.

Tsuruta, Dorothy Randall. "I Ain't About to Be Non-violent, Honey." *Black Scholar* 29, no. 2–3 (1999): 54–58.

Vaillant, George E. *Adaptation to Life*. 1977. Cambridge, MA: Harvard University Press, 1995.

van der Kolk, Bessel. *The Body Keeps the Score: Brain, Mind, and Body in the Healing of Trauma*. New York: Penguin, 2014.

Veal, Michael E. *Dub: Soundscapes and Shattered Songs in Jamaican Reggae*. Middleton, CT: Wesleyan University Press, 2007.

Vogel, Shane. *The Scene of Harlem Cabaret: Race, Sexuality, Performance*. Chicago: University of Chicago Press, 2009.

Vogel, Shane. *Stolen Time: Black Fad Performance and the Calypso Craze*. Chicago: University of Chicago Press, 2018.

Vogue. "Filmmaker and Activist Tourmaline on How to Freedom Dream." July 2, 2020. https://www.vogue.com/article/filmmaker-and-activist-tourmaline-on-how-to-freedom-dream.

Vološinov, V. N. *Marxism and the Philosophy of Language*. 1929. Translated by Ladislav Matejka and I. R. Titunik. Cambridge, MA: Harvard University Press, 1986.

Walcott, Rinaldo. *The Long Emancipation: Toward Black Freedom*. Durham, NC: Duke University Press, 2021.

Walsh, Alan. "The Fantasy World of Nina Simone." *Melody Maker*, December 21, 1968.

Walsh, Alan, and Jack Hutton. "Antibes Jazz Festival Report: Miles, Peterson, and Nina on Form." *Melody Maker*, August 2, 1969.

Ward, Brian. *Just My Soul Responding: Rhythm and Blues, Black Consciousness, and Race Relations*. Berkeley: University of California Press, 1998.

Warner, Jennifer. *Keeper of the Flame: A Biography of Nina Simone*. Anaheim, CA: Golgotha Press, 2014.

Warner, Michael. "Publics and Counterpublics." *Public Culture* 14, no. 1 (2002): 49–90.

Warren, Calvin L. *Ontological Terror: Blackness, Nihilism, and Emancipation*. Durham, NC: Duke University Press, 2018.

Weheliye, Alexander G. *Habeas Viscus: Racializing Assemblages, Biopolitics, and Black Feminist Theories of the Human*. Durham, NC: Duke University Press, 2014.

West, Hollie I. "A Closer Look at the Styles of Nina and Aretha." *Washington Post*, March 22, 1970.

West, Hollie I. "The Return of Nina Simone." *Washington Post*, June 7, 1980.

White, Timothy. *Catch a Fire: The Life of Bob Marley*. New York: Holt, Rinehart and Winston, 1983.

Wilderson, Frank B., III. *Red, White, and Black: Cinema and the Structures of US Antagonisms*. Durham, NC: Duke University Press, 2010.

Wilson, Carl. *Let's Talk about Love: A Journey to the End of Taste*. New York: Bloomsbury, 2007.

Wilson, John S. "Museums in Tune with Nina Simone." *New York Times*, February 5, 1969.

Wilson, John S. "Nina Simone and Trio, at Hunter, Blend Jazz, Pop and Stage Music." *New York Times*, October 22, 1960.

Wilson, John S. "The Two Faces of Nina Simone." *New York Times*, December 31, 1967.

Wilson, Sheryl C., and Theodore X. Barber. "The Fantasy-Prone Personality: Implications for Understanding Imagery, Hypnosis, and Parapsychological Phenomena." In *Imagery: Current Theory, Research and Application*, edited by A. A. Sheikh, 340–90. New York: Wiley, 1983.

Winnicott, D. W. *The Child, the Family and the Outside World*. London: Pelican Books, 1964.

Winnicott, D. W. "Ego Distortion in Terms of True and False Self." 1960. In *The Maturational Process and the Facilitating Environment: Studies in the Theory of Emotional Development*, 140–57. New York: International Universities Press, 1965.

Winnicott, D. W. *Home Is Where We Start From: Essays by a Psychoanalyst*. New York: W. W. Norton, 1986.

Winnicott, D. W. "Transitional Objects and Transitional Phenomena." 1951. In *Playing and Reality*, 1–34. London: Routledge, 2005.

Winston, Brian. "A Whole Technology of Dyeing: A Note on Ideology and the Apparatus of the Chromatic Moving Image." *Daedalus* 114, no. 4 (1985): 105–23.

Wright, Nazera Sadiq. *Black Girlhood in the Nineteenth Century*. Urbana: University of Illinois Press, 2016.

Wynter, Sylvia. "No Humans Involved: An Open Letter to My Colleagues." *Forum N.H.I.: Knowledge for the 21st Century* 1, no. 1 (1994): 42–73.

Wynter, Sylvia. "Towards the Sociogenic Principle: Fanon, Identity, the Puzzle of Conscious Experience, and What It Is Like to Be 'Black.'" In *National Identities and Socio-Political Changes in Latin America*, edited by Mercedes F. Durán-Cogan and Antonio Gómez-Moriana, 30–66. New York: Routledge, 2001.

Wynter, Sylvia. "Unsettling the Coloniality of Being/Power/Truth/Freedom: Towards the Human, after Man, Its Overrepresentation—An Argument." *Centennial Review* 3, no. 3 (2003): 257–337.

Yablonsky, Linda. "Nina Simone at the Village Gate." In *The Show I'll Never Forget: 50 Writers Relive Their Most Memorable Concertgoing Experience*, edited by Sean Manning, 58–68. Cambridge, MA: Da Capo Press, 2007.

Yaffe, David. *Reckless Daughter: A Portrait of Joni Mitchell*. New York: Farrar, Straus and Giroux, 2017.

Youcef, Abdeldjalil Larbi. "Nina Simone in Algiers: Singing Revolution in the Land of Revolutionaries." Unpublished typescript, 2018.

Zaborowska, Magdelena J. *James Baldwin's Turkish Decade: Erotics of Exile*. Durham, NC: Duke University Press, 2009.

Zaborowska, Magdelena J. *Me and My House: James Baldwin's Last Decade in France*. Durham, NC: Duke University Press, 2018.

Žižek, Slavoj. *The Sublime Object of Ideology*. London: Verso, 1989.

Earle, William, 122
Edwards, Brent Hayes, 131
ekphrasis, 195–97
Ellington, Duke, 75, 100, 101
Elliott, Richard, 64, 150
Ellis, Warren, 183–84, 270n42
emotion. *See* affect
Evans, Kellylee, 200
Everly Brothers, 101
Evers, Medgar, 71, 139
expression. *See* fantasy: and performance
Exuma, 27, 115, 125, 133, 142, 145

fandom, 110, 152 174–175, 224
Fanon, Frantz, 58–59, 110, 247n69
fantasy: and agency, 5, 152, 172, 206; and
   ambivalence, 4, 10, 19, 29, 74, 162, 181;
   author's own, 16, 22, 29, 162–63, 224; of
   belonging, 117–21, 186–88; of conversation, 191–94; cross-racial identifications,
   27, 29–30; as defense, 11; definition of,
   7–14; expansiveness of, 73, 98; expressed
   through clothes, 7, 92–94, 215–18; haunting as, 215–18; historically determined,
   12–14, 24, 35, 53, 109, 118, 121, 130, 141,
   143, 178, 185, 193, 209, 213, 215–20,
   238n44; honesty of, 6, 17, 45; and literalness, 4, 6, 10, 36, 42–46, 57, 62–64, 77,
   88, 102, 107, 185, 203; meaningfulness of,
   7, 28, 43–44; multiple positions in, 49–51,
   55–56, 73–74, 102, 109, 218, 246n54
   (*see also* voicing); of origins, 118, 194;
   of politics, 213–14; and performance,
   3–4, 36–37, 48, 49, 55–56, 85, 87–88,
   102–7, 124, 141–45, 148–68, 181, 194, 203,
   220–21, 225; psychoanalytic conception
   of, 5–6, 9–11; public v. private life, 17; and
   satisfaction, 5, 9–10, 55, 73, 86, 98, 163;
   spatial metaphors for, 10, 50, 147; and
   thinking, 95–98; unconscious aspect, 6,
   233n7; violent aspect, 52–53; and writing,
   29, 37, 162–63, 224
Farrakhan, Louis, 191
Fashawn, 201
Faulkner, William, 219
Feldstein, Ruth, 87
Felix Da Housecat, 201
Ferreira da Silva, Denise, 221

Fields, Dorothy, 75
50 Cent, 201
Fitzgerald, Ella, 77
the Five Stairsteps, 101
Flack, Roberta, 80–81, 105, 252n19,
   253n22
The Flamethrowers, 208–9
Flatley, Jonathan, 206, 234n15
flirtation, 191–93
Flo Rider, 201
Flying Lotus, 201
folk music, 27, 77, 101, 166–67, 255n72
Fonda, Bridget, 209–10
For Colored Girls (film), 195
Four Women (film), 195
Foye, Hope, 83
France, 32, 135–36, 213
François, Claude, 101
Franklin, Aretha, 120, 213
Freud, Sigmund, 9, 10, 12, 52, 102, 147,
   234n10, 234n13, 237n29; cathexis
   (*Besetzung*), 147; deferred action
   (*Nachträglichkeit*), 92; identification,
   246n54; Oedipus complex, 53, 201;
   origin of writing, 266n45; negation, 6,
   234n12; phylogeny, 247n65; primal scene
   (*Urszene*), 237n29; projection, 264n17;
   regression, 67; repetition, 236n25; seduc-
   tion theory (*Verführungsszene*), 236n24,
   237n29; transference, 242n79
Frudakis, Zenos, 186
The Fugees, 80

Gaines, Malik, 55, 88
Gallagher, Ellen, 185
Garfunkel, Art, 82
Garland, Phyl, 110, 167
Garza, Alicia, 18
Gazaway, Amerigo, 201
Gershwin, George, 32, 36, 75, 76,
   101
Gibb, Barry, 3, 4
Ginsberg, Allen, 190
Giovanni, Nikki, 107, 189–91
Glissant, Édouard, 171
Glück, Robert, 109
graphomania, 243n92
Guccione, Bob, 174

Vološinov, V. N., 21
vodun, 122–24, 128, 133. *See also* obeah

The Walkabouts, 200
Warner, Jennifer, 33
Waymon, John Divine "J. D.," 31, 40, 42, 45, 49, 52
Waymon, Mary Kate, 31, 40, 42, 52
Waymon, Samuel, 42, 76, 161
Weheliye, Alexander, 19, 221
Weill, Kurt, 86–88
We're Here, 215–18
West, Kanye, 201
What Happened, Miss Simone? (film), 2, 17, 33, 66

whiteness, 19, 35, 48, 58–60, 61, 79, 82, 90, 101, 110, 121, 122, 134, 154–56, 164, 182, 208–11, 225, 252n12, 258n1
white womanhood, 208–11
Wilson, Al, 81
Wilson, Nancy, 81
Winfrey, Oprah, 197
Winnicott, D. W., 9, 52, 236n19
Wright, Letitia, 212
Wynter, Sylvia, 19

Xiu Xiu, 200

Yablonsky, Linda, 148
Young, Linda, 195